BIGHEAD

BY JEFFREY BROWN

TOP SHELF PRODUCTIONS

·CHICAGO · GEORGIA · PORTLAND·

INDICIA

By Jeffrey Brown

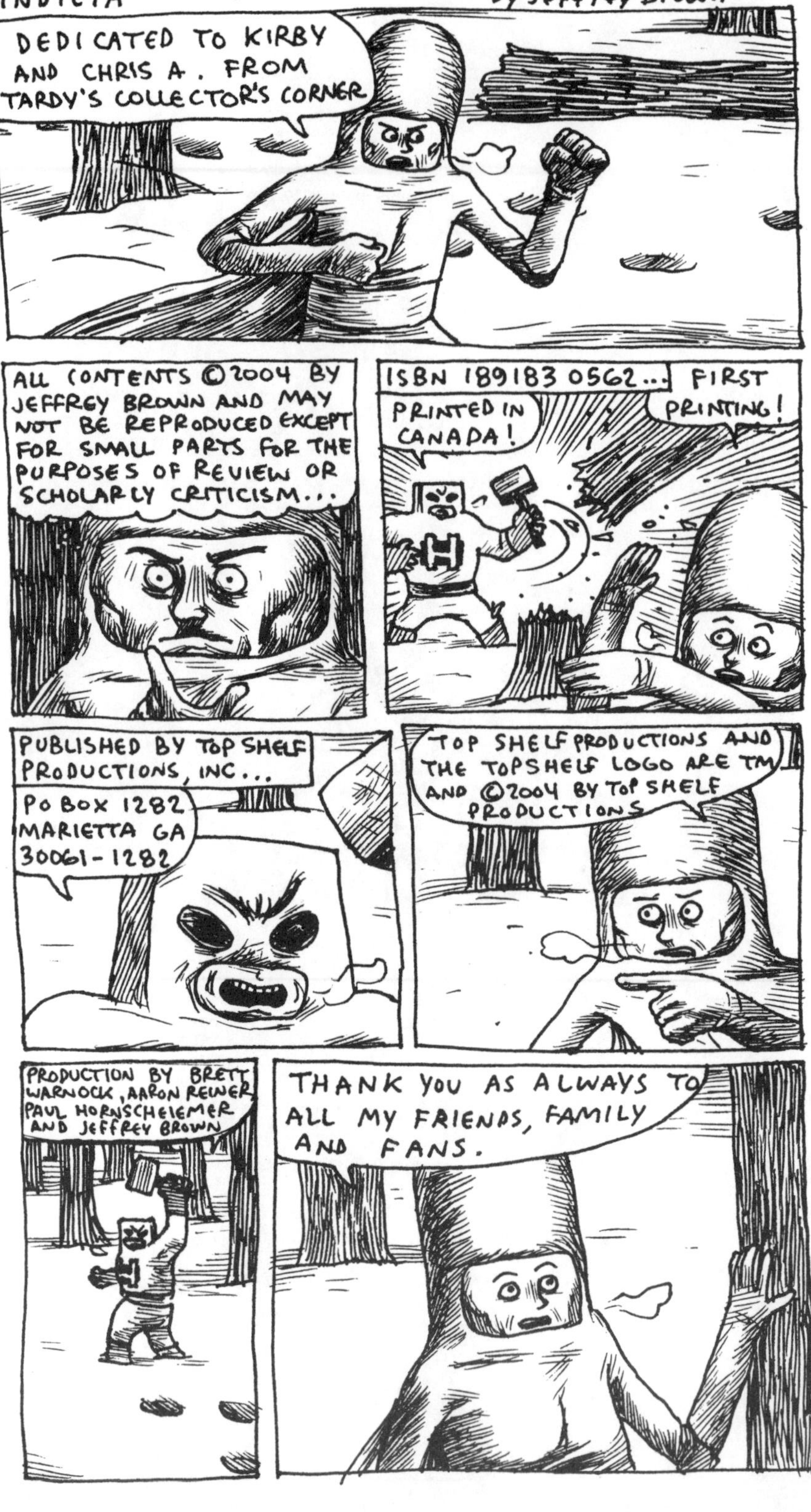
DEDICATED TO KIRBY AND CHRIS A. FROM TARDY'S COLLECTOR'S CORNER
ALL CONTENTS ©2004 BY JEFFREY BROWN AND MAY NOT BE REPRODUCED EXCEPT FOR SMALL PARTS FOR THE PURPOSES OF REVIEW OR SCHOLARLY CRITICISM...
ISBN 189183 0562...
PRINTED IN CANADA!
FIRST PRINTING!
PUBLISHED BY TOP SHELF PRODUCTIONS, INC...
PO BOX 1282 MARIETTA GA 30061-1282
TOP SHELF PRODUCTIONS AND THE TOPSHELF LOGO ARE TM AND ©2004 BY TOP SHELF PRODUCTIONS
PRODUCTION BY BRETT WARNOCK, AARON REINER PAUL HORNSCHEIEMER AND JEFFREY BROWN
THANK YOU AS ALWAYS TO ALL MY FRIENDS, FAMILY AND FANS.

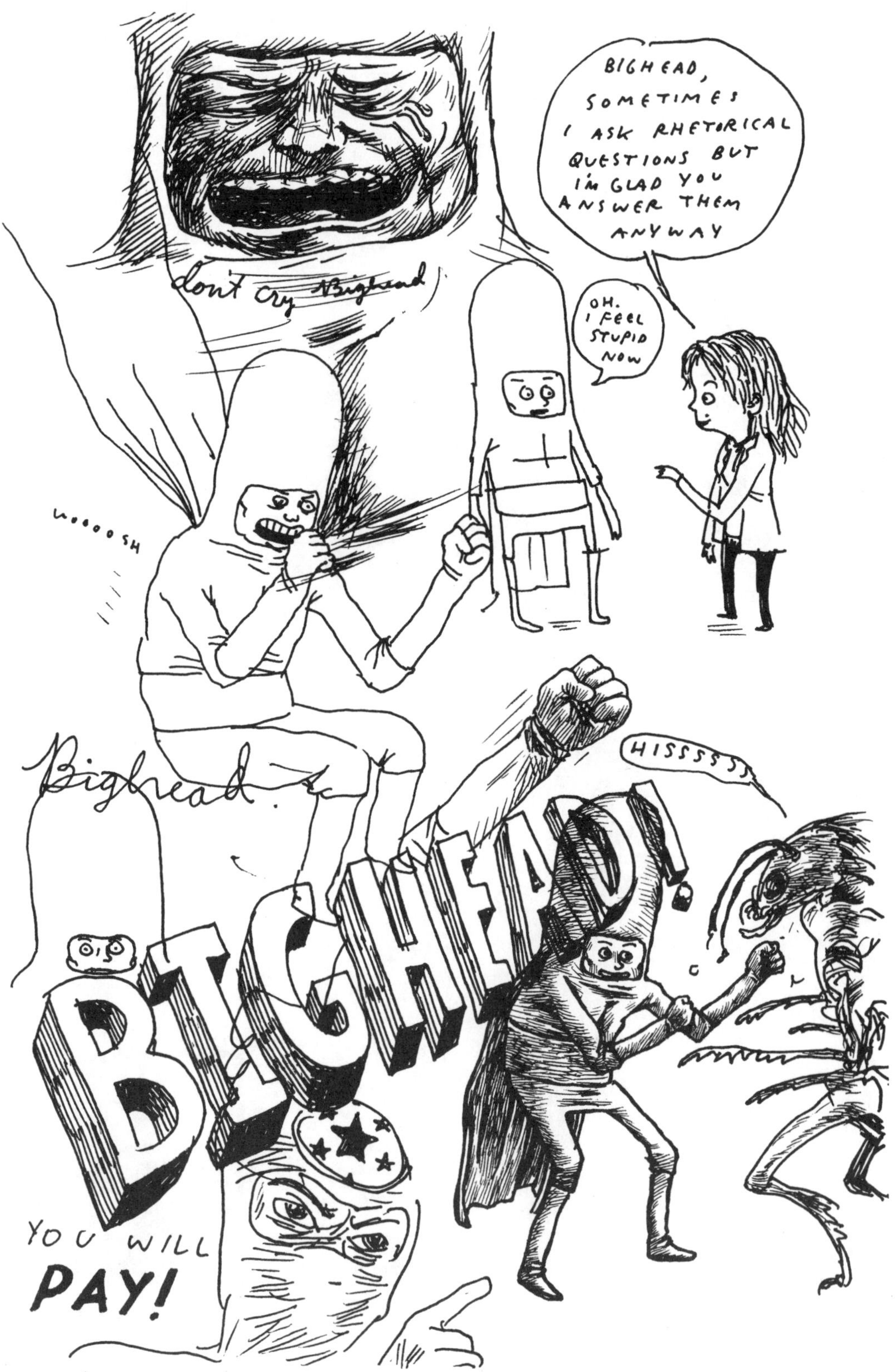

don't cry Bighead
BIGHEAD, SOMETIMES I ASK RHETORICAL QUESTIONS BUT I'M GLAD YOU ANSWER THEM ANYWAY
OH. I FEEL STUPID NOW
WOOOOSH
Bighead
HISSSSS
BIGHEAD!
YOU WILL PAY!

SUSPECTED POWERS OF BIGHEAD

ALTHOUGH IT IS NOT CLEAR EXACTLY WHAT SUPER POWERS BIGHEAD MAY POSSESS, VARIOUS NERD AND GEEK INTELLECTUALS HAVE LONG GUESSED AT THE EXACT ABILITIES. HERE IS A SUMMARY DESCRIPTION COMPILED FROM A NUMBER OF SOURCES:

MYSTERIOUS AND ALLURING

INQUISITIVE MIND, LIKE A KITTEN, OR SMALL CHILD

ENLARGED CRANIUM ENABLES SUPERIOR DEDUCTIVE REASONING AS WELL AS NON-LINEAR PROBLEM SOLVING

CAPE = CAN FLY

EYES SHOOT LASER BEAMS

MELODIC VOICE CAN SMOOTH TALK EVEN THE COLDEST OF HEARTS

MASSIVELY POWERFUL FIST

WELL DEFINED MUSCLES

BIG HEART

CAN LIFT EXTREMELY HEAVY OBJECTS

AMBIDEXTOROUS

STICKY FEET- CAN CLIMB WALLS BY 'WALKING' UP THEM

DEADLY STEEL-TOED KICKING ABILITY

HAS ADDITIONAL KNEECAPS

SUPER-FAST RUNNING SPEED

LACKS ACHILLES HEEL

ABOVE AVERAGE STAMINA

NAME: BIGHEAD
SECRET IDENTITY: UNKNOWN
AGE: APX. 30-35
LOCATION: VARIES; USUALLY LARGE CITIES
ORIGIN: REPEATEDLY TAUNTED BY SCHOOLMATES, BIGHEAD BECAME EMOTIONALLY SCARRED, CAUSING HIS HEAD TO SWELL WITH POWER.
FIRST APPEARANCE: UNBELIEVABLE SUPER STORIES #176, AS "HUGE HEAD"
ARCH ENEMY: SMALLHEAD
TEAM AFFILIATION: SCARLET FLYING APPENDAGES OF MICHIGAN
TURN-OFFS: SMOKING, ANNOYING LAUGH, THICK ANKLES

HEROIC SYMBOL:

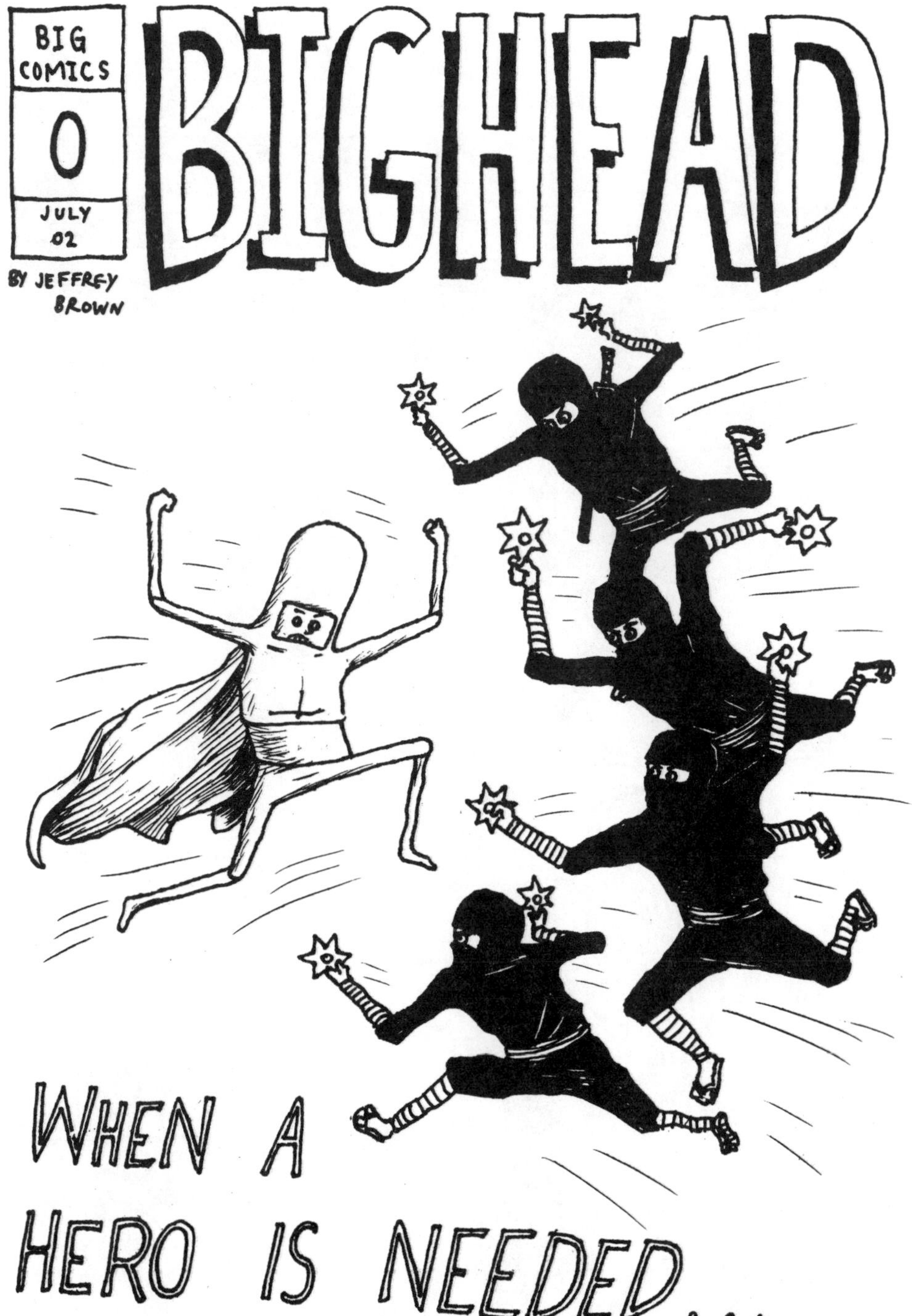
BIG COMICS
0
JULY 02
BIGHEAD
BY JEFFREY BROWN
WHEN A HERO IS NEEDED...

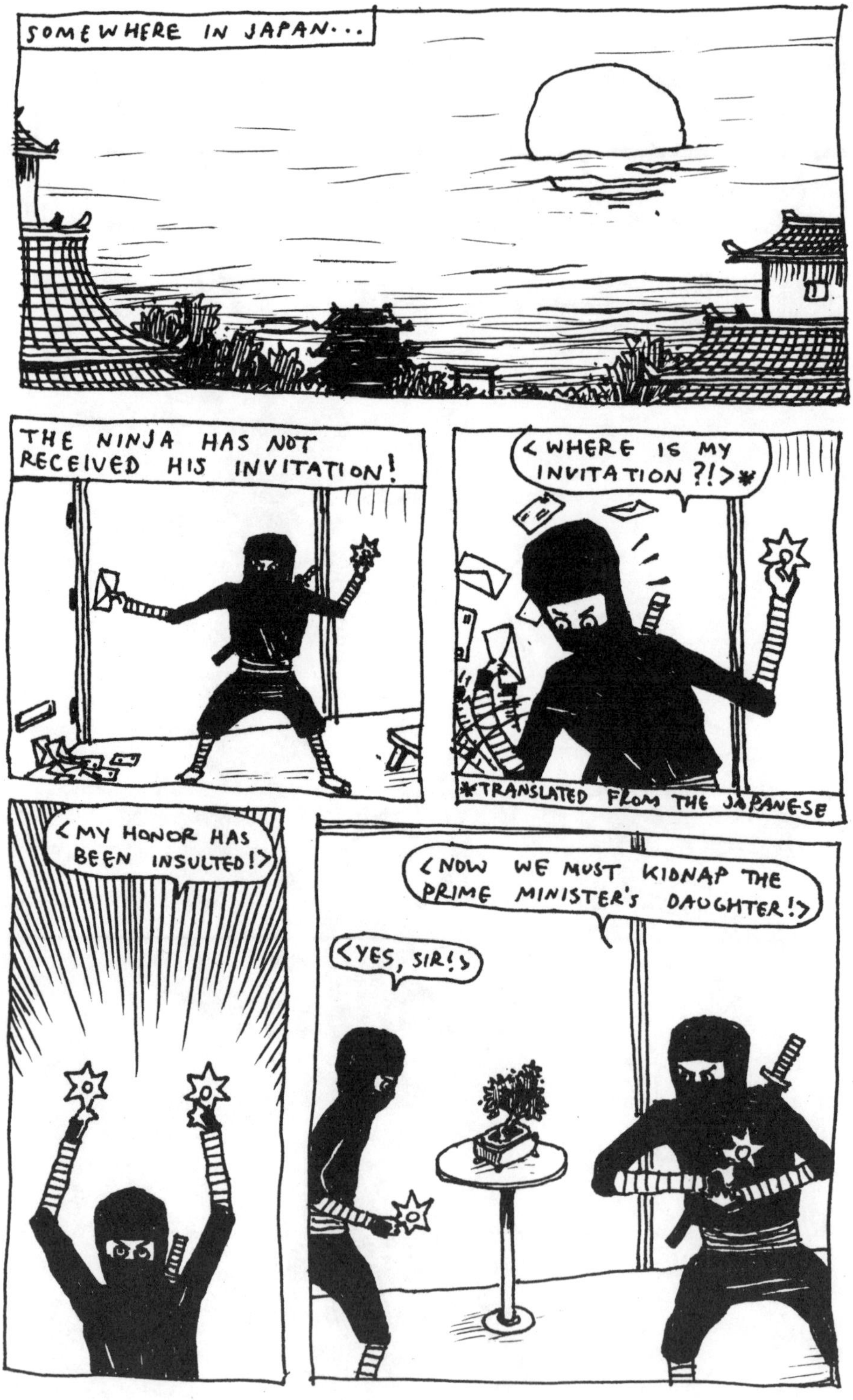
SOMEWHERE IN JAPAN...
THE NINJA HAS NOT RECEIVED HIS INVITATION!
<WHERE IS MY INVITATION?!>*
*TRANSLATED FROM THE JAPANESE
<MY HONOR HAS BEEN INSULTED!>
<NOW WE MUST KIDNAP THE PRIME MINISTER'S DAUGHTER!>
<YES, SIR!>

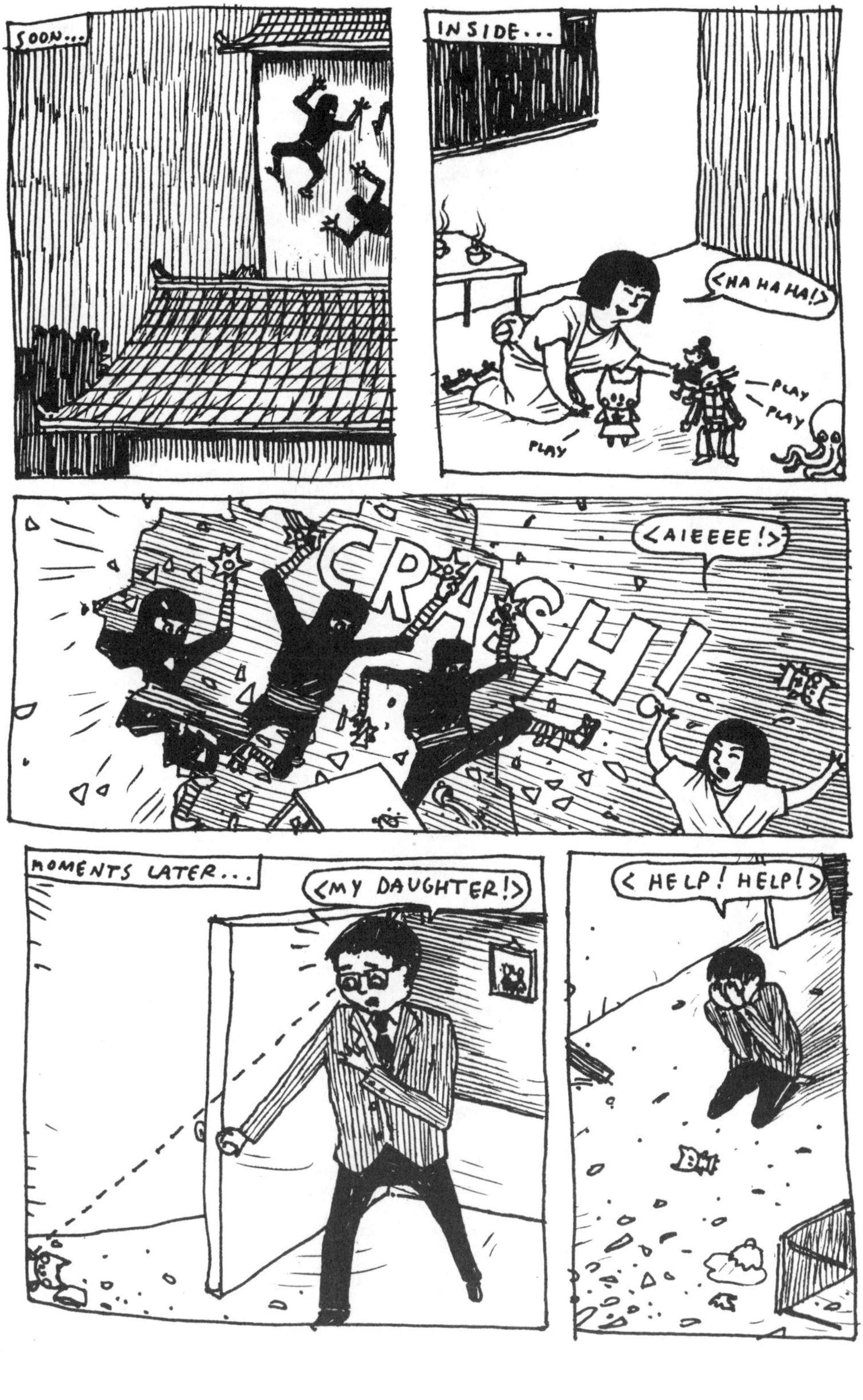
SOON...
INSIDE...
<HA HA HA!>
PLAY
PLAY
PLAY
<AIEEEEE!>
CRASH!
MOMENTS LATER...
<MY DAUGHTER!>
< HELP! HELP!>

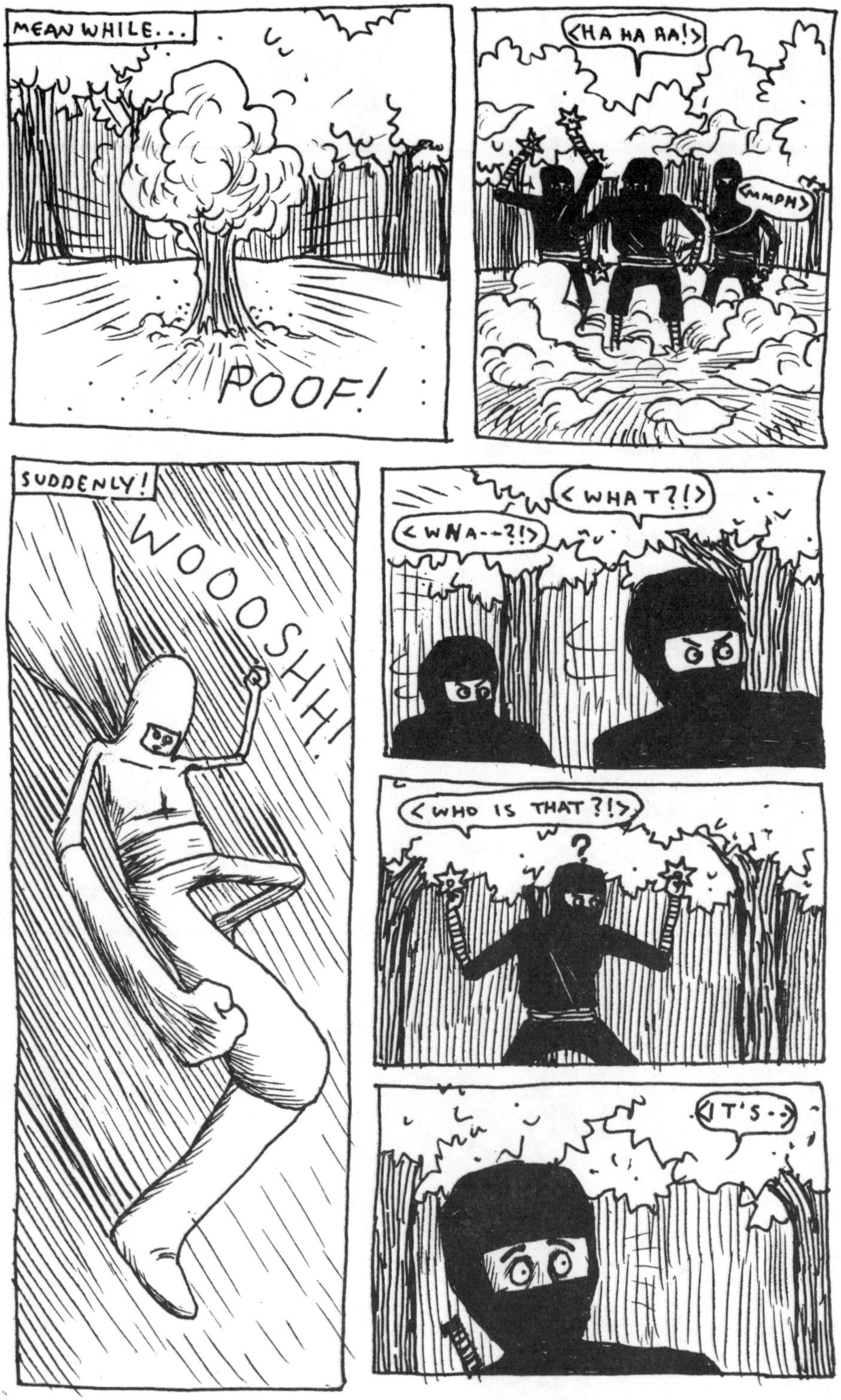
MEANWHILE...
POOF!
<HA HA HA!>
<MMPH>
SUDDENLY!
WOOOOSHH!
<WHAT?!>
<WNA--?!>
<WHO IS THAT?!>
?
<IT'S-->

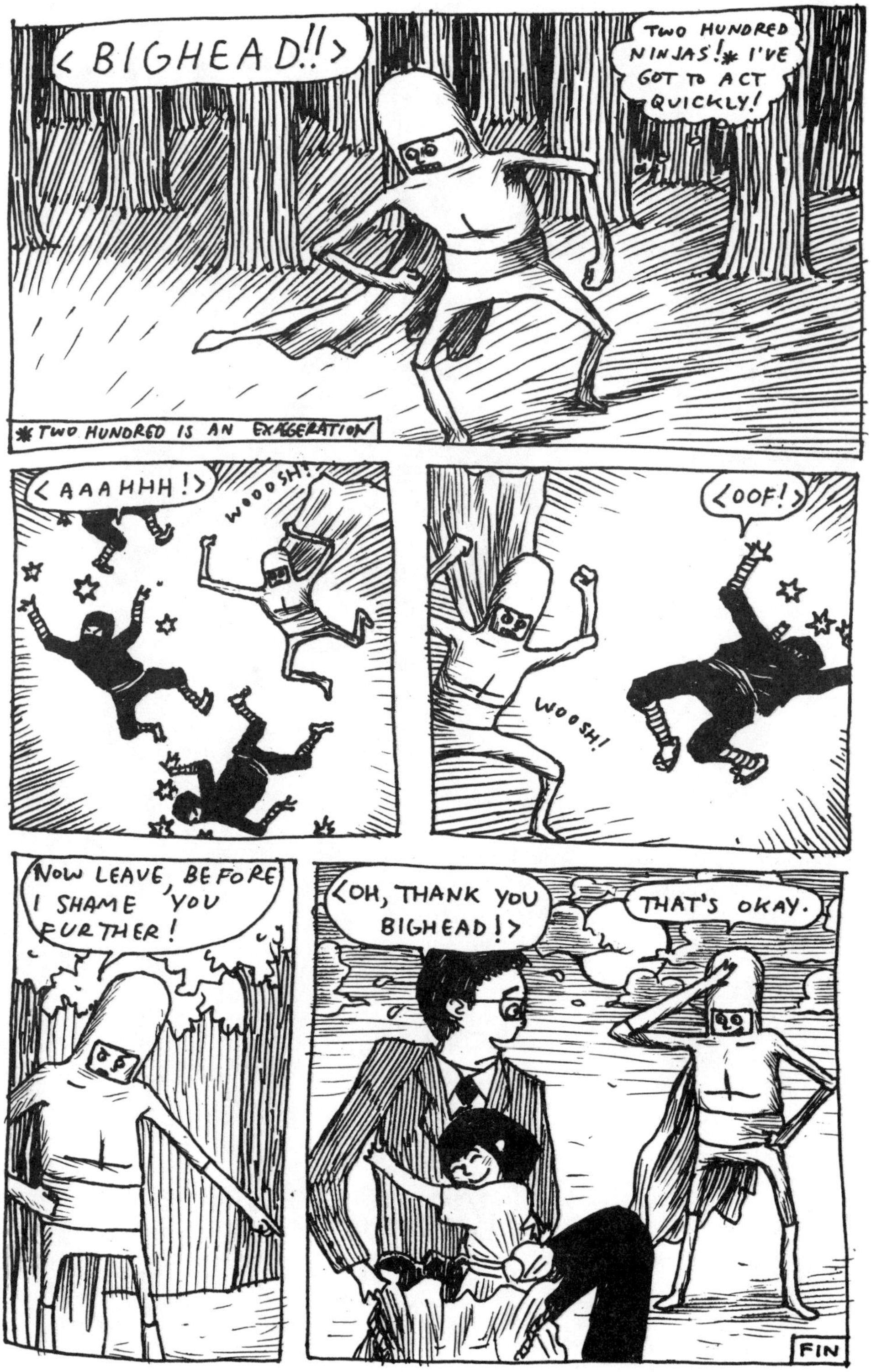
< BIGHEAD!! >
TWO HUNDRED NINJAS!* I'VE GOT TO ACT QUICKLY!
* TWO HUNDRED IS AN EXAGGERATION
<AAAHHH!>
WOOOSH!
<OOF!>
WOOSH!
NOW LEAVE, BEFORE I SHAME YOU FURTHER!
<OH, THANK YOU BIGHEAD!>
THAT'S OKAY.
FIN

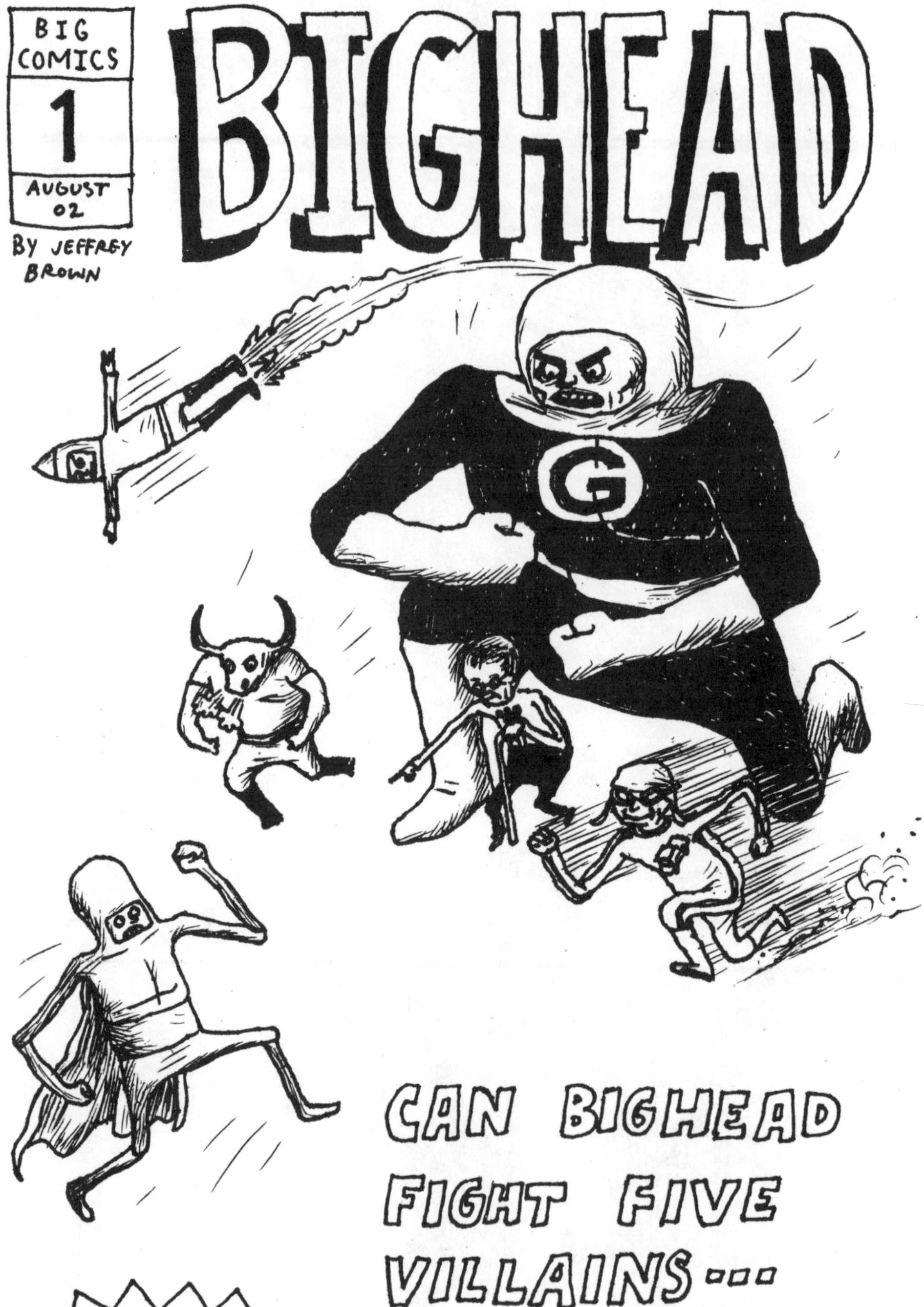
BIG COMICS
1
AUGUST 02
BIGHEAD
BY JEFFREY BROWN
G
CAN BIGHEAD FIGHT FIVE VILLAINS...
...AT ONCE?!
DOUBLE SIZED PREMIERE ISSUE!

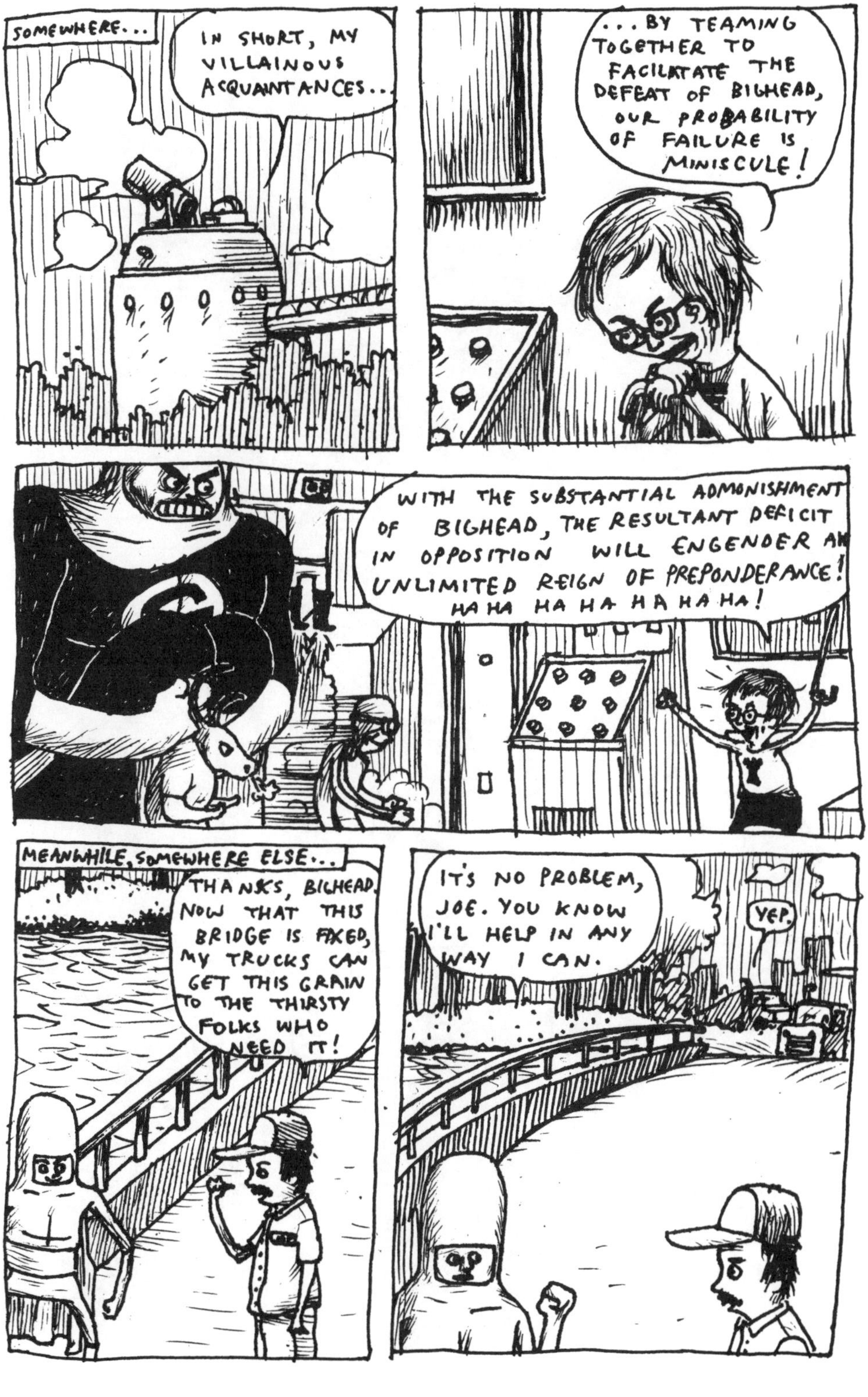
SOMEWHERE...
IN SHORT, MY VILLAINOUS ACQUAINTANCES...
...BY TEAMING TOGETHER TO FACILATATE THE DEFEAT OF BIGHEAD, OUR PROBABILITY OF FAILURE IS MINISCULE!
WITH THE SUBSTANTIAL ADMONISHMENT OF BIGHEAD, THE RESULTANT DEFICIT IN OPPOSITION WILL ENGENDER AN UNLIMITED REIGN OF PREPONDERANCE! HA HA HA HA HA HA HA!
MEANWHILE, SOMEWHERE ELSE...
THANKS, BIGHEAD. NOW THAT THIS BRIDGE IS FIXED, MY TRUCKS CAN GET THIS GRAIN TO THE THIRSTY FOLKS WHO NEED IT!
IT'S NO PROBLEM, JOE. YOU KNOW I'LL HELP IN ANY WAY I CAN.
YEP.

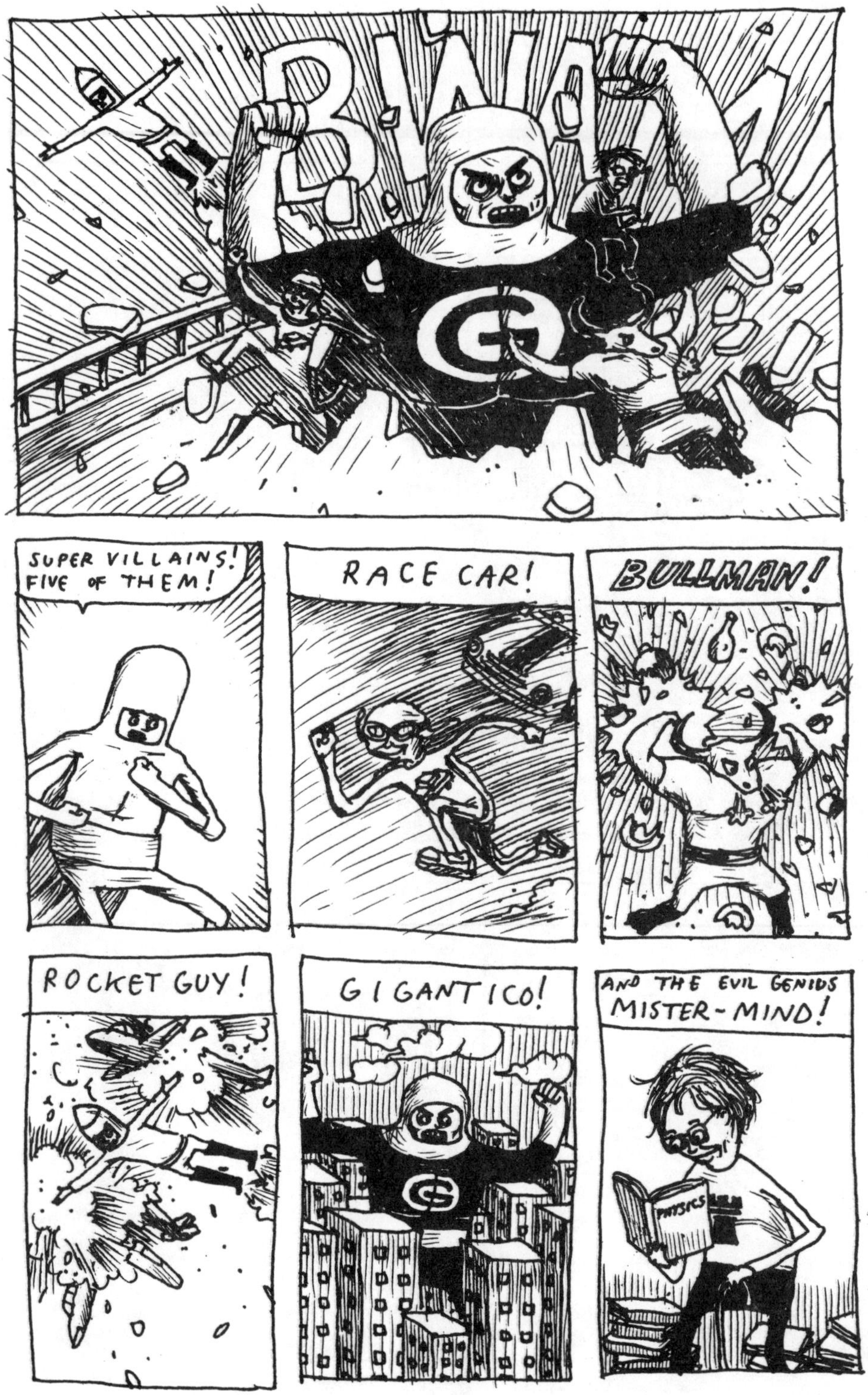
BWAM!
SUPER VILLAINS! FIVE OF THEM!
RACE CAR!
BULLMAN!
ROCKET GUY!
GIGANTICO!
AND THE EVIL GENIUS MISTER-MIND!
PHYSICS

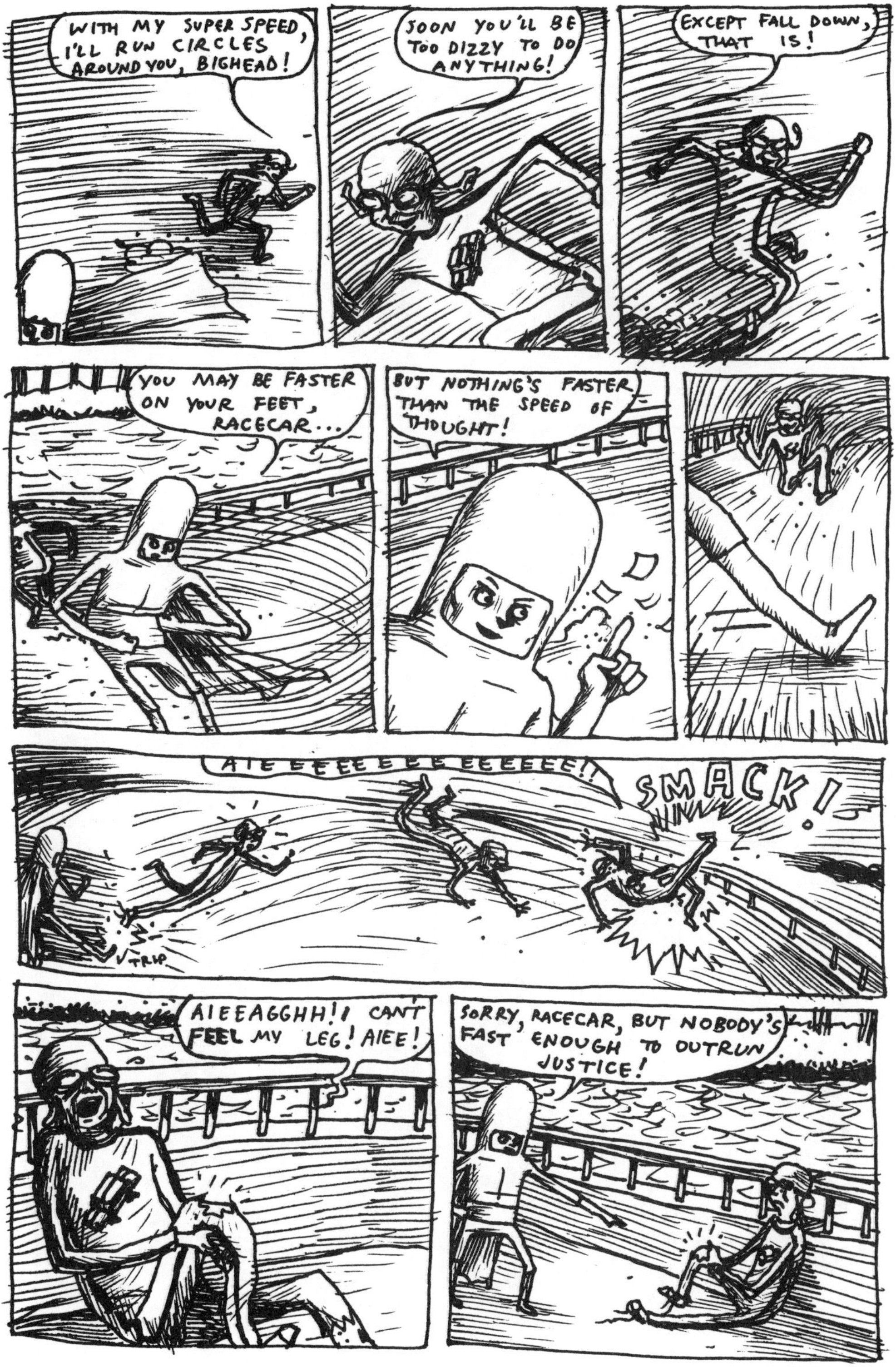
WITH MY SUPER SPEED, I'LL RUN CIRCLES AROUND YOU, BIGHEAD!
SOON YOU'LL BE TOO DIZZY TO DO ANYTHING!
EXCEPT FALL DOWN, THAT IS!
YOU MAY BE FASTER ON YOUR FEET, RACECAR...
BUT NOTHING'S FASTER THAN THE SPEED OF THOUGHT!
AIEEEEEEEEEEEEEEEEE!!
SMACK!
TRIP
AIEEAGGHH!! I CAN'T FEEL MY LEG! AIEE!
SORRY, RACECAR, BUT NOBODY'S FAST ENOUGH TO OUTRUN JUSTICE!

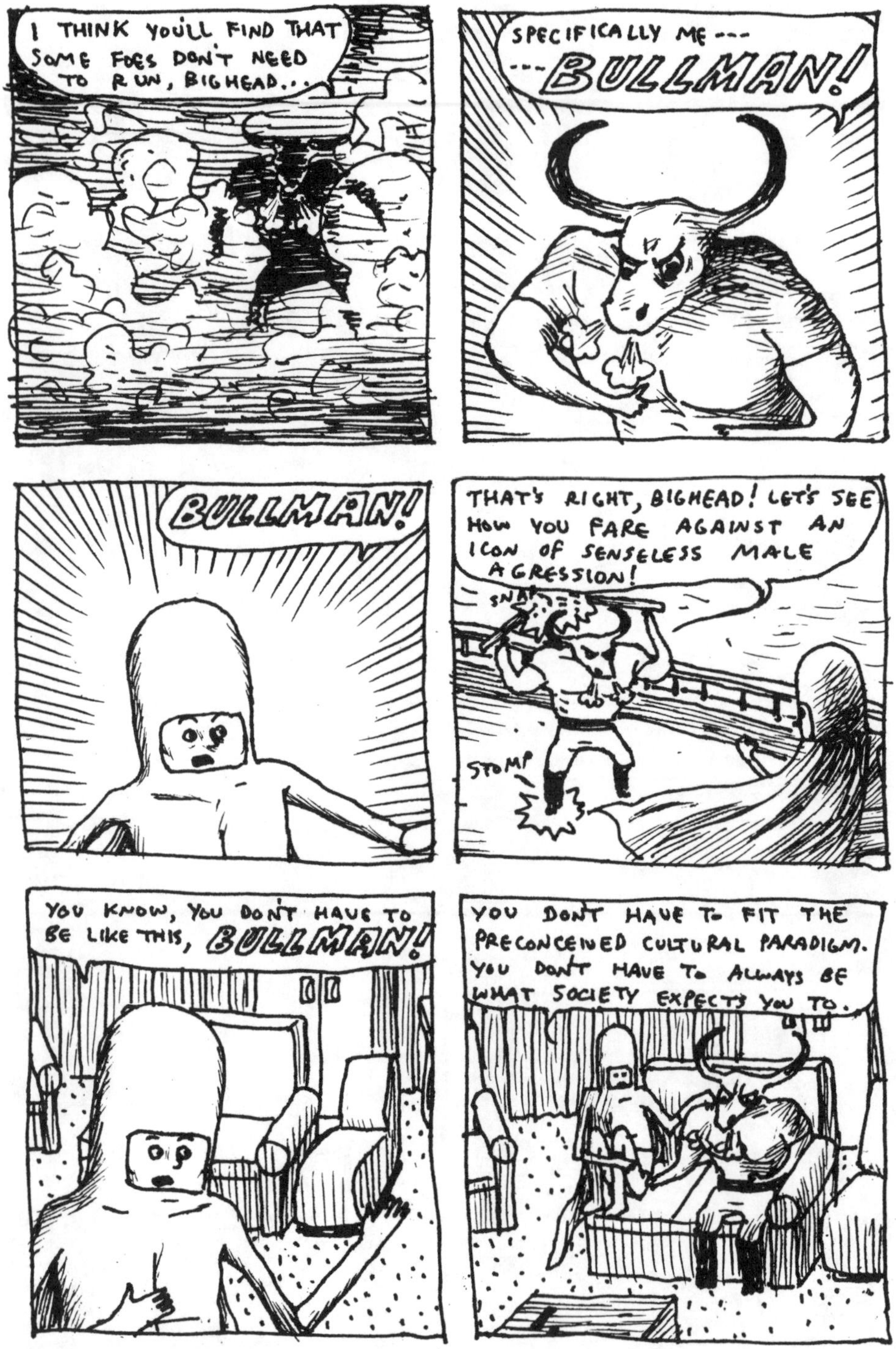
I THINK YOU'LL FIND THAT SOME FOES DON'T NEED TO RUN, BIGHEAD...
SPECIFICALLY ME--- ---BULLMAN!
BULLMAN!
THAT'S RIGHT, BIGHEAD! LET'S SEE HOW YOU FARE AGAINST AN ICON OF SENSELESS MALE AGRESSION!
SNAP
STOMP
YOU KNOW, YOU DON'T HAVE TO BE LIKE THIS, BULLMAN!
YOU DONT HAVE TO FIT THE PRECONCEIVED CULTURAL PARADIGM. YOU DON'T HAVE TO ALWAYS BE WHAT SOCIETY EXPECTS YOU TO.

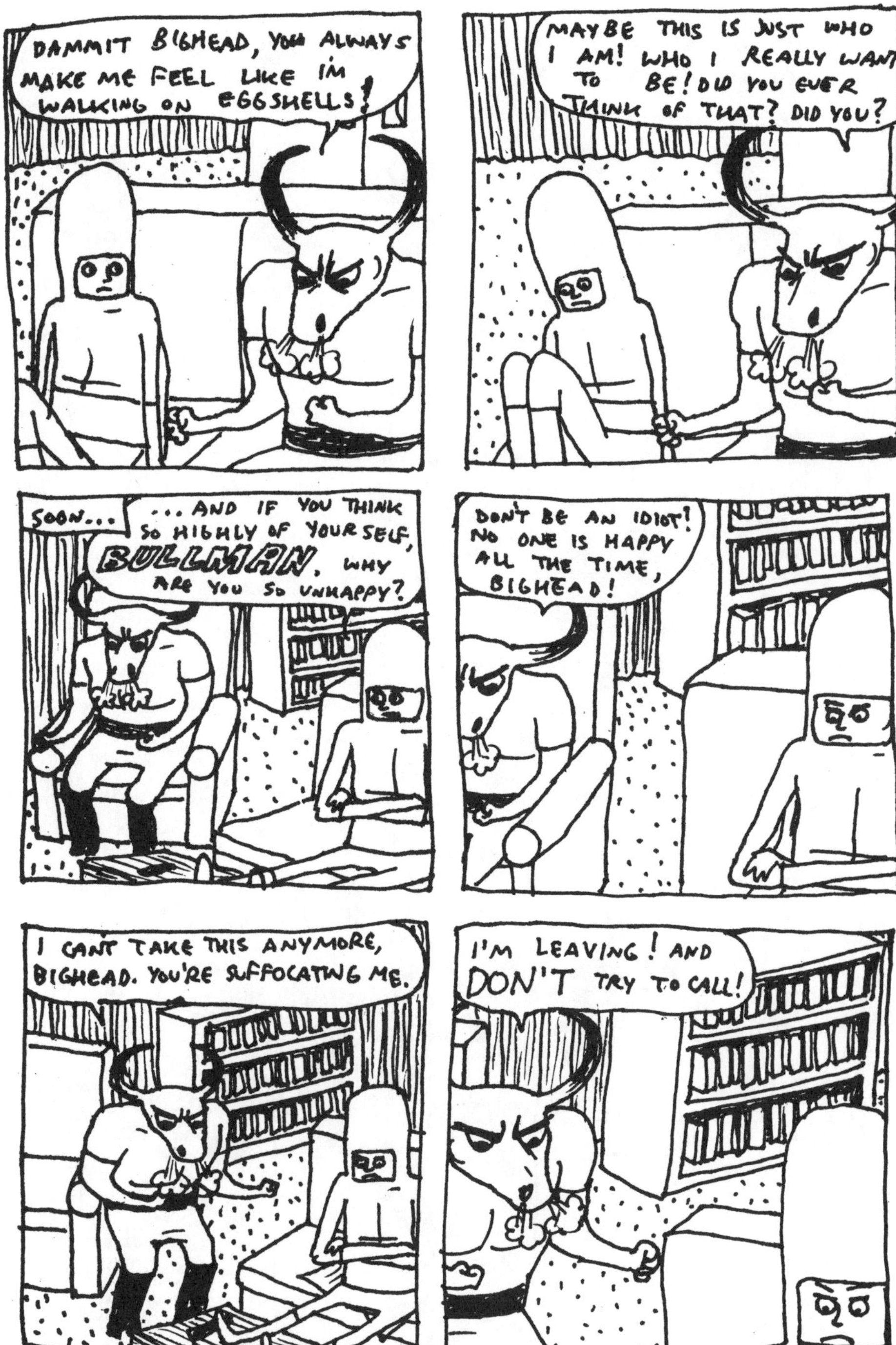
DAMMIT BIGHEAD, YOU ALWAYS MAKE ME FEEL LIKE I'M WALKING ON EGGSHELLS!
MAYBE THIS IS JUST WHO I AM! WHO I REALLY WANT TO BE! DID YOU EVER THINK OF THAT? DID YOU?
SOON...
...AND IF YOU THINK SO HIGHLY OF YOURSELF, BULLMAN, WHY ARE YOU SO UNHAPPY?
DON'T BE AN IDIOT! NO ONE IS HAPPY ALL THE TIME, BIGHEAD!
I CANT TAKE THIS ANYMORE, BIGHEAD. YOU'RE SUFFOCATING ME.
I'M LEAVING! AND DON'T TRY TO CALL!

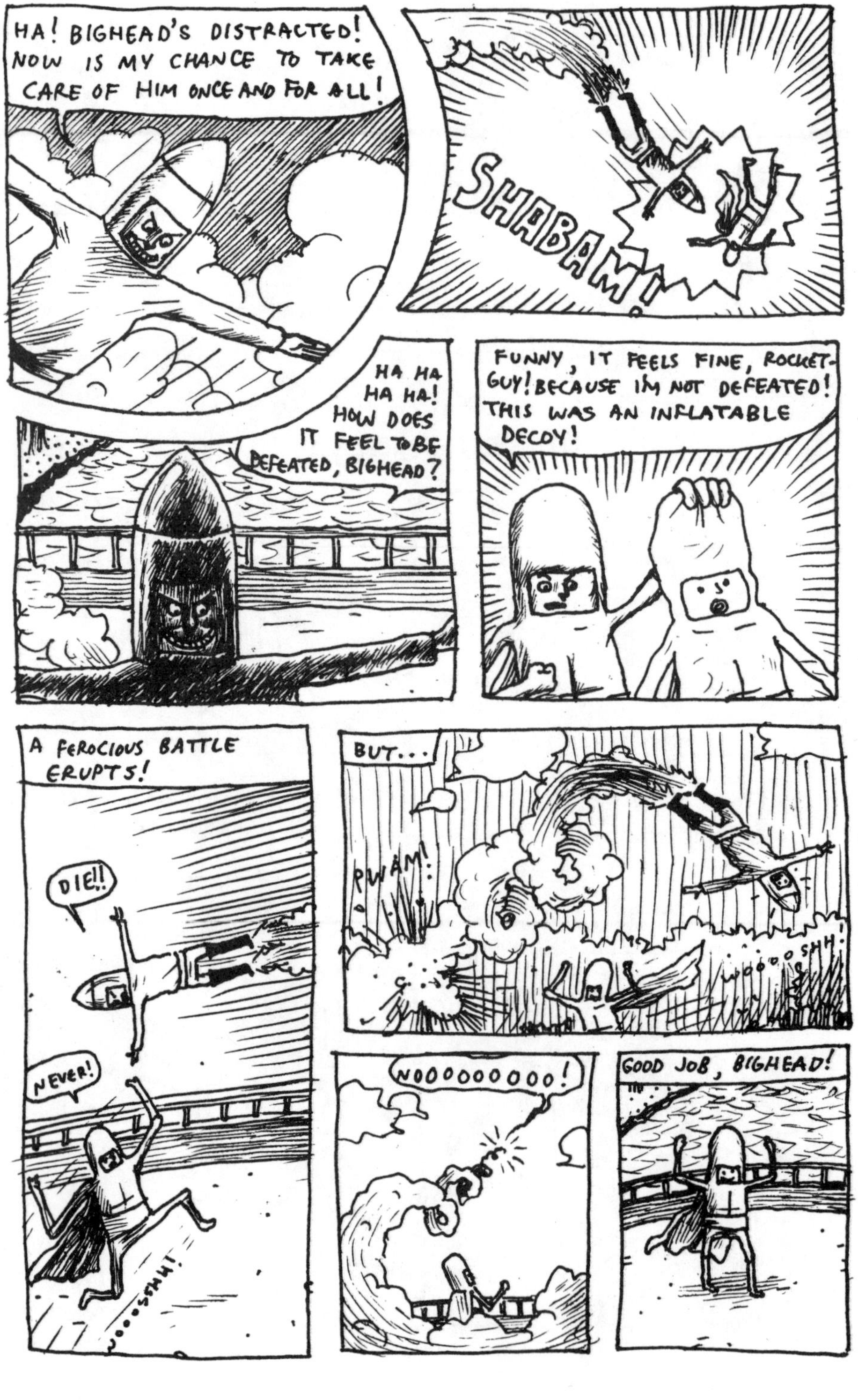
HA! BIGHEAD'S DISTRACTED! NOW IS MY CHANCE TO TAKE CARE OF HIM ONCE AND FOR ALL!
SHABAM!
HA HA HA HA! HOW DOES IT FEEL TO BE DEFEATED, BIGHEAD?
FUNNY, IT FEELS FINE, ROCKET-GUY! BECAUSE I'M NOT DEFEATED! THIS WAS AN INFLATABLE DECOY!
A FEROCIOUS BATTLE ERUPTS!
DIE!!
NEVER!
WOOOSHH!
BUT...
PWAM!
WOOOOOOSHH!
NOOOOOOOOO!
GOOD JOB, BIGHEAD!

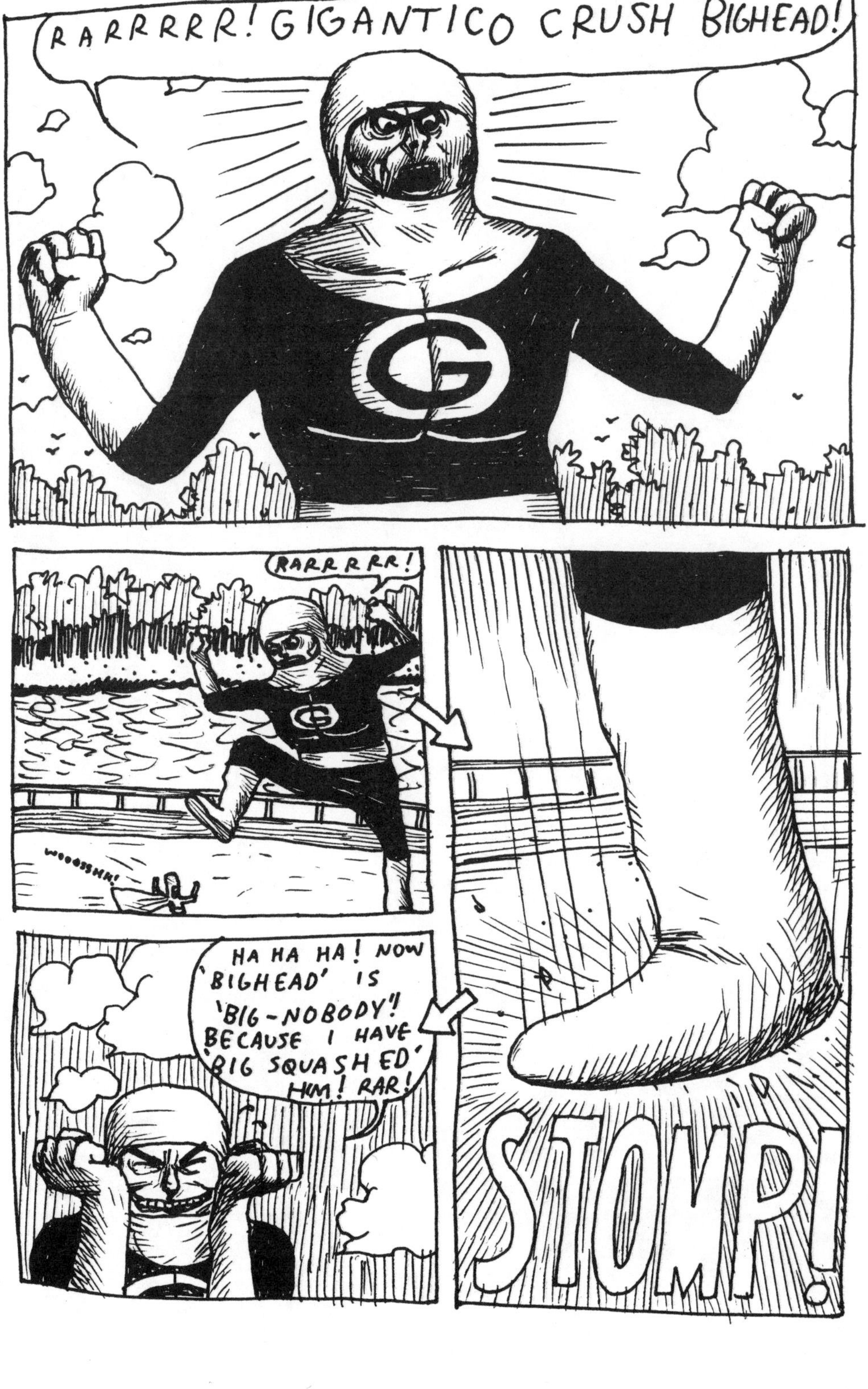
RARRRRRR! GIGANTICO CRUSH BIGHEAD!
RARRRRR!
WOOOSSHH!
STOMP!
HA HA HA! NOW 'BIGHEAD' IS 'BIG-NOBODY'! BECAUSE I HAVE 'BIG SQUASHED' HIM! RAR!

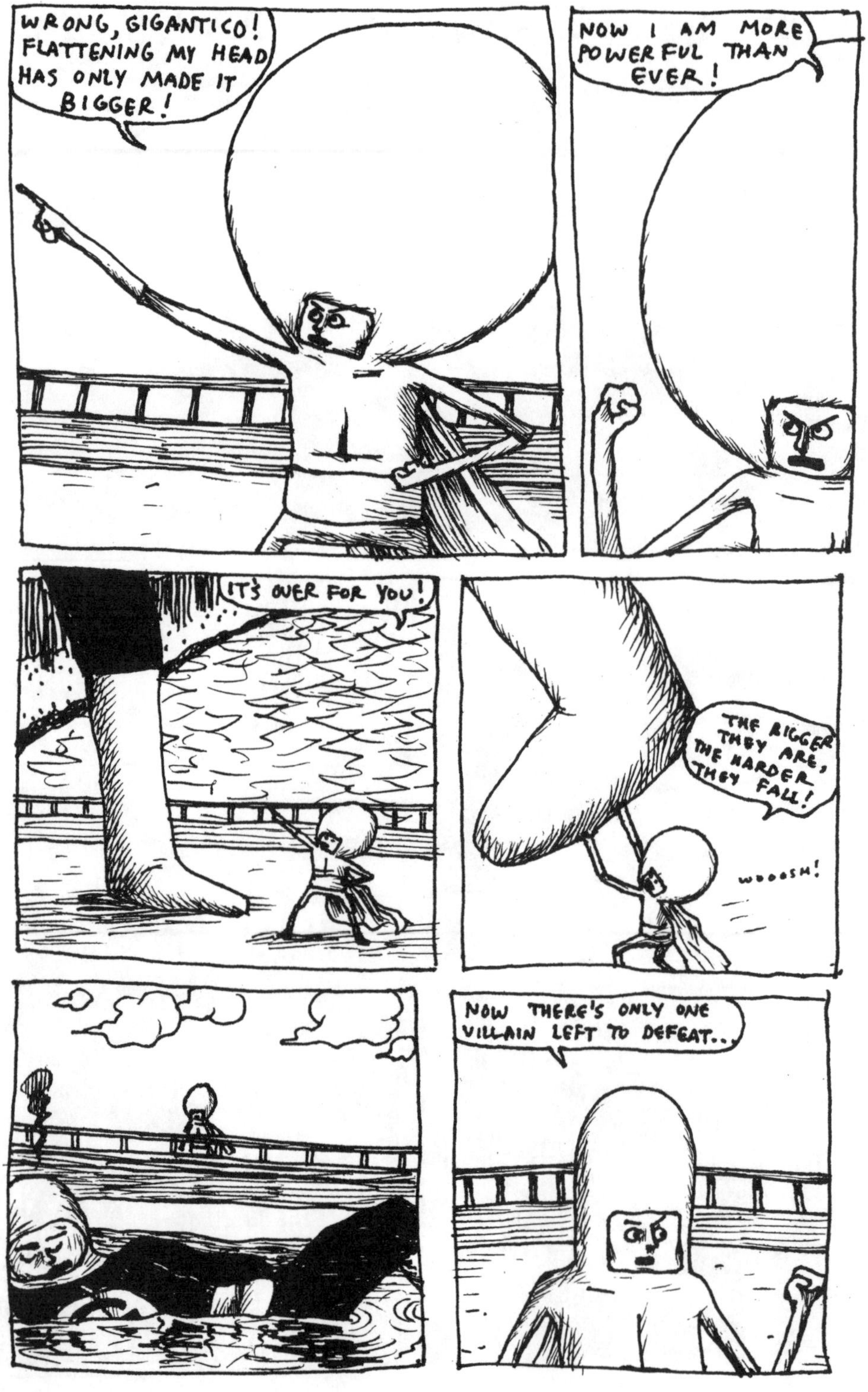
WRONG, GIGANTICO! FLATTENING MY HEAD HAS ONLY MADE IT BIGGER!
NOW I AM MORE POWERFUL THAN EVER!
IT'S OVER FOR YOU!
THE BIGGER THEY ARE, THE HARDER THEY FALL!
WOOOSH!
NOW THERE'S ONLY ONE VILLAIN LEFT TO DEFEAT..

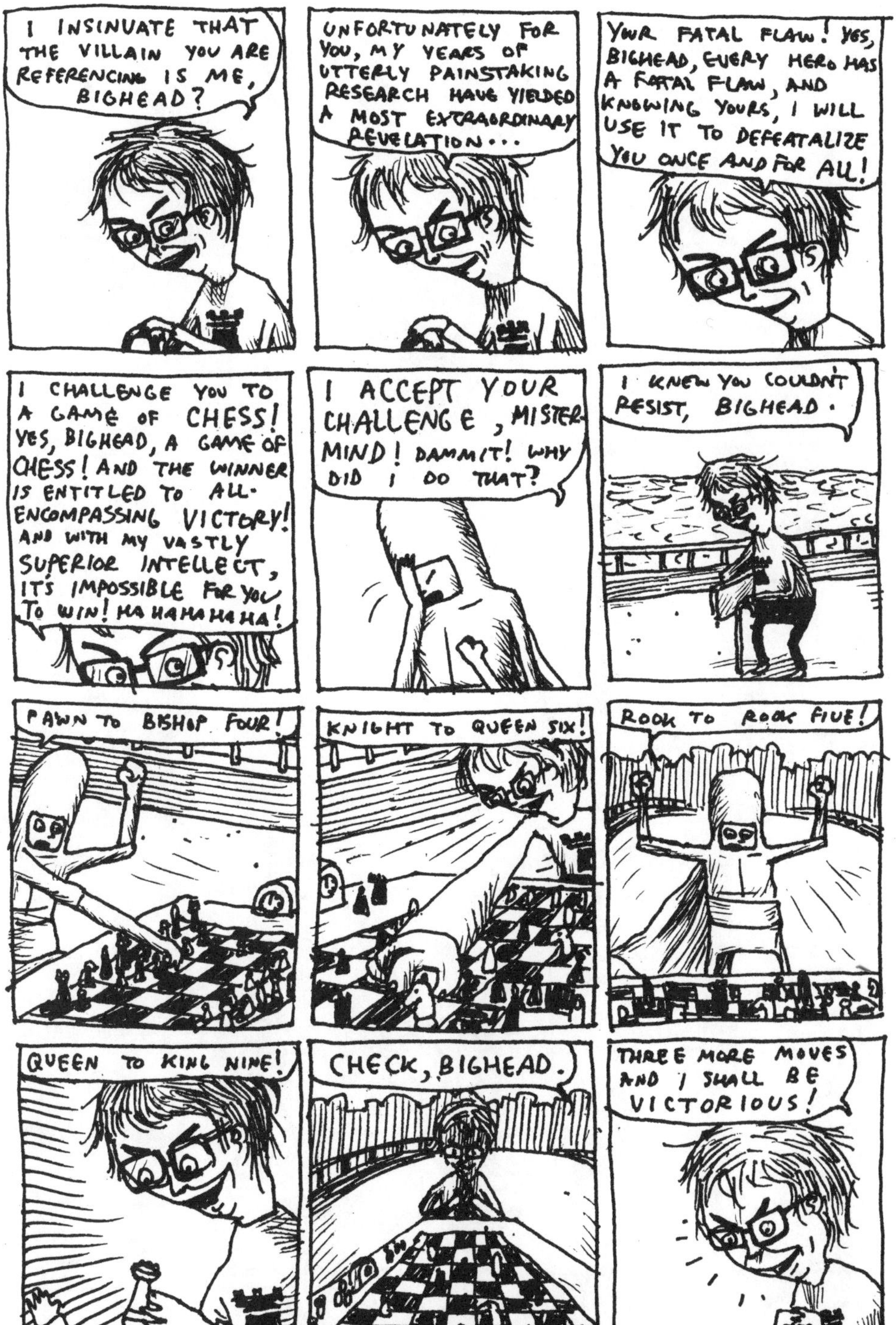
I INSINUATE THAT THE VILLAIN YOU ARE REFERENCING IS ME, BIGHEAD?
UNFORTUNATELY FOR YOU, MY YEARS OF UTTERLY PAINSTAKING RESEARCH HAVE YIELDED A MOST EXTRAORDINARY REVELATION...
YOUR FATAL FLAW! YES, BIGHEAD, EVERY HERO HAS A FATAL FLAW, AND KNOWING YOURS, I WILL USE IT TO DEFEATALIZE YOU ONCE AND FOR ALL!
I CHALLENGE YOU TO A GAME OF CHESS! YES, BIGHEAD, A GAME OF CHESS! AND THE WINNER IS ENTITLED TO ALL-ENCOMPASSING VICTORY! AND WITH MY VASTLY SUPERIOR INTELLECT, IT'S IMPOSSIBLE FOR YOU TO WIN! HAHAHAHAHAHA!
I ACCEPT YOUR CHALLENGE, MISTER-MIND! DAMMIT! WHY DID I DO THAT?
I KNEW YOU COULDN'T RESIST, BIGHEAD.
PAWN TO BISHOP FOUR!
KNIGHT TO QUEEN SIX!
ROOK TO ROOK FIVE!
QUEEN TO KING NINE!
CHECK, BIGHEAD.
THREE MORE MOVES AND I SHALL BE VICTORIOUS!

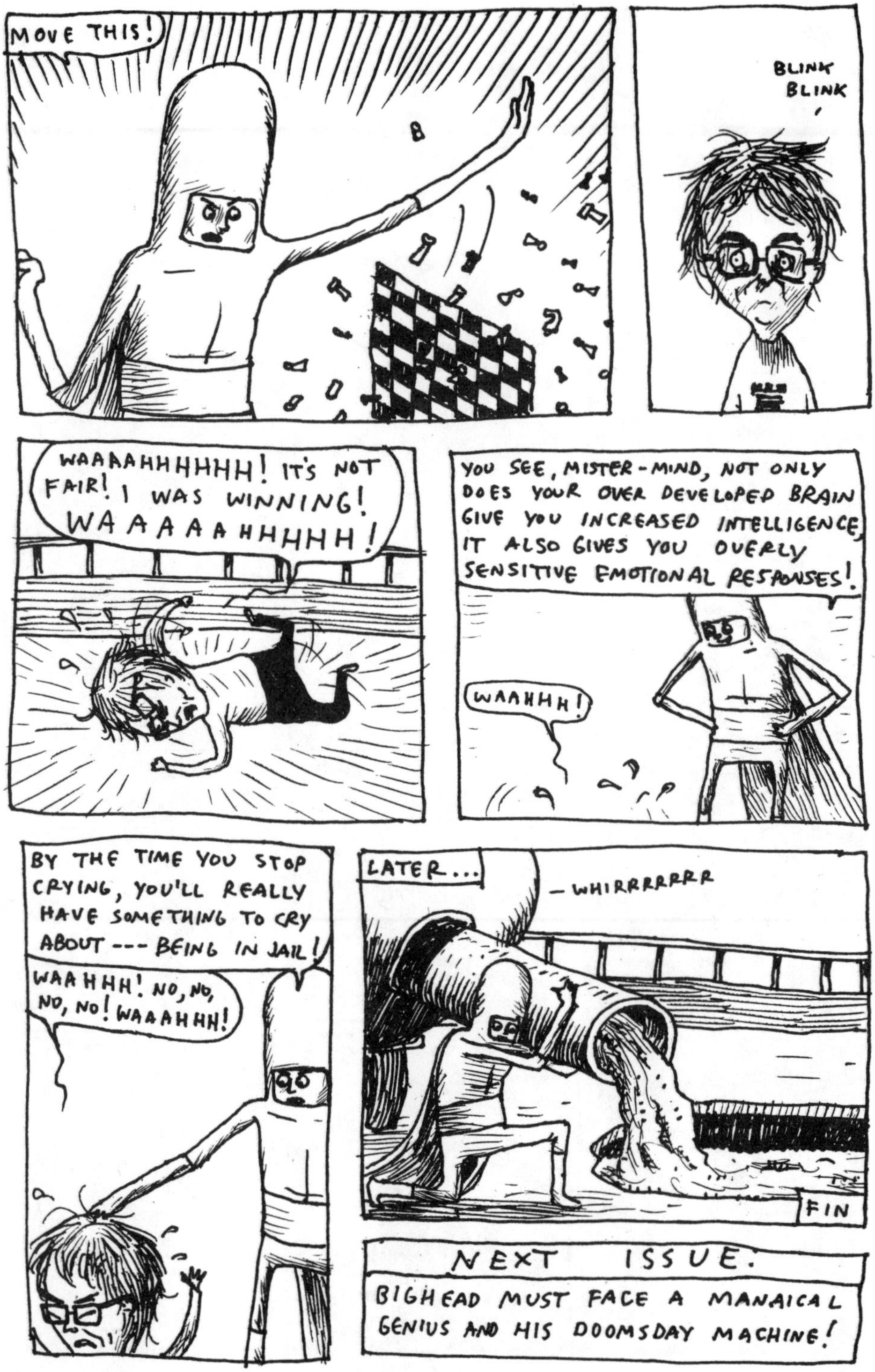
MOVE THIS!
BLINK BLINK
WAAAAHHHHHH! IT'S NOT FAIR! I WAS WINNING! WAAAAAHHHHH!
YOU SEE, MISTER-MIND, NOT ONLY DOES YOUR OVER DEVELOPED BRAIN GIVE YOU INCREASED INTELLIGENCE, IT ALSO GIVES YOU OVERLY SENSITIVE EMOTIONAL RESPONSES!
WAAHHH!
BY THE TIME YOU STOP CRYING, YOU'LL REALLY HAVE SOMETHING TO CRY ABOUT --- BEING IN JAIL!
WAAHHH! NO, NO, NO, NO! WAAAHHH!
LATER...
-WHIRRRRRRR
FIN
NEXT ISSUE:
BIGHEAD MUST FACE A MANAICAL GENIUS AND HIS DOOMSDAY MACHINE!

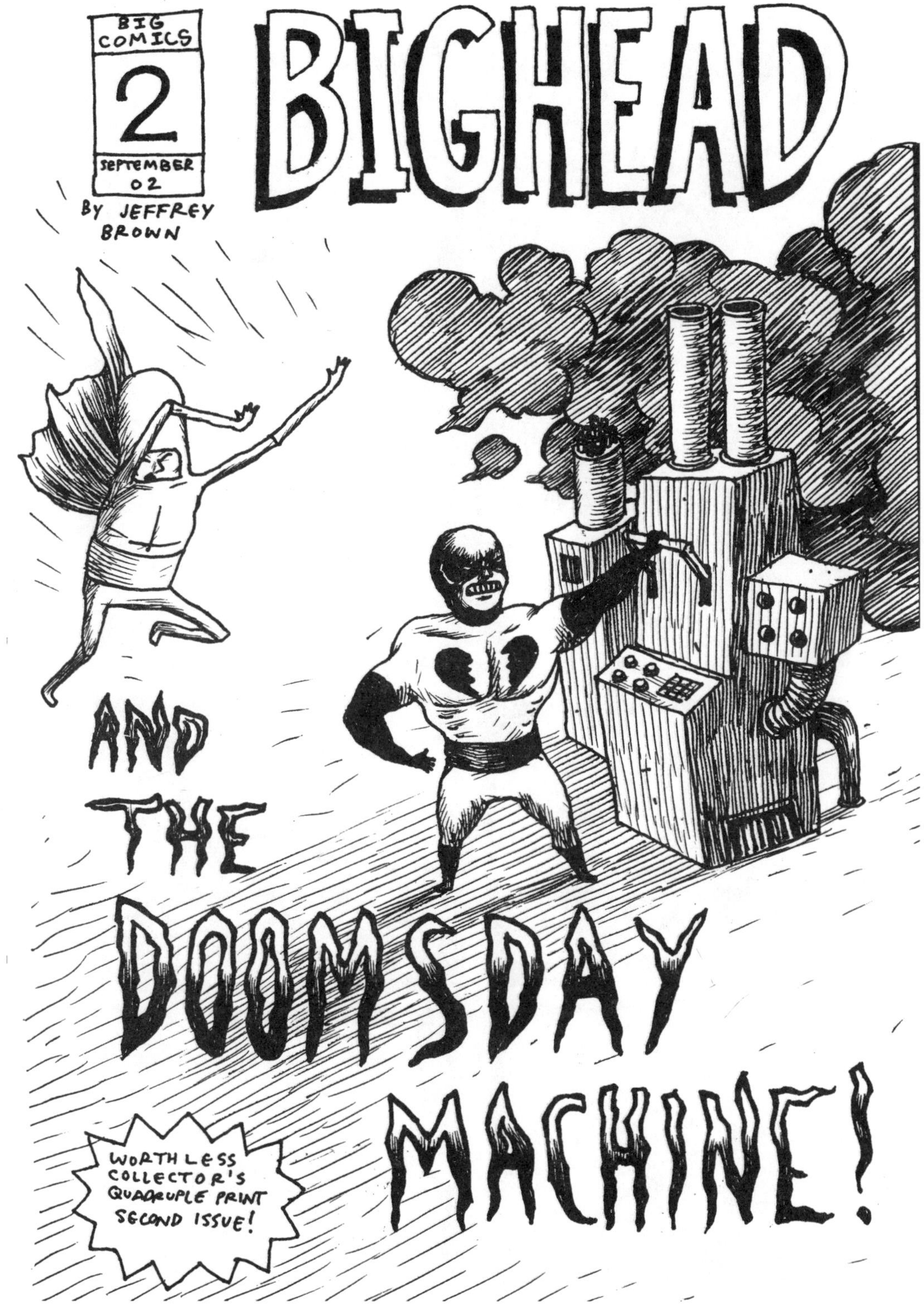
BIG COMICS
2
SEPTEMBER 02
BY JEFFREY BROWN
BIGHEAD
AND THE DOOMSDAY MACHINE!
WORTHLESS COLLECTOR'S QUADRUPLE PRINT SECOND ISSUE!

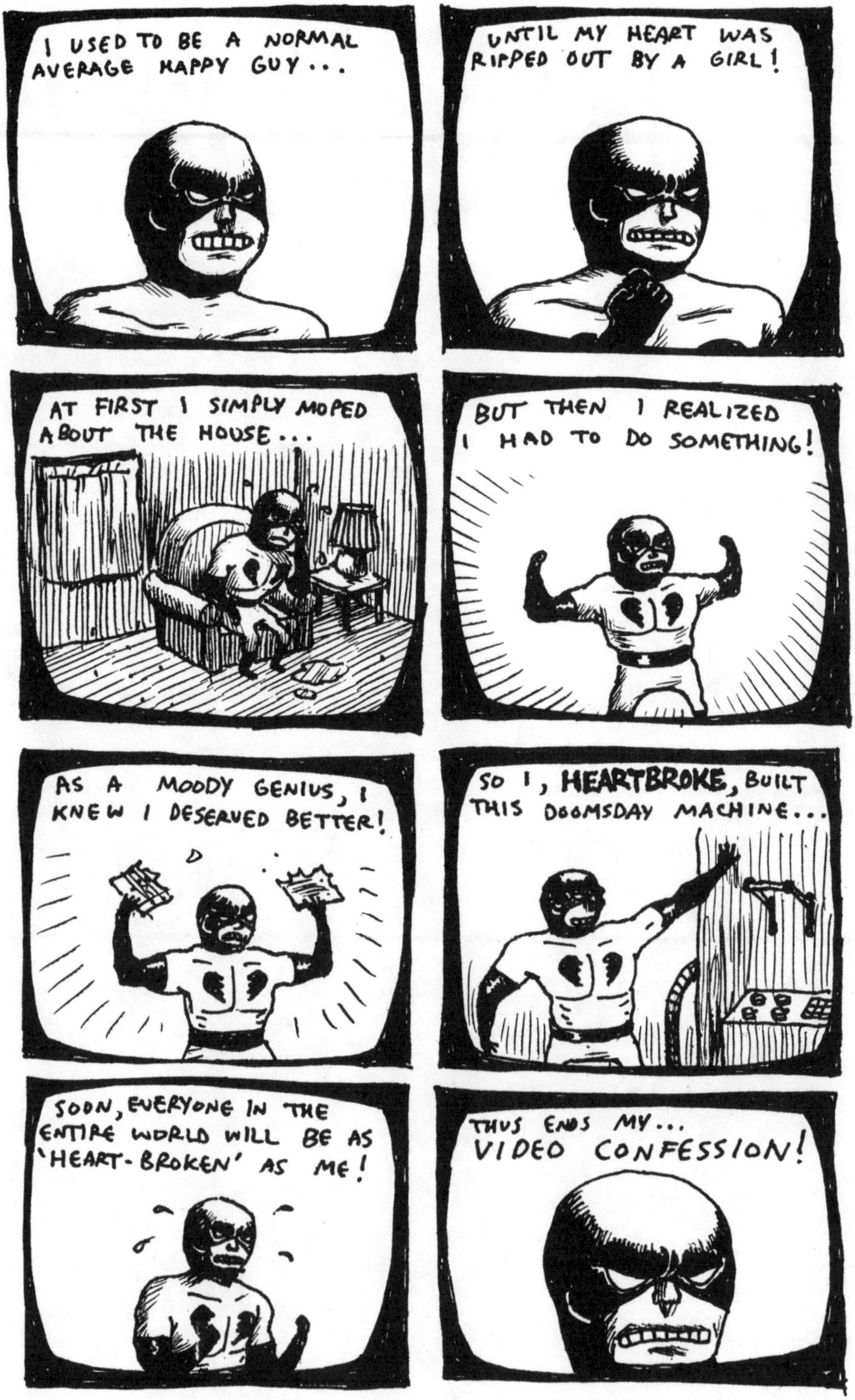
I USED TO BE A NORMAL AVERAGE HAPPY GUY...
UNTIL MY HEART WAS RIPPED OUT BY A GIRL!
AT FIRST I SIMPLY MOPED ABOUT THE HOUSE...
BUT THEN I REALIZED I HAD TO DO SOMETHING!
AS A MOODY GENIUS, I KNEW I DESERVED BETTER!
SO I, HEARTBROKE, BUILT THIS DOOMSDAY MACHINE...
SOON, EVERYONE IN THE ENTIRE WORLD WILL BE AS 'HEART-BROKEN' AS ME!
THUS ENDS MY... VIDEO CONFESSION!

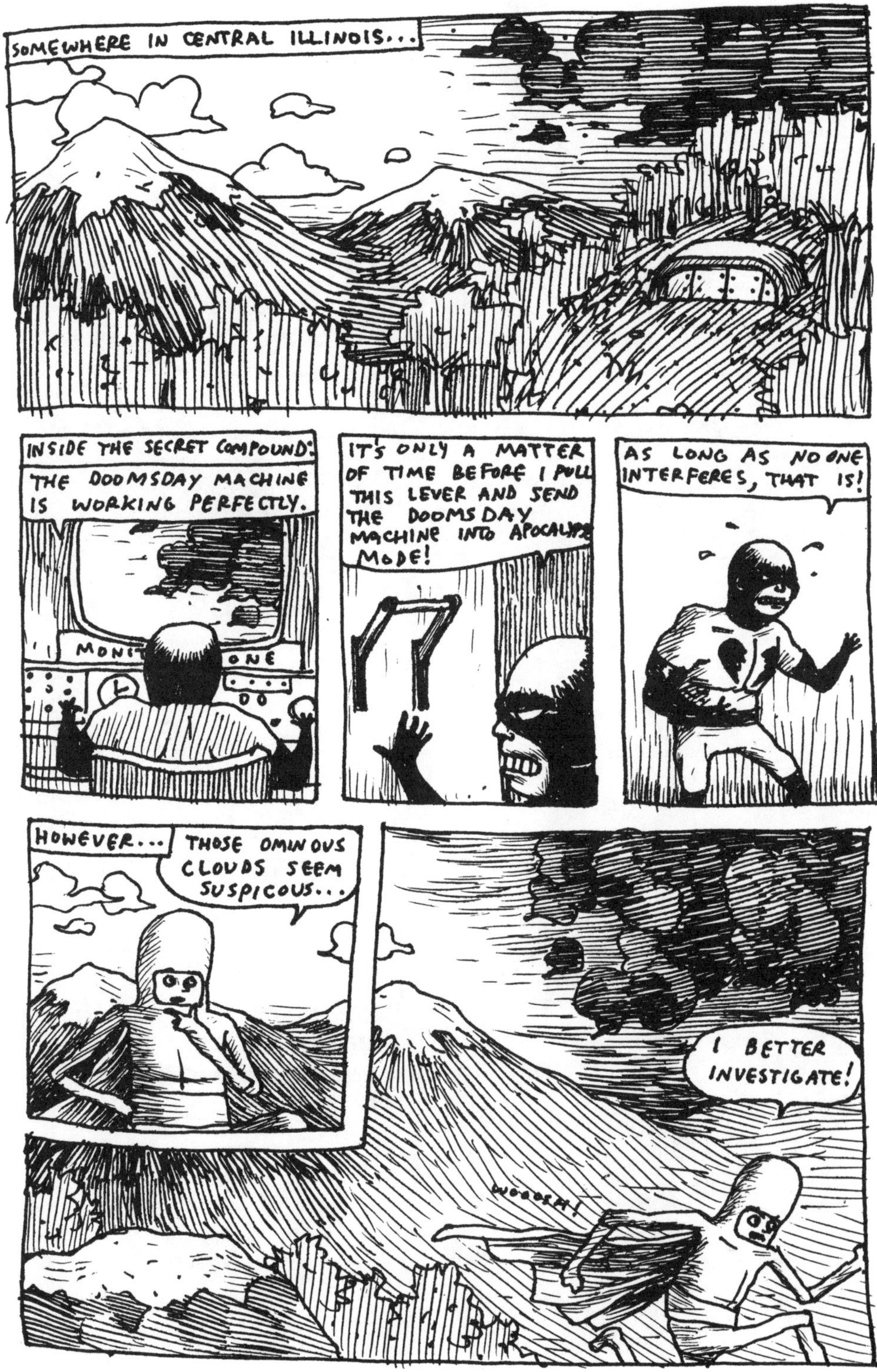
SOMEWHERE IN CENTRAL ILLINOIS...
INSIDE THE SECRET COMPOUND:
THE DOOMSDAY MACHINE IS WORKING PERFECTLY.
IT'S ONLY A MATTER OF TIME BEFORE I PULL THIS LEVER AND SEND THE DOOMSDAY MACHINE INTO APOCALYPSE MODE!
AS LONG AS NO ONE INTERFERES, THAT IS!
HOWEVER...
THOSE OMINOUS CLOUDS SEEM SUSPICOUS...
I BETTER INVESTIGATE!
WOOOSH!

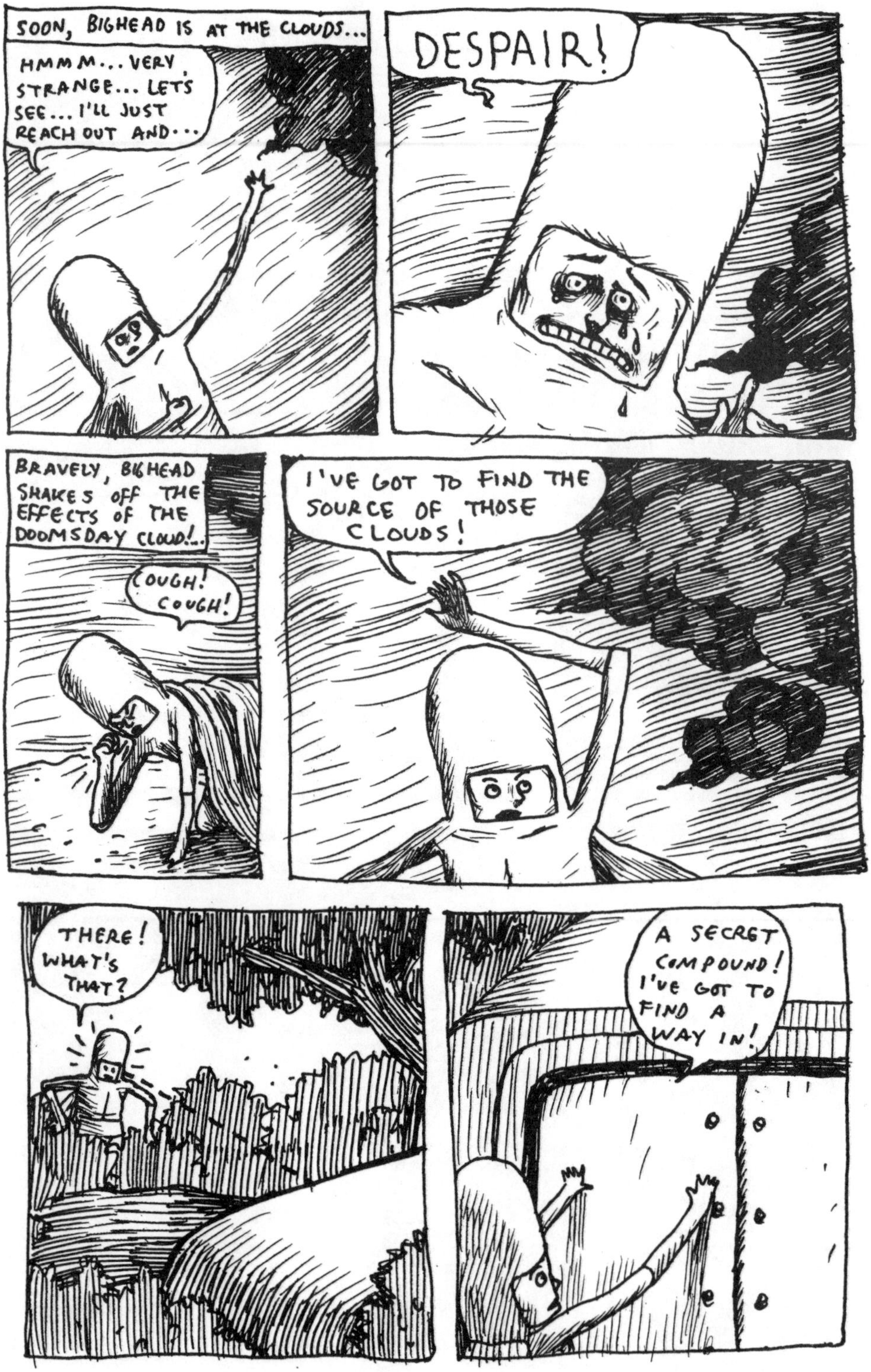
SOON, BIGHEAD IS AT THE CLOUDS...
HMMM... VERY STRANGE... LET'S SEE... I'LL JUST REACH OUT AND...
DESPAIR!
BRAVELY, BIGHEAD SHAKES OFF THE EFFECTS OF THE DOOMSDAY CLOUD!..
COUGH! COUGH!
I'VE GOT TO FIND THE SOURCE OF THOSE CLOUDS!
THERE! WHAT'S THAT?
A SECRET COMPOUND! I'VE GOT TO FIND A WAY IN!

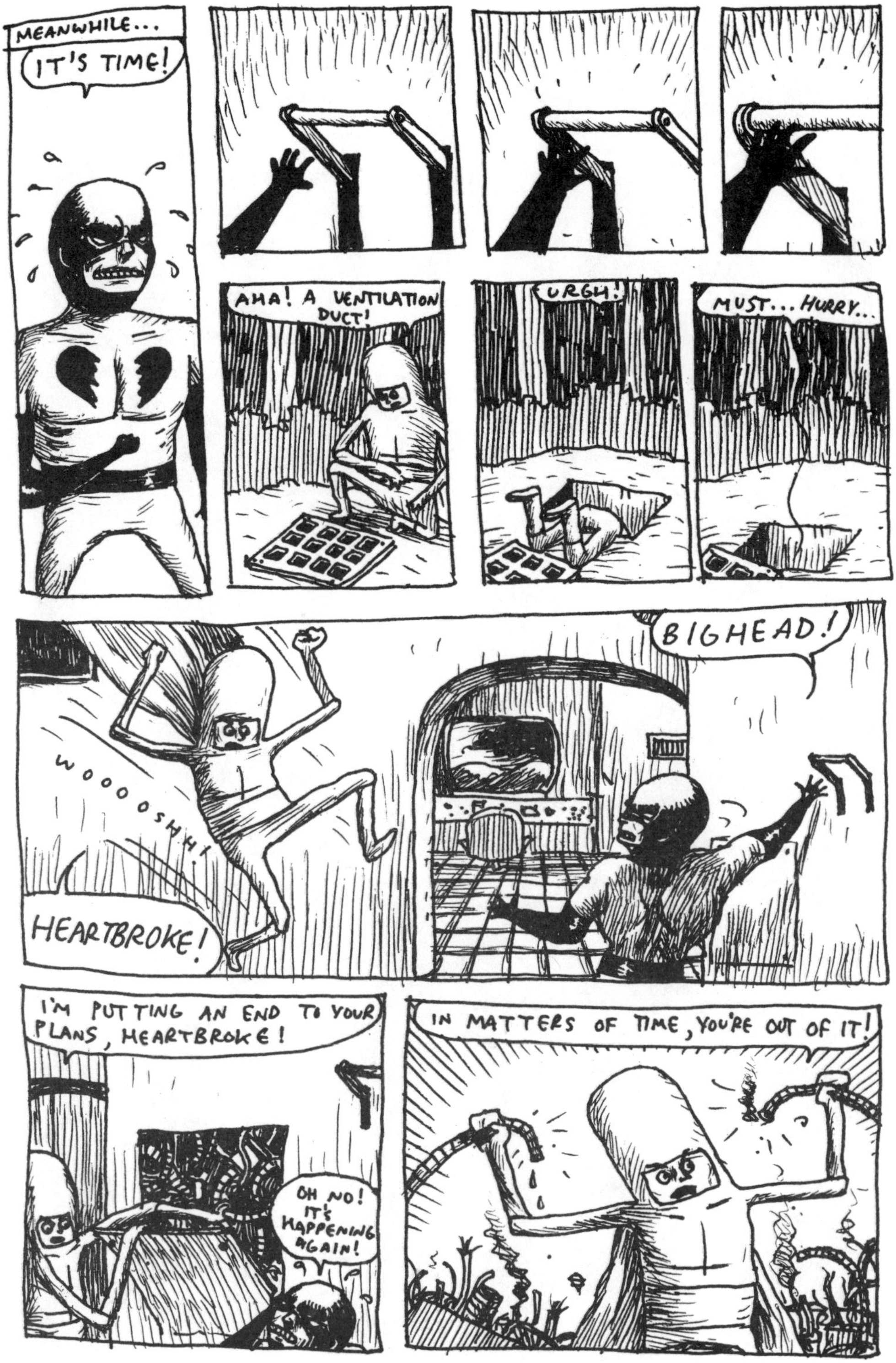
MEANWHILE...
IT'S TIME!
AHA! A VENTILATION DUCT!
URGH!
MUST... HURRY...
WOOOOOSHH!
HEARTBROKE!
BIGHEAD!
I'M PUTTING AN END TO YOUR PLANS, HEARTBROKE!
OH NO! IT'S HAPPENING AGAIN!
IN MATTERS OF TIME, YOU'RE OUT OF IT!

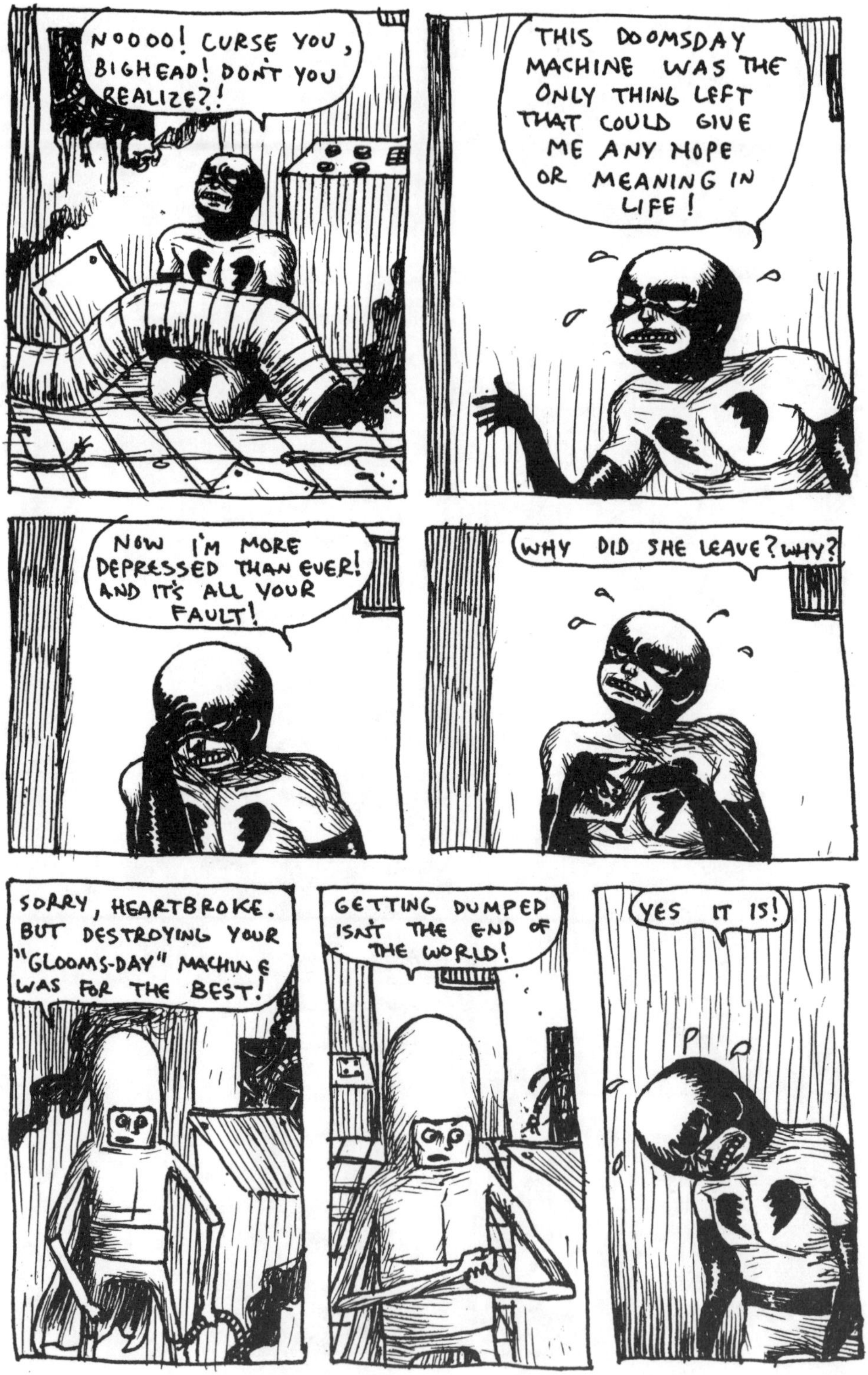
NOOOO! CURSE YOU, BIGHEAD! DON'T YOU REALIZE?!
THIS DOOMSDAY MACHINE WAS THE ONLY THING LEFT THAT COULD GIVE ME ANY HOPE OR MEANING IN LIFE!
NOW I'M MORE DEPRESSED THAN EVER! AND IT'S ALL YOUR FAULT!
WHY DID SHE LEAVE? WHY?
SORRY, HEARTBROKE. BUT DESTROYING YOUR "GLOOMS-DAY" MACHINE WAS FOR THE BEST!
GETTING DUMPED ISN'T THE END OF THE WORLD!
YES IT IS!

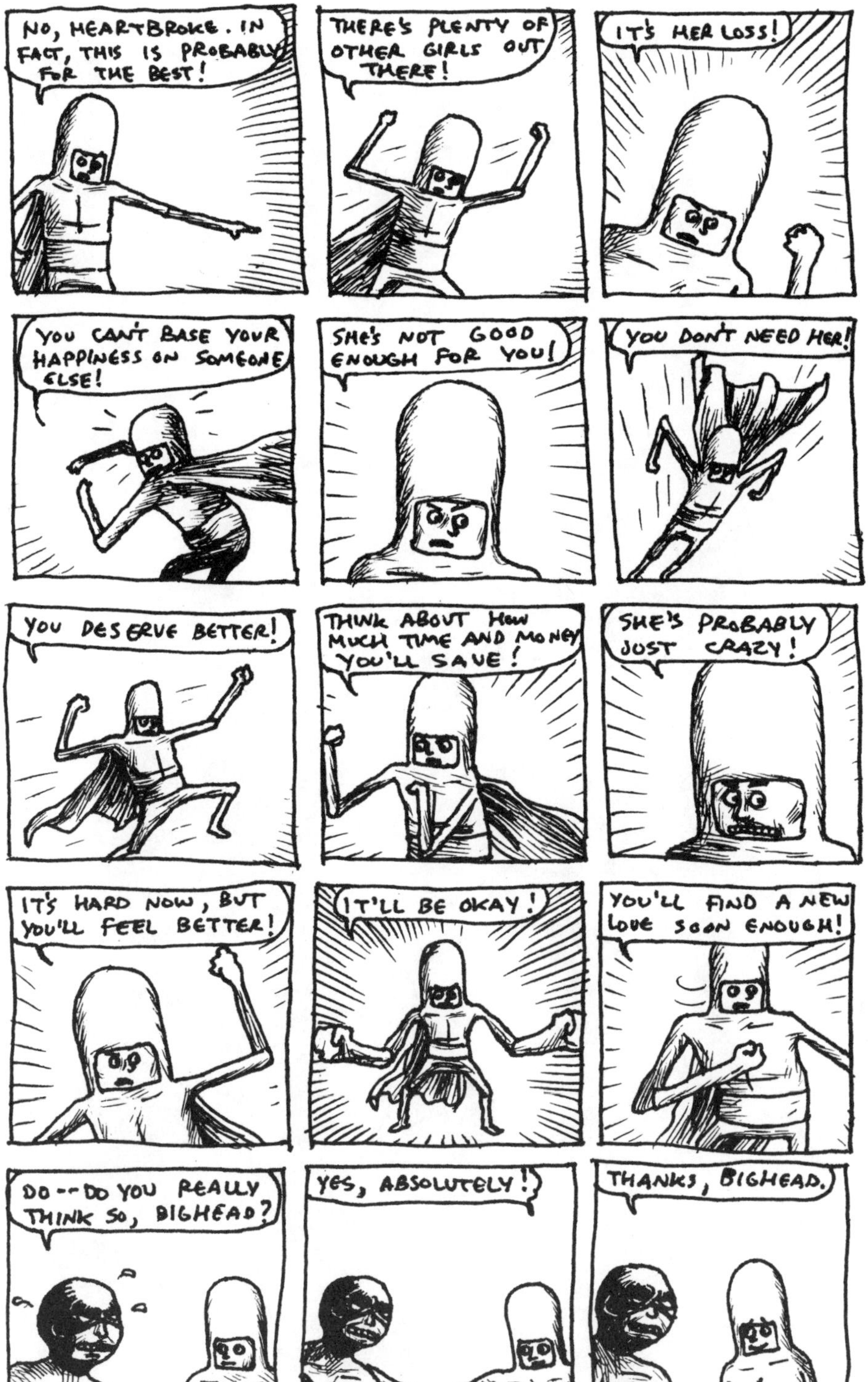
NO, HEARTBROKE. IN FACT, THIS IS PROBABLY FOR THE BEST!
THERE'S PLENTY OF OTHER GIRLS OUT THERE!
IT'S HER LOSS!
YOU CAN'T BASE YOUR HAPPINESS ON SOMEONE ELSE!
SHE'S NOT GOOD ENOUGH FOR YOU!
YOU DON'T NEED HER!
YOU DESERVE BETTER!
THINK ABOUT HOW MUCH TIME AND MONEY YOU'LL SAVE!
SHE'S PROBABLY JUST CRAZY!
IT'S HARD NOW, BUT YOU'LL FEEL BETTER!
IT'LL BE OKAY!
YOU'LL FIND A NEW LOVE SOON ENOUGH!
DO--DO YOU REALLY THINK SO, BIGHEAD?
YES, ABSOLUTELY!
THANKS, BIGHEAD.
FIN

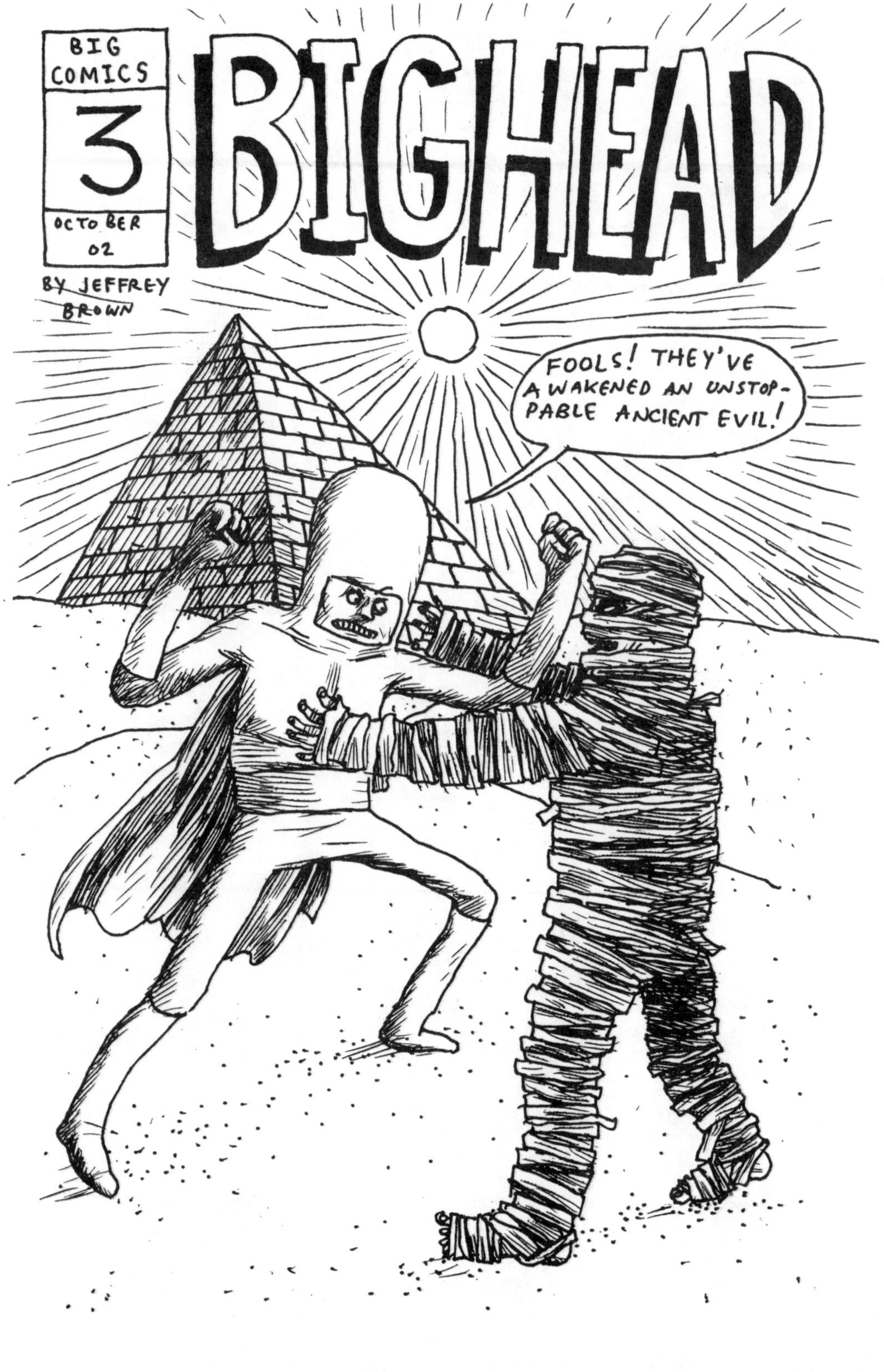
BIG COMICS
3
OCTOBER 02
BIGHEAD
BY JEFFREY BROWN
FOOLS! THEY'VE AWAKENED AN UNSTOP-PABLE ANCIENT EVIL!

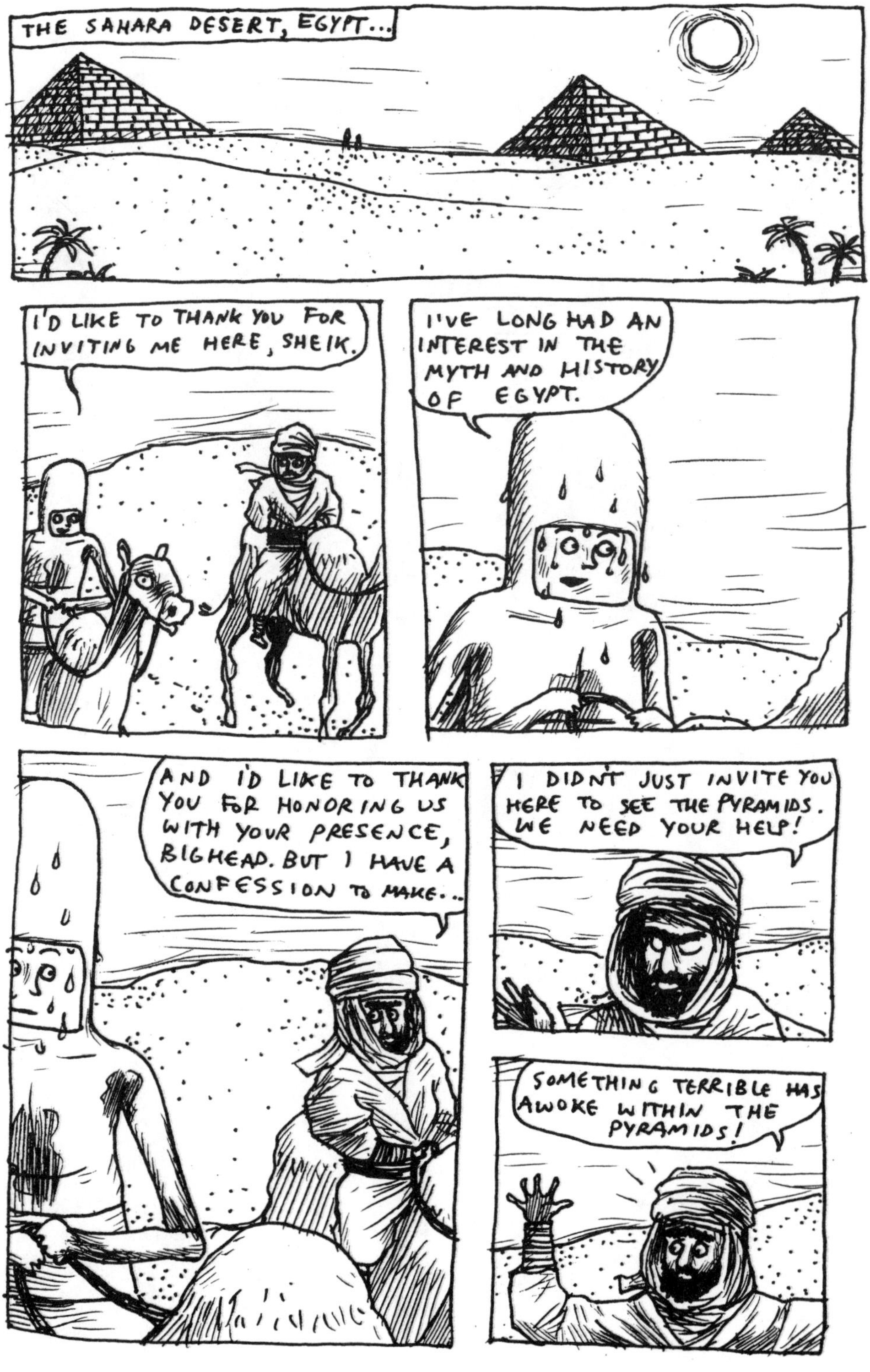
THE SAHARA DESERT, EGYPT...
I'D LIKE TO THANK YOU FOR INVITING ME HERE, SHEIK.
I'VE LONG HAD AN INTEREST IN THE MYTH AND HISTORY OF EGYPT.
AND I'D LIKE TO THANK YOU FOR HONORING US WITH YOUR PRESENCE, BIGHEAD. BUT I HAVE A CONFESSION TO MAKE...
I DIDN'T JUST INVITE YOU HERE TO SEE THE PYRAMIDS. WE NEED YOUR HELP!
SOMETHING TERRIBLE HAS AWOKE WITHIN THE PYRAMIDS!

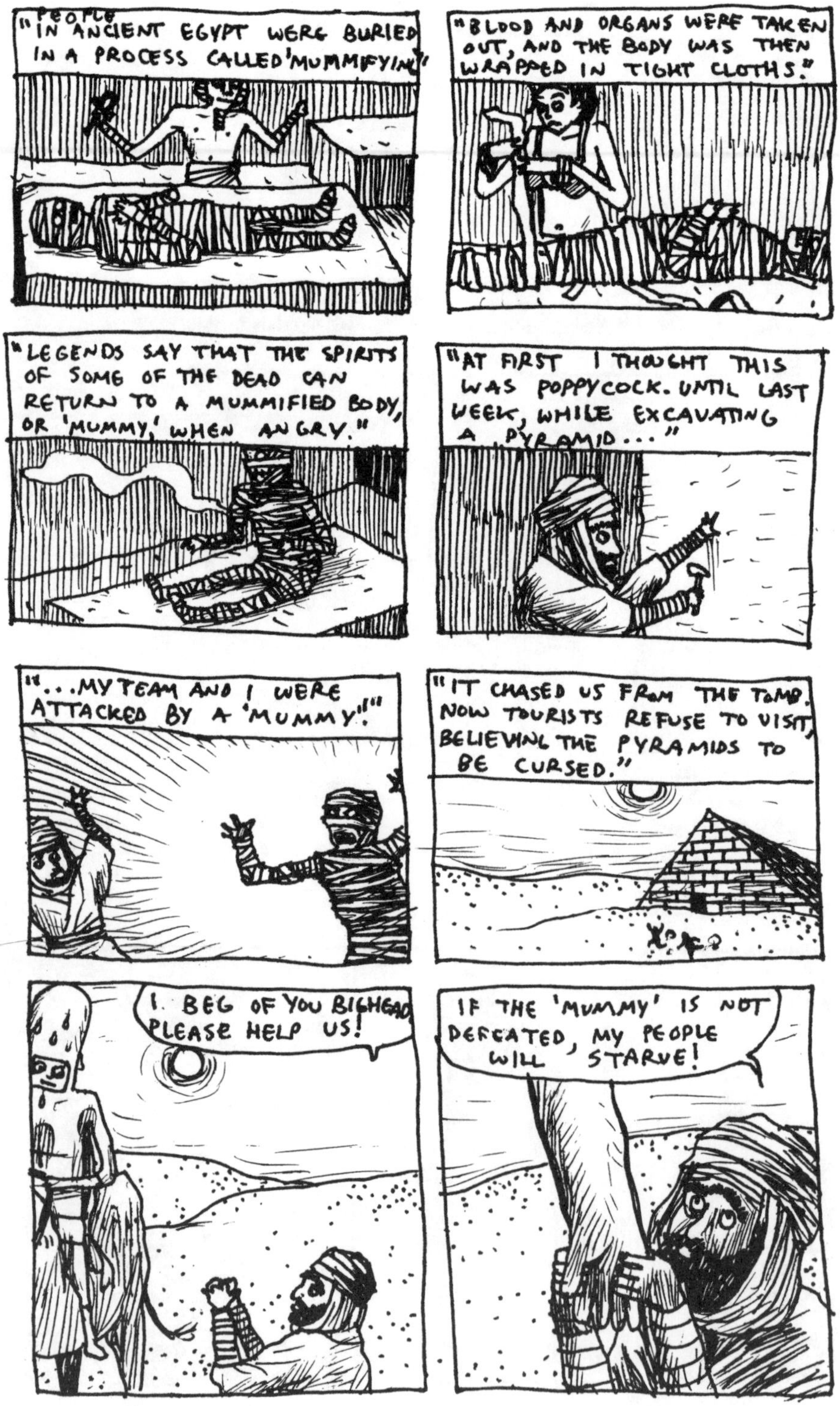
"PEOPLE IN ANCIENT EGYPT WERE BURIED IN A PROCESS CALLED 'MUMMIFYIN'"
"BLOOD AND ORGANS WERE TAKEN OUT, AND THE BODY WAS THEN WRAPPED IN TIGHT CLOTHS."
"LEGENDS SAY THAT THE SPIRITS OF SOME OF THE DEAD CAN RETURN TO A MUMMIFIED BODY, OR 'MUMMY,' WHEN ANGRY."
"AT FIRST I THOUGHT THIS WAS POPPYCOCK. UNTIL LAST WEEK, WHILE EXCAVATING A PYRAMID..."
"...MY TEAM AND I WERE ATTACKED BY A 'MUMMY'!"
"IT CHASED US FROM THE TOMB. NOW TOURISTS REFUSE TO VISIT, BELIEVING THE PYRAMIDS TO BE CURSED."
I BEG OF YOU BIGHEAD PLEASE HELP US!
IF THE 'MUMMY' IS NOT DEFEATED, MY PEOPLE WILL STARVE!

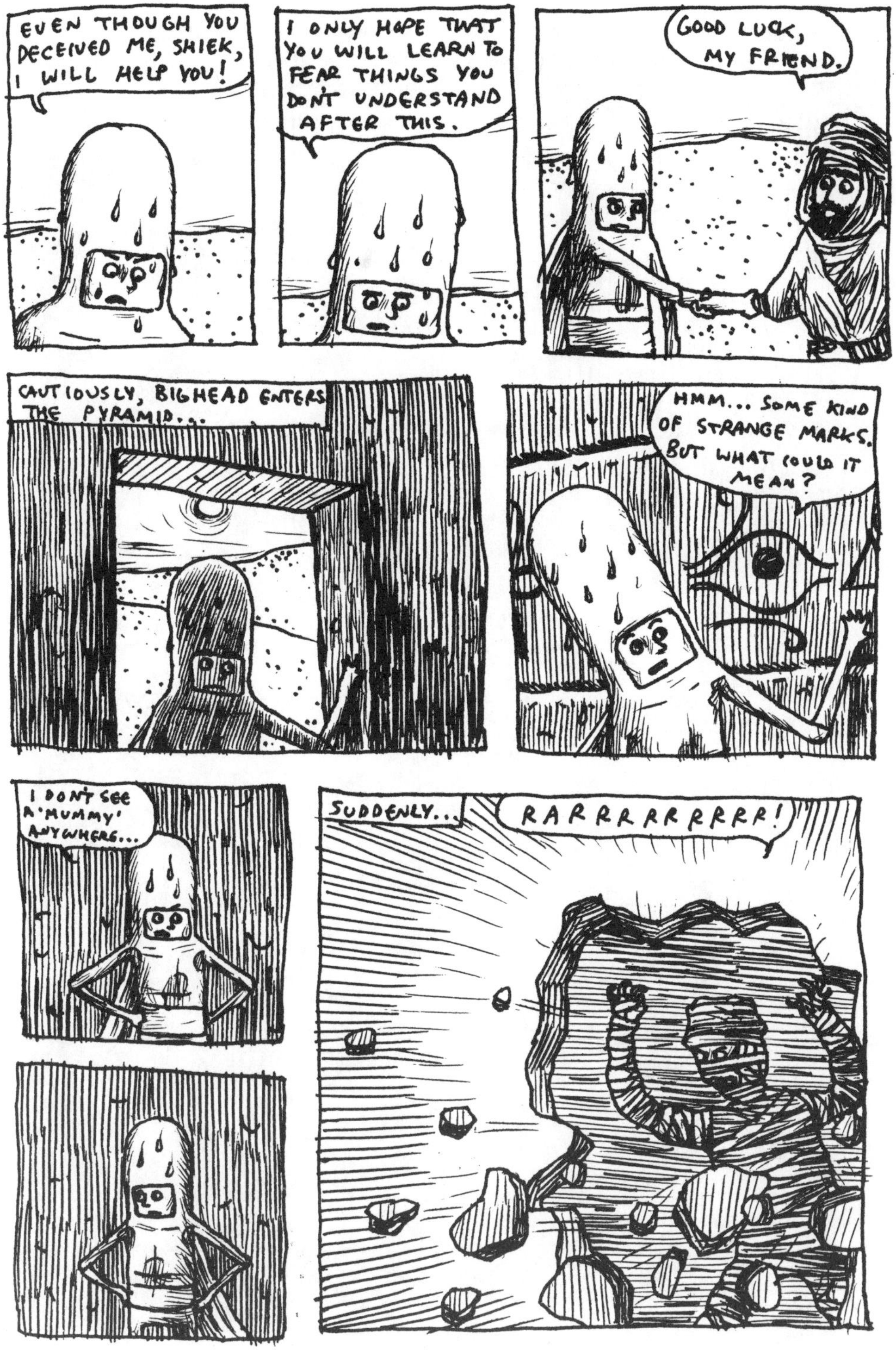

EVEN THOUGH YOU DECEIVED ME, SHIEK, I WILL HELP YOU!
I ONLY HOPE THAT YOU WILL LEARN TO FEAR THINGS YOU DON'T UNDERSTAND AFTER THIS.
GOOD LUCK, MY FRIEND.
CAUTIOUSLY, BIGHEAD ENTERS THE PYRAMID...
HMM... SOME KIND OF STRANGE MARKS. BUT WHAT COULD IT MEAN?
I DON'T SEE A 'MUMMY' ANYWHERE...
SUDDENLY...
RARRRRRRRRRR!

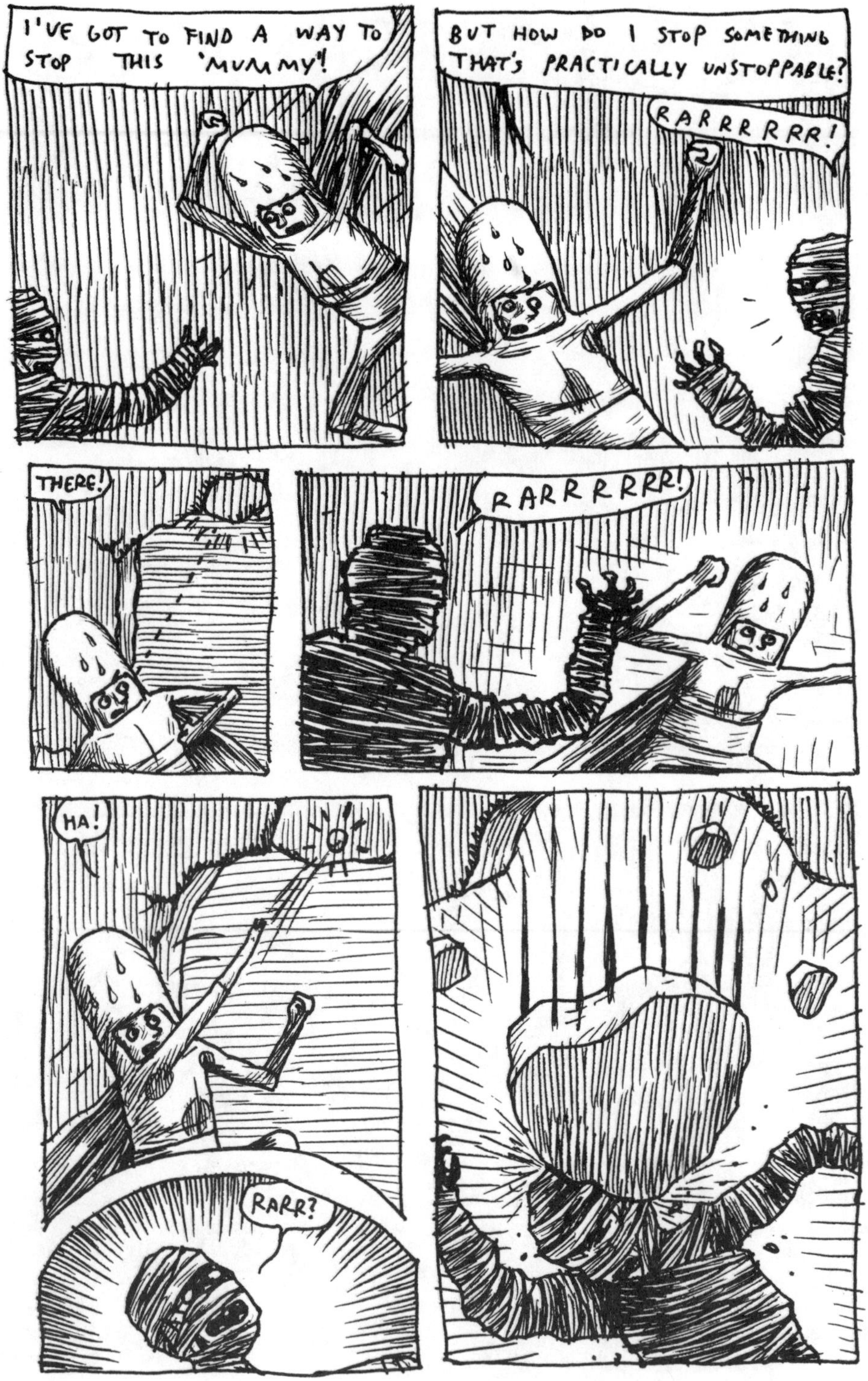
I'VE GOT TO FIND A WAY TO STOP THIS 'MUMMY'!
BUT HOW DO I STOP SOMETHING THAT'S PRACTICALLY UNSTOPPABLE?
RARRRRRR!
THERE!
RARRRRRR!
HA!
RARR?

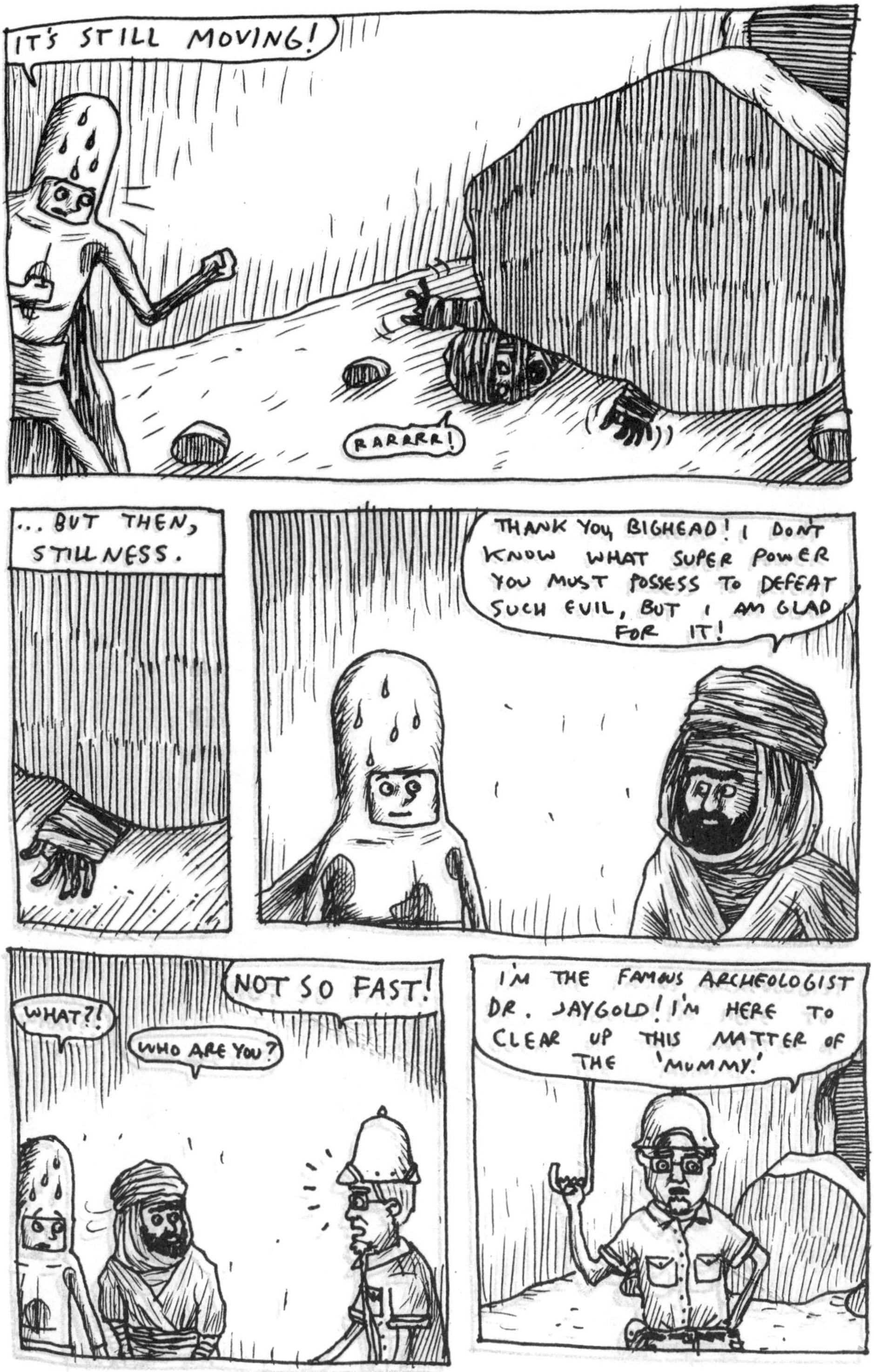
IT'S STILL MOVING!
RARRRR!
... BUT THEN, STILLNESS.
THANK YOU, BIGHEAD! I DONT KNOW WHAT SUPER POWER YOU MUST POSSESS TO DEFEAT SUCH EVIL, BUT I AM GLAD FOR IT!
NOT SO FAST!
WHAT?!
WHO ARE YOU?
I'M THE FAMOUS ARCHEOLOGIST DR. JAYGOLD! I'M HERE TO CLEAR UP THIS MATTER OF THE 'MUMMY.'

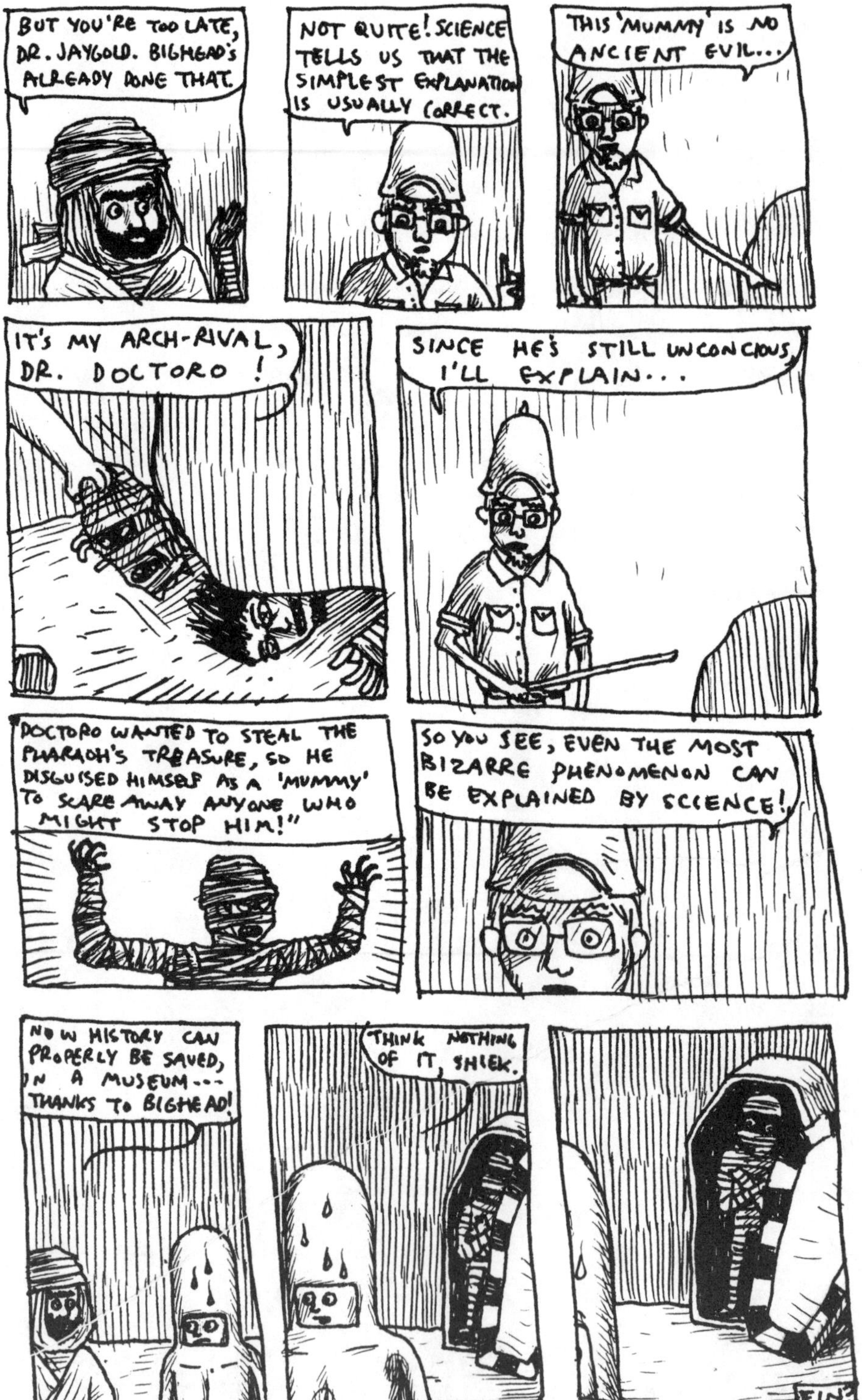
BUT YOU'RE TOO LATE, DR. JAYGOLD. BIGHEAD'S ALREADY DONE THAT.
NOT QUITE! SCIENCE TELLS US THAT THE SIMPLEST EXPLANATION IS USUALLY CORRECT.
THIS 'MUMMY' IS NO ANCIENT EVIL...
IT'S MY ARCH-RIVAL, DR. DOCTORO!
SINCE HE'S STILL UNCONCIOUS, I'LL EXPLAIN...
DOCTORO WANTED TO STEAL THE PHARAOH'S TREASURE, SO HE DISGUISED HIMSELF AS A 'MUMMY' TO SCARE AWAY ANYONE WHO MIGHT STOP HIM!"
SO YOU SEE, EVEN THE MOST BIZARRE PHENOMENON CAN BE EXPLAINED BY SCIENCE!
NOW HISTORY CAN PROPERLY BE SAVED, IN A MUSEUM... THANKS TO BIGHEAD!
THINK NOTHING OF IT, SHIEK.
FIN?

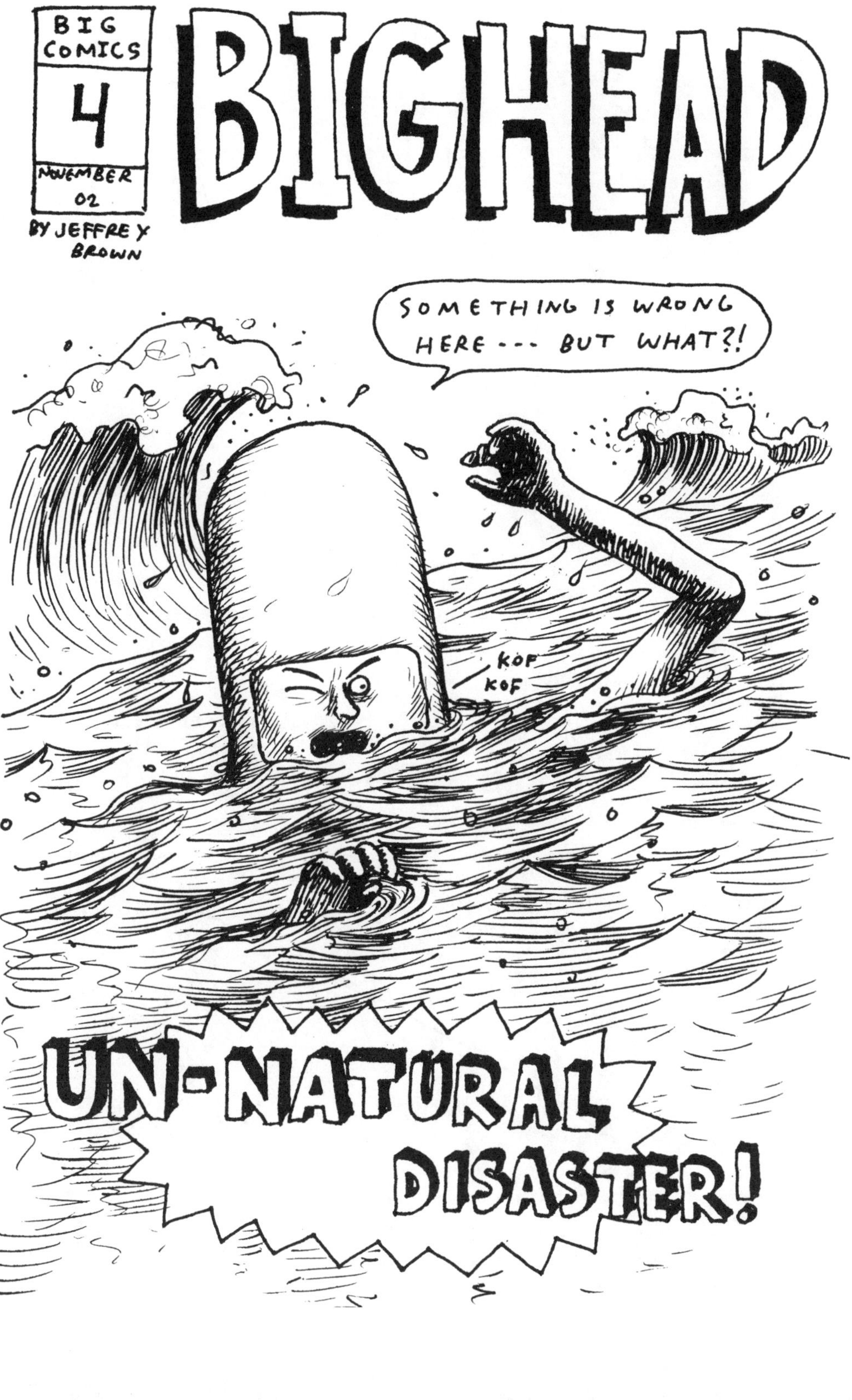
BIG COMICS
4
NOVEMBER 02
BY JEFFREY BROWN
BIGHEAD
SOMETHING IS WRONG HERE --- BUT WHAT?!
KOF KOF
UN-NATURAL DISASTER!

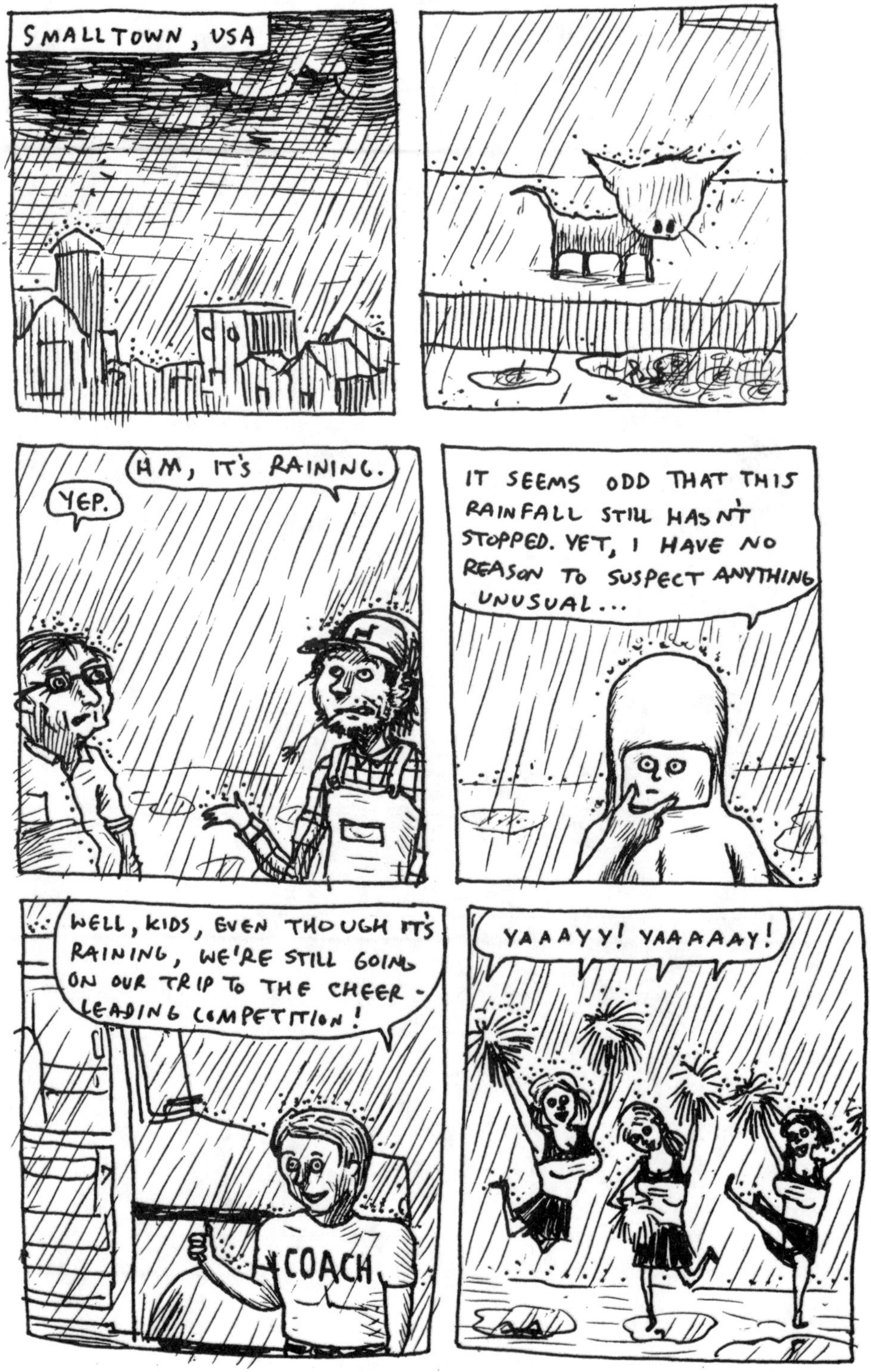
SMALLTOWN, USA
HM, IT'S RAINING.
YEP.
IT SEEMS ODD THAT THIS RAINFALL STILL HASN'T STOPPED. YET, I HAVE NO REASON TO SUSPECT ANYTHING UNUSUAL...
WELL, KIDS, EVEN THOUGH IT'S RAINING, WE'RE STILL GOING ON OUR TRIP TO THE CHEER-LEADING COMPETITION!
COACH
YAAAYY! YAAAAAY!

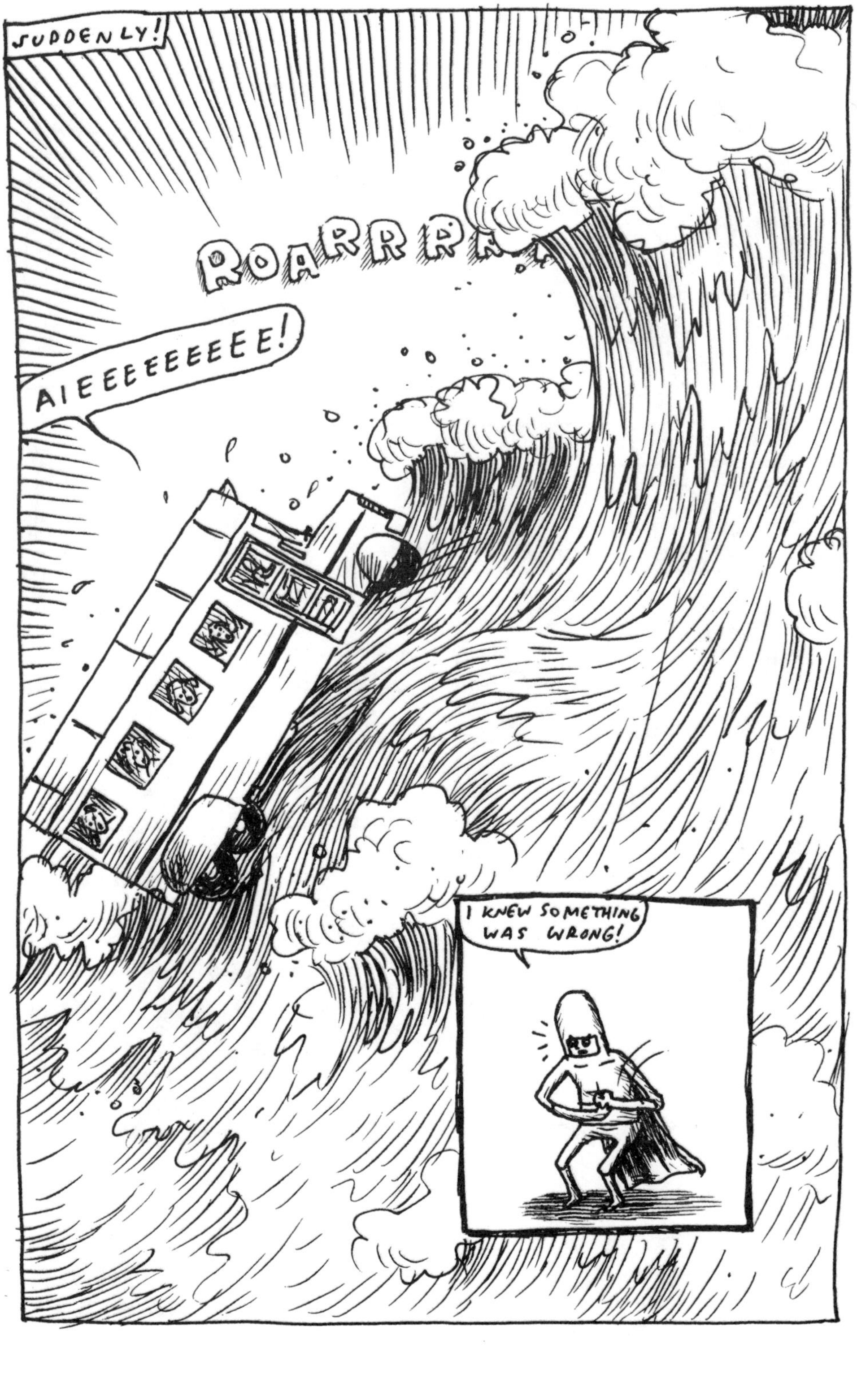
SUDDENLY!
ROARRRR
AIEEEEEEEEEE!
I KNEW SOMETHING WAS WRONG!

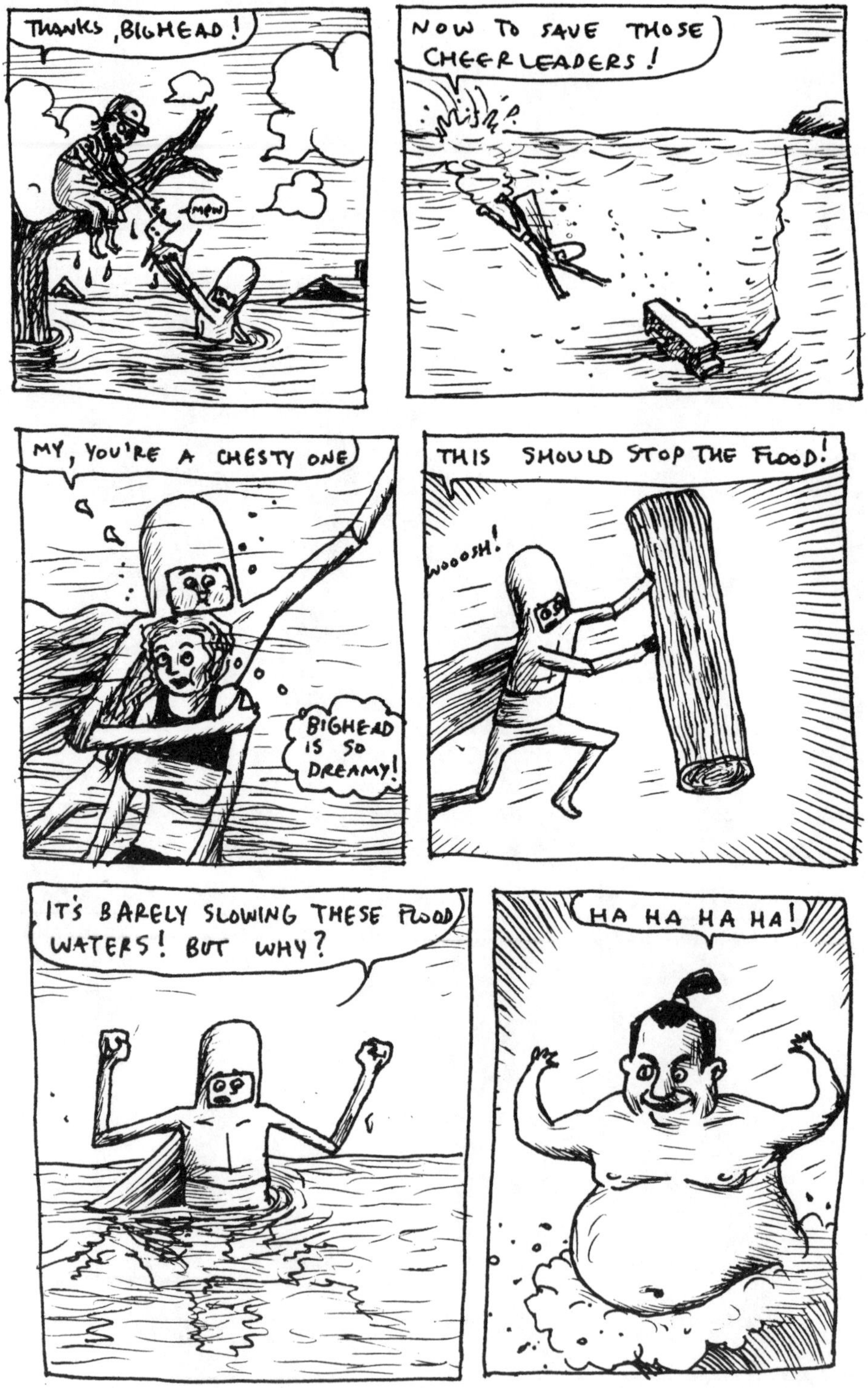
THANKS, BIGHEAD!
MEW
NOW TO SAVE THOSE CHEERLEADERS!
MY, YOU'RE A CHESTY ONE
BIGHEAD IS SO DREAMY!
THIS SHOULD STOP THE FLOOD!
WOOOSH!
IT'S BARELY SLOWING THESE FLOOD WATERS! BUT WHY?
HA HA HA HA!

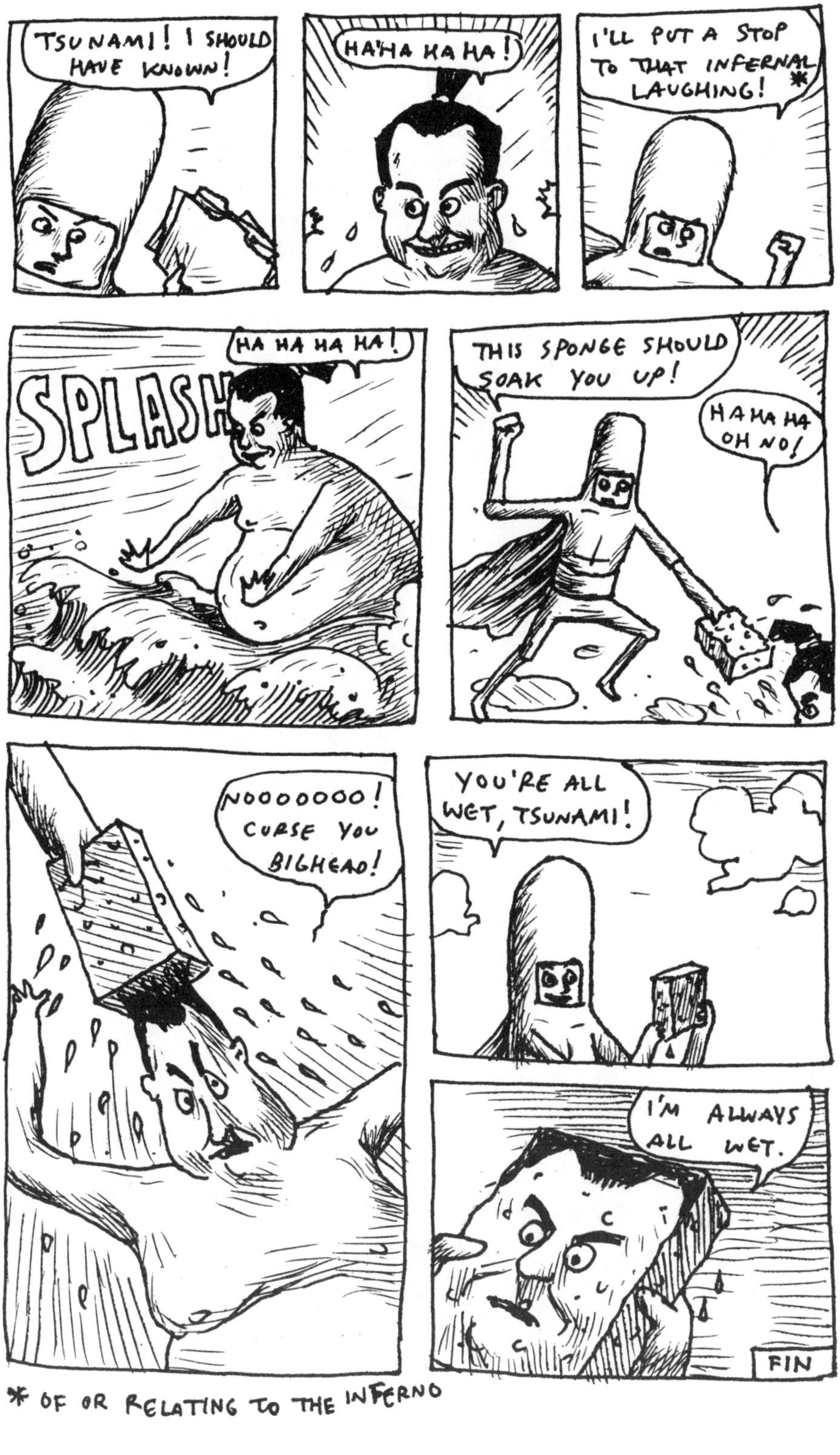
TSUNAMI! I SHOULD HAVE KNOWN!
HA'HA HA HA!
I'LL PUT A STOP TO THAT INFERNAL* LAUGHING!
HA HA HA HA!
SPLASH
THIS SPONGE SHOULD SOAK YOU UP!
HA HA HA OH NO!
NOOOOOOO! CURSE YOU BIGHEAD!
YOU'RE ALL WET, TSUNAMI!
I'M ALWAYS ALL WET.
FIN

* OF OR RELATING TO THE INFERNO

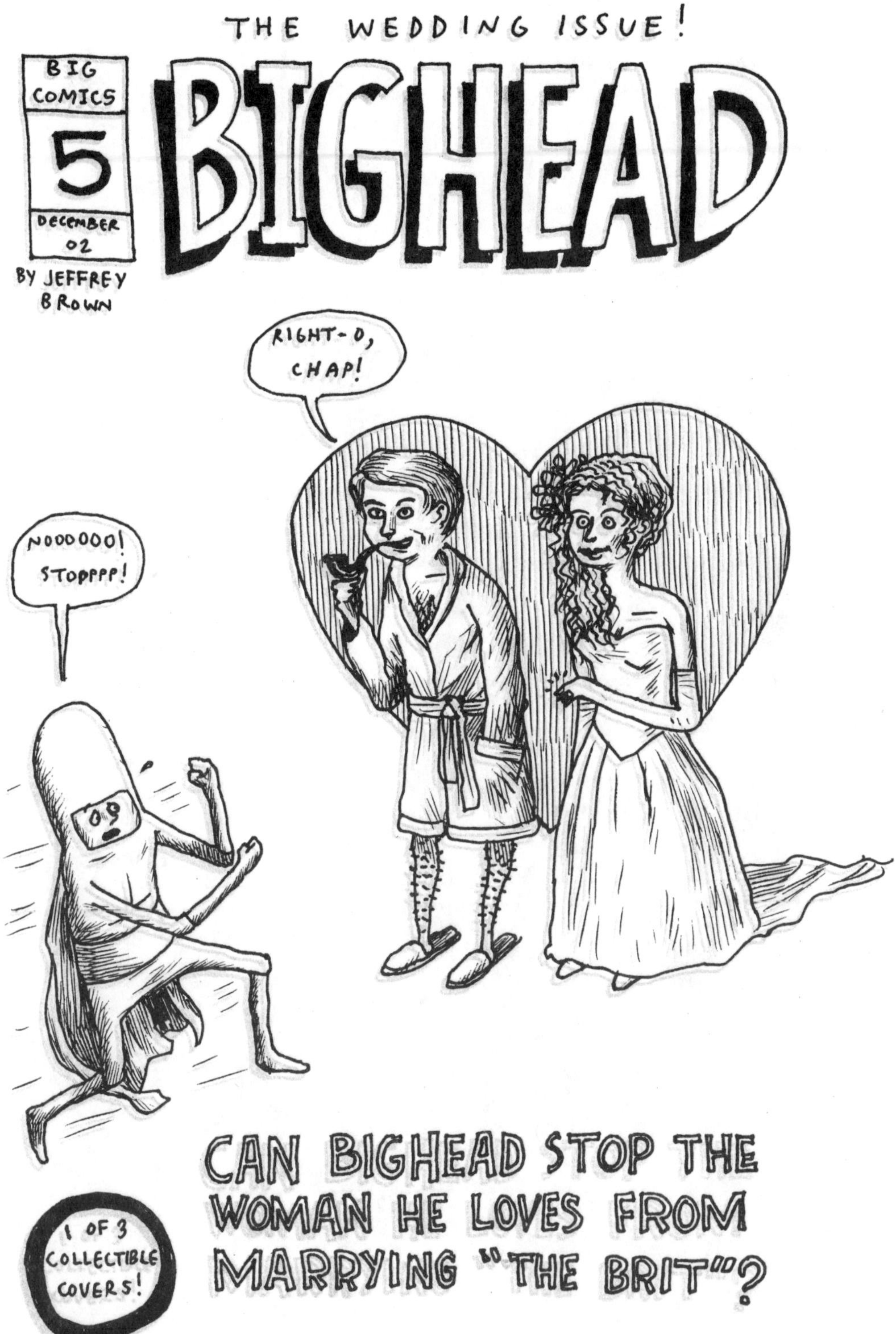
THE WEDDING ISSUE!
BIG COMICS
5
DECEMBER 02
BIGHEAD
BY JEFFREY BROWN
RIGHT-O, CHAP!
NOOOOOO! STOPPPP!
CAN BIGHEAD STOP THE WOMAN HE LOVES FROM MARRYING "THE BRIT"?
1 OF 3 COLLECTIBLE COVERS!

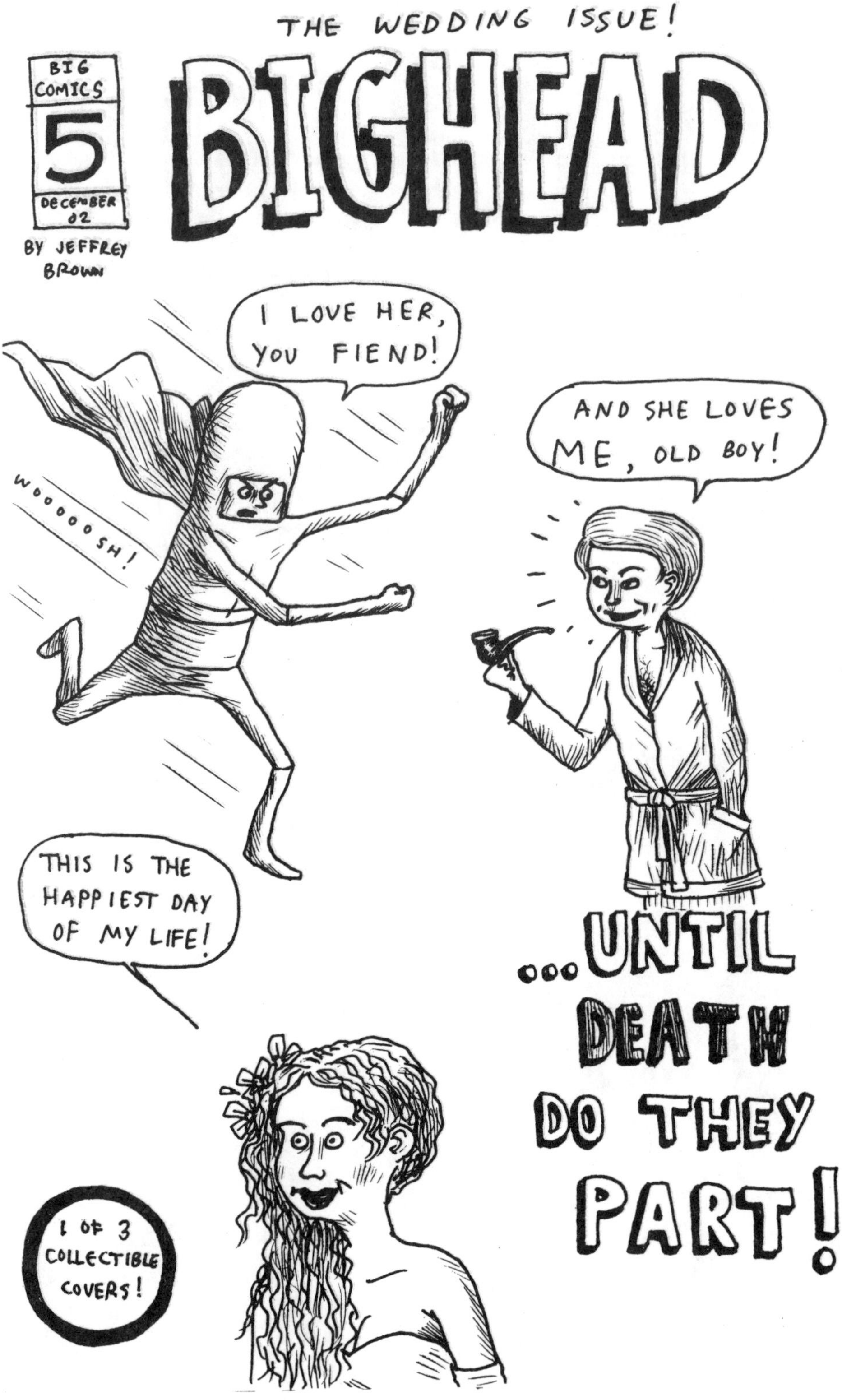
THE WEDDING ISSUE!
BIG COMICS
5
DECEMBER 02
BIGHEAD
BY JEFFREY BROWN
I LOVE HER, YOU FIEND!
WOOOOOOOSH!
AND SHE LOVES ME, OLD BOY!
THIS IS THE HAPPIEST DAY OF MY LIFE!
...UNTIL DEATH DO THEY PART!
1 OF 3 COLLECTIBLE COVERS!

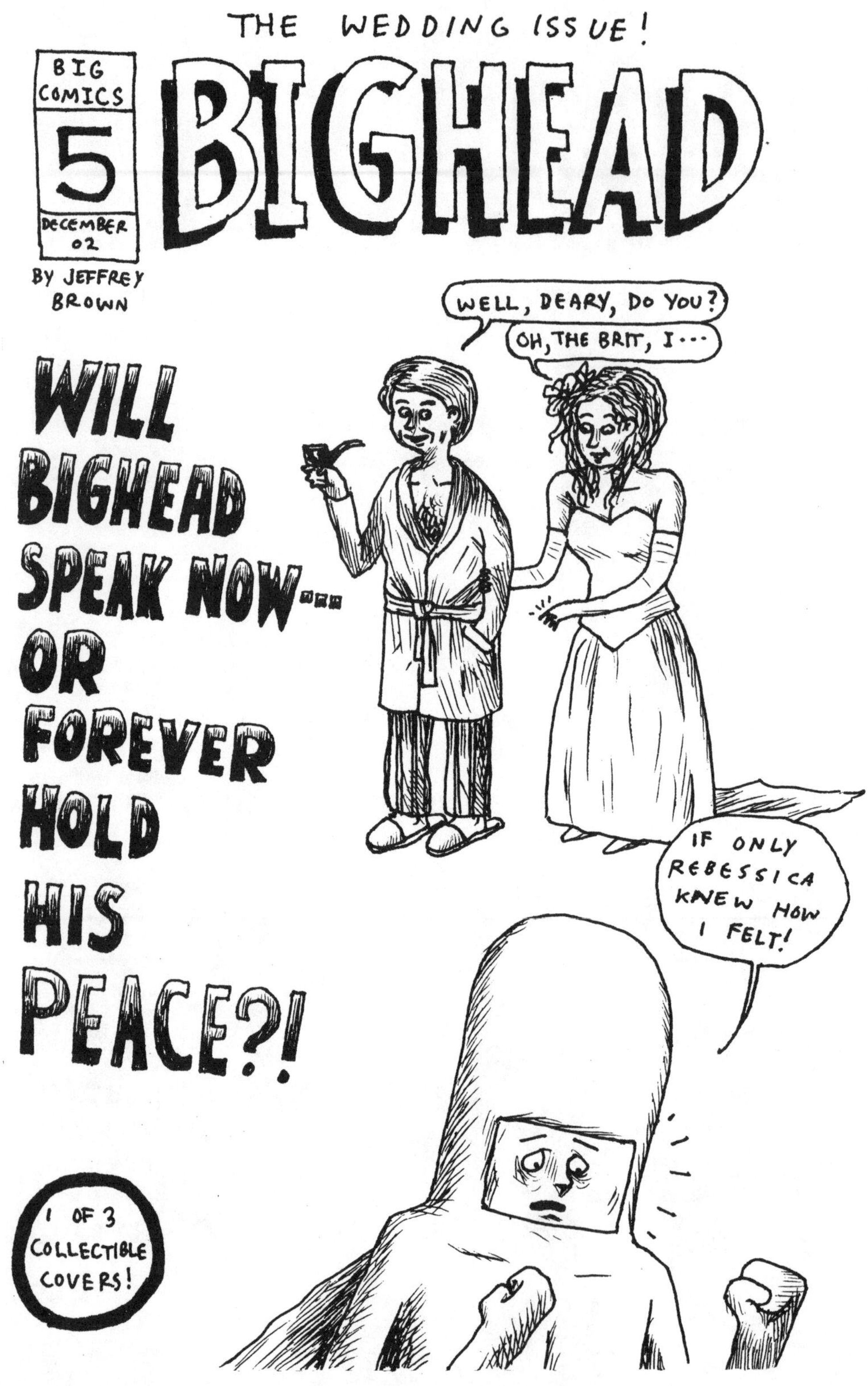
THE WEDDING ISSUE!
BIG COMICS
5
DECEMBER 02
BIGHEAD
BY JEFFREY BROWN
WELL, DEARY, DO YOU?
OH, THE BRIT, I···
WILL BIGHEAD SPEAK NOW... OR FOREVER HOLD HIS PEACE?!
IF ONLY REBESSICA KNEW HOW I FELT!
1 OF 3 COLLECTIBLE COVERS!

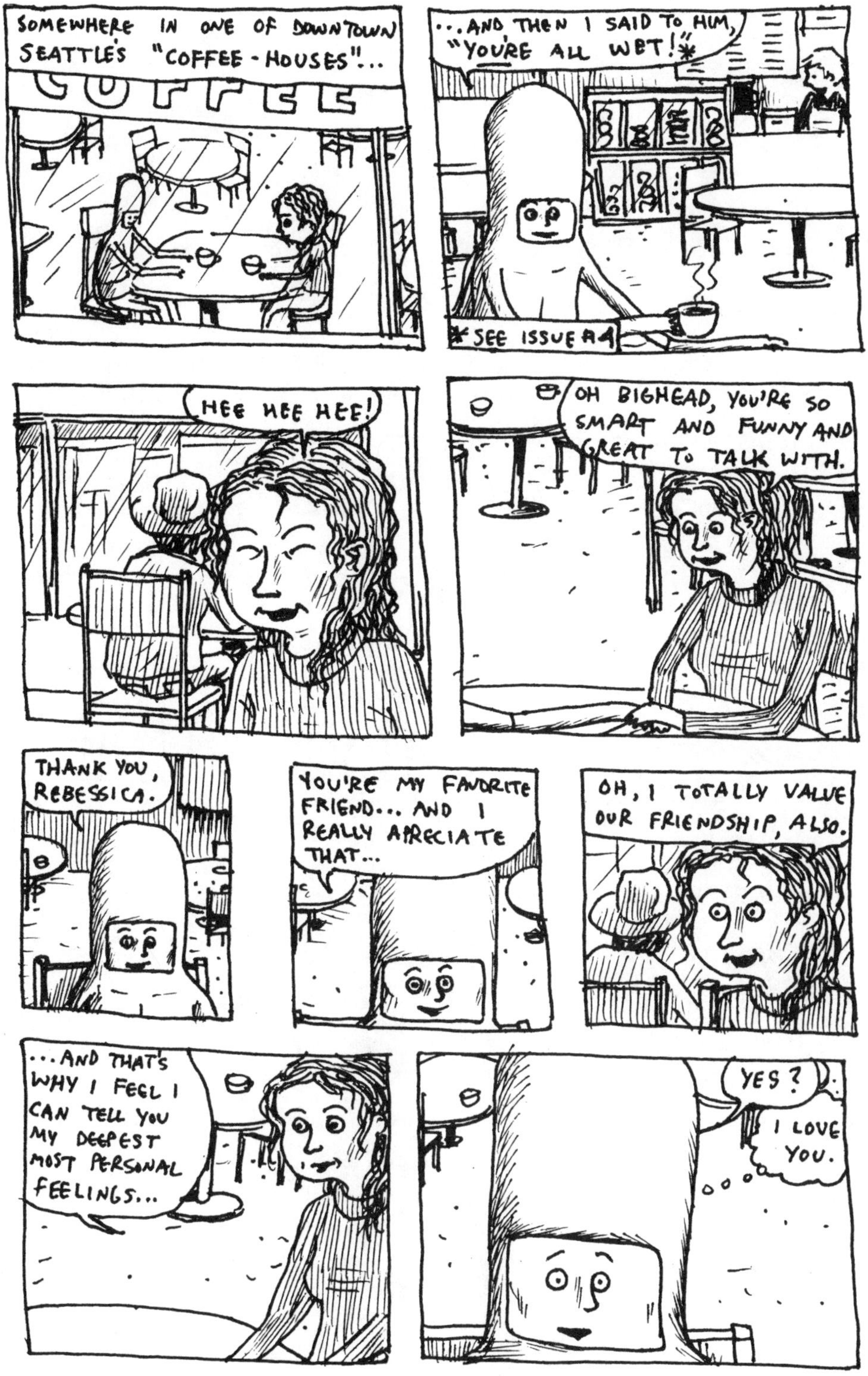
SOMEWHERE IN ONE OF DOWNTOWN SEATTLE'S "COFFEE-HOUSES"...
COFFEE
...AND THEN I SAID TO HIM, "YOU'RE ALL WET!"*
*SEE ISSUE #4
HEE HEE HEE!
OH BIGHEAD, YOU'RE SO SMART AND FUNNY AND GREAT TO TALK WITH.
THANK YOU, REBESSICA.
YOU'RE MY FAVORITE FRIEND... AND I REALLY APRECIATE THAT...
OH, I TOTALLY VALUE OUR FRIENDSHIP, ALSO.
...AND THAT'S WHY I FEEL I CAN TELL YOU MY DEEPEST MOST PERSONAL FEELINGS...
YES?
I LOVE YOU.

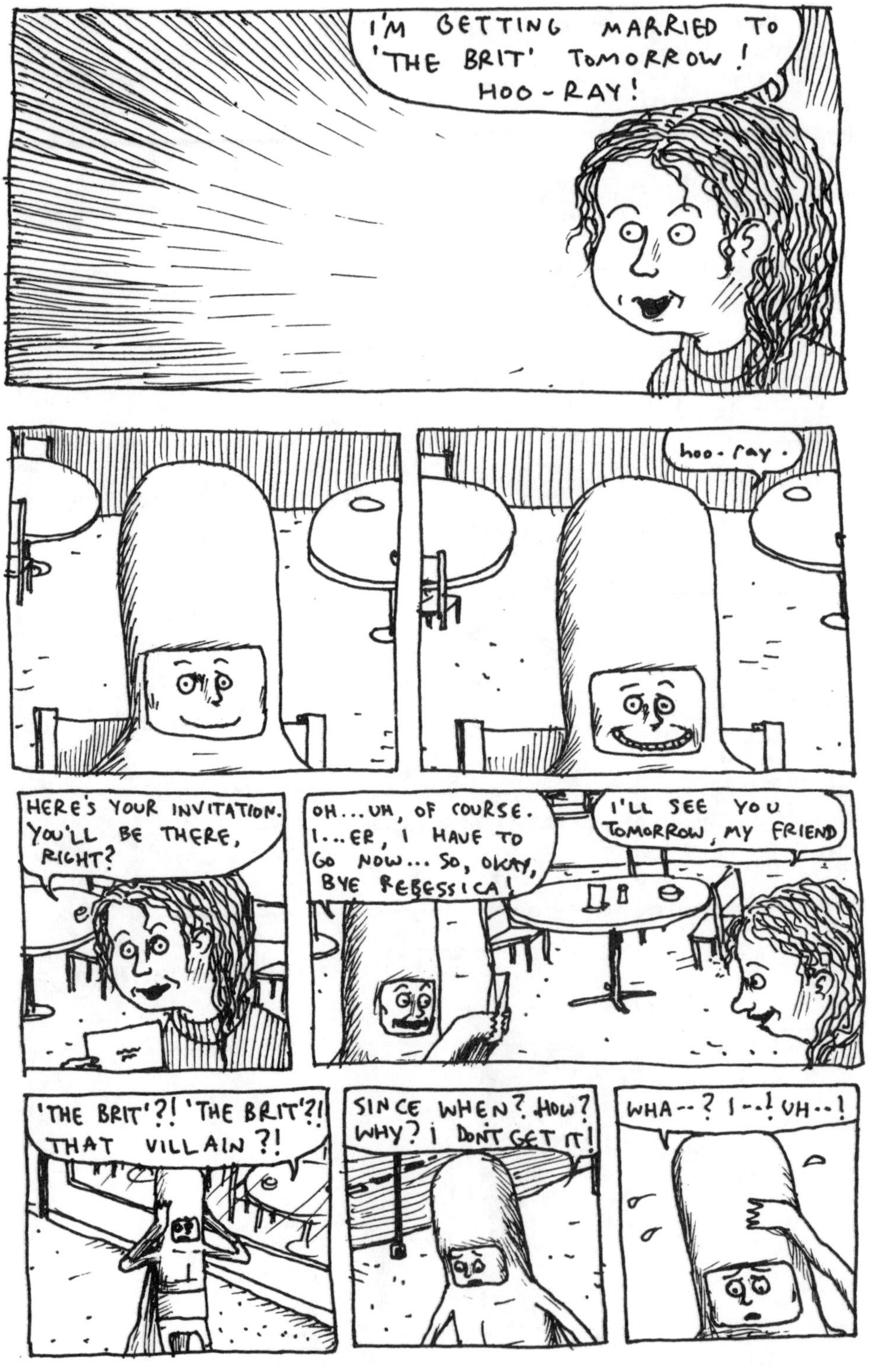
I'M GETTING MARRIED TO 'THE BRIT' TOMORROW! HOO-RAY!
hoo-ray.
HERE'S YOUR INVITATION. YOU'LL BE THERE, RIGHT?
OH...UH, OF COURSE. I...ER, I HAVE TO GO NOW... SO, OKAY, BYE REBESSICA!
I'LL SEE YOU TOMORROW, MY FRIEND
'THE BRIT'?! 'THE BRIT'?! THAT VILLAIN?!
SINCE WHEN? HOW? WHY? I DON'T GET IT!
WHA--? I--! UH--!

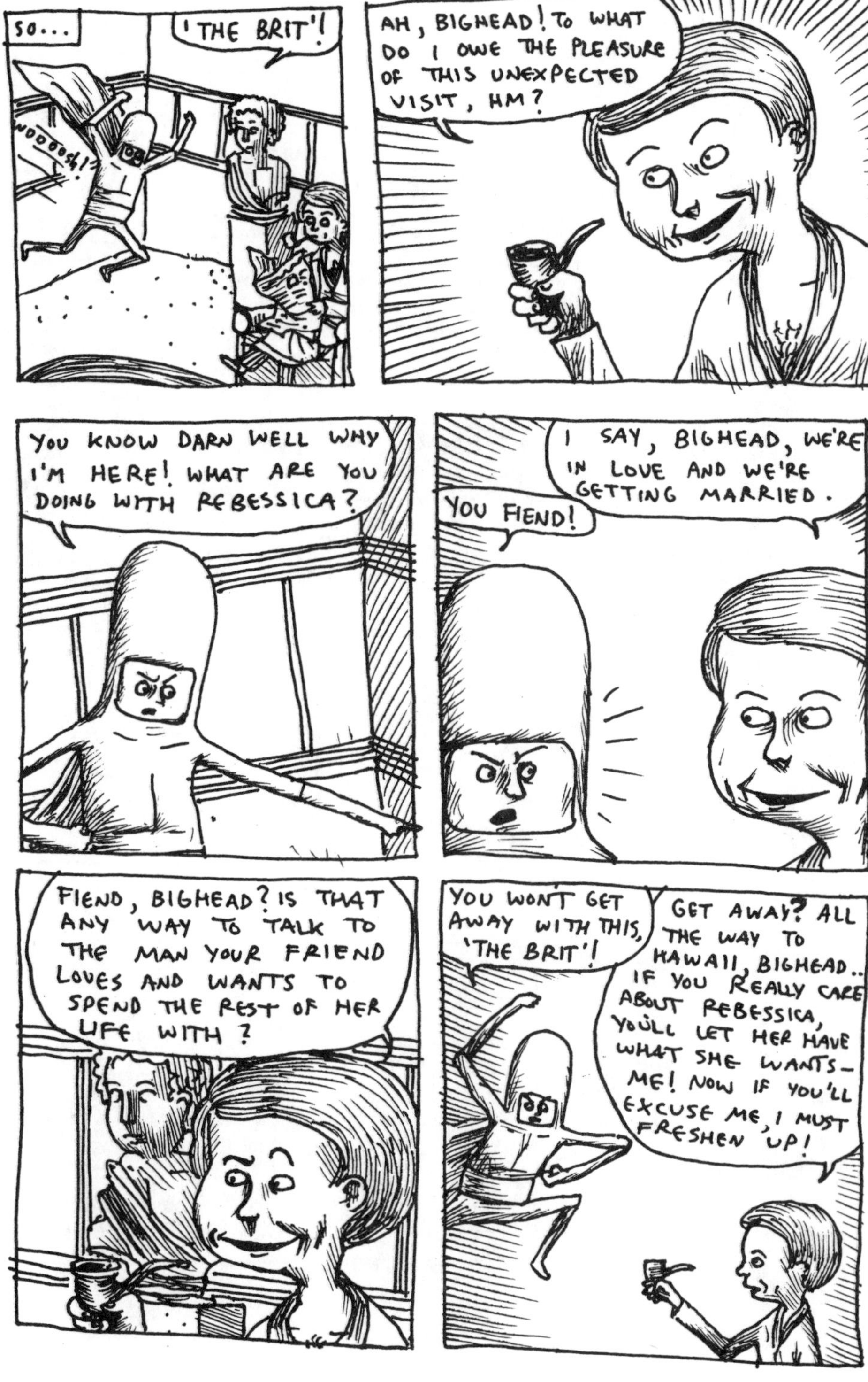
SO...
'THE BRIT'!
WOOOOSH!
AH, BIGHEAD! TO WHAT DO I OWE THE PLEASURE OF THIS UNEXPECTED VISIT, HM?
YOU KNOW DARN WELL WHY I'M HERE! WHAT ARE YOU DOING WITH REBESSICA?
YOU FIEND!
I SAY, BIGHEAD, WE'RE IN LOVE AND WE'RE GETTING MARRIED.
FIEND, BIGHEAD? IS THAT ANY WAY TO TALK TO THE MAN YOUR FRIEND LOVES AND WANTS TO SPEND THE REST OF HER LIFE WITH?
YOU WON'T GET AWAY WITH THIS, 'THE BRIT'!
GET AWAY? ALL THE WAY TO HAWAII, BIGHEAD... IF YOU REALLY CARE ABOUT REBESSICA, YOU'LL LET HER HAVE WHAT SHE WANTS– ME! NOW IF YOU'LL EXCUSE ME, I MUST FRESHEN UP!

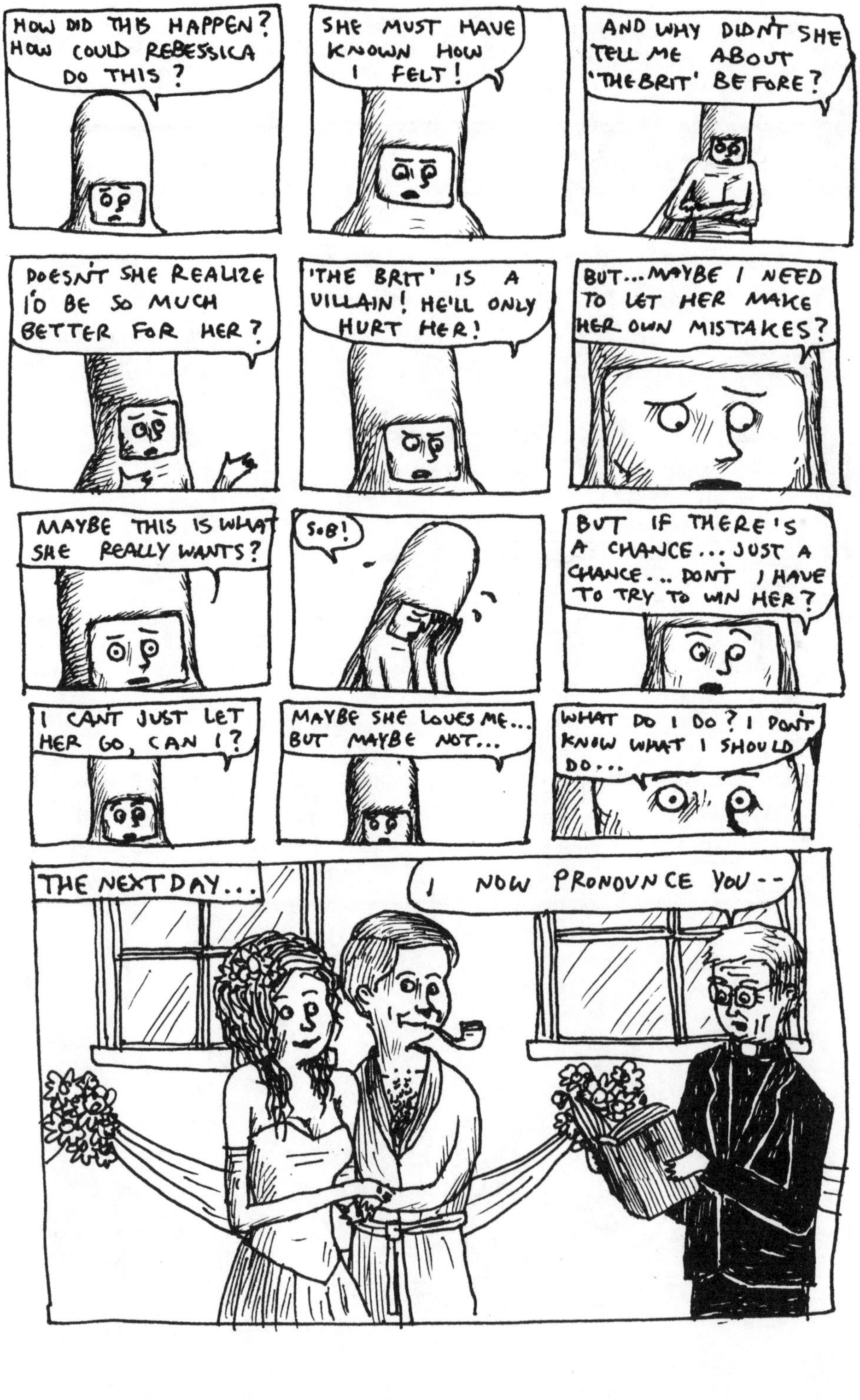
HOW DID THIS HAPPEN? HOW COULD REBESSICA DO THIS?
SHE MUST HAVE KNOWN HOW I FELT!
AND WHY DIDN'T SHE TELL ME ABOUT 'THE BRIT' BEFORE?
DOESN'T SHE REALIZE I'D BE SO MUCH BETTER FOR HER?
'THE BRIT' IS A VILLAIN! HE'LL ONLY HURT HER!
BUT... MAYBE I NEED TO LET HER MAKE HER OWN MISTAKES?
MAYBE THIS IS WHAT SHE REALLY WANTS?
SOB!
BUT IF THERE'S A CHANCE... JUST A CHANCE... DON'T I HAVE TO TRY TO WIN HER?
I CAN'T JUST LET HER GO, CAN I?
MAYBE SHE LOVES ME... BUT MAYBE NOT...
WHAT DO I DO? I DON'T KNOW WHAT I SHOULD DO...
THE NEXT DAY...
I NOW PRONOUNCE YOU--

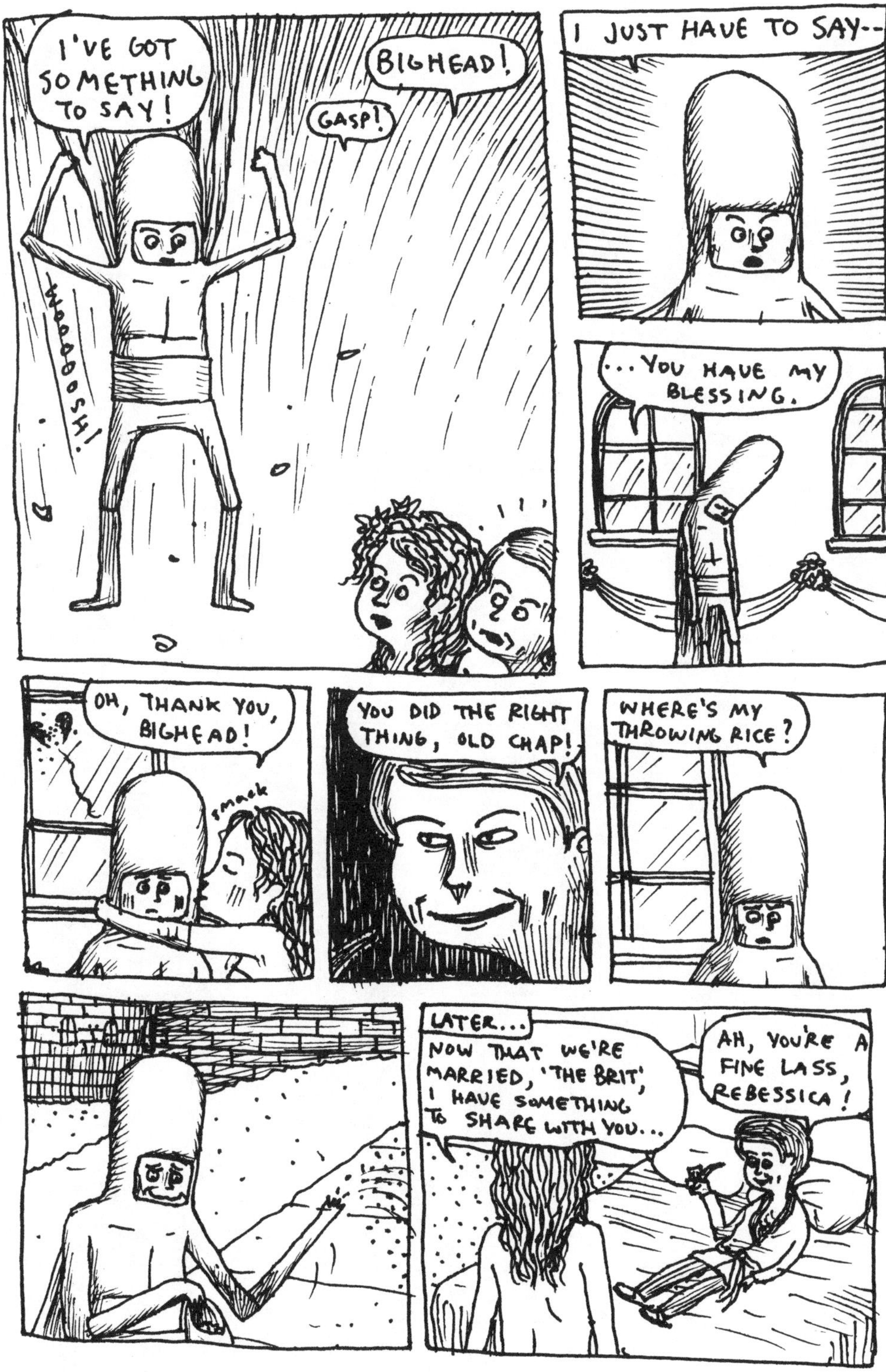
I'VE GOT SOMETHING TO SAY!
BIGHEAD!
GASP!
WOOOOOSH!
I JUST HAVE TO SAY--
...YOU HAVE MY BLESSING.
OH, THANK YOU, BIGHEAD!
smack
YOU DID THE RIGHT THING, OLD CHAP!
WHERE'S MY THROWING RICE?
LATER...
NOW THAT WE'RE MARRIED, 'THE BRIT', I HAVE SOMETHING TO SHARE WITH YOU...
AH, YOU'RE A FINE LASS, REBESSICA!

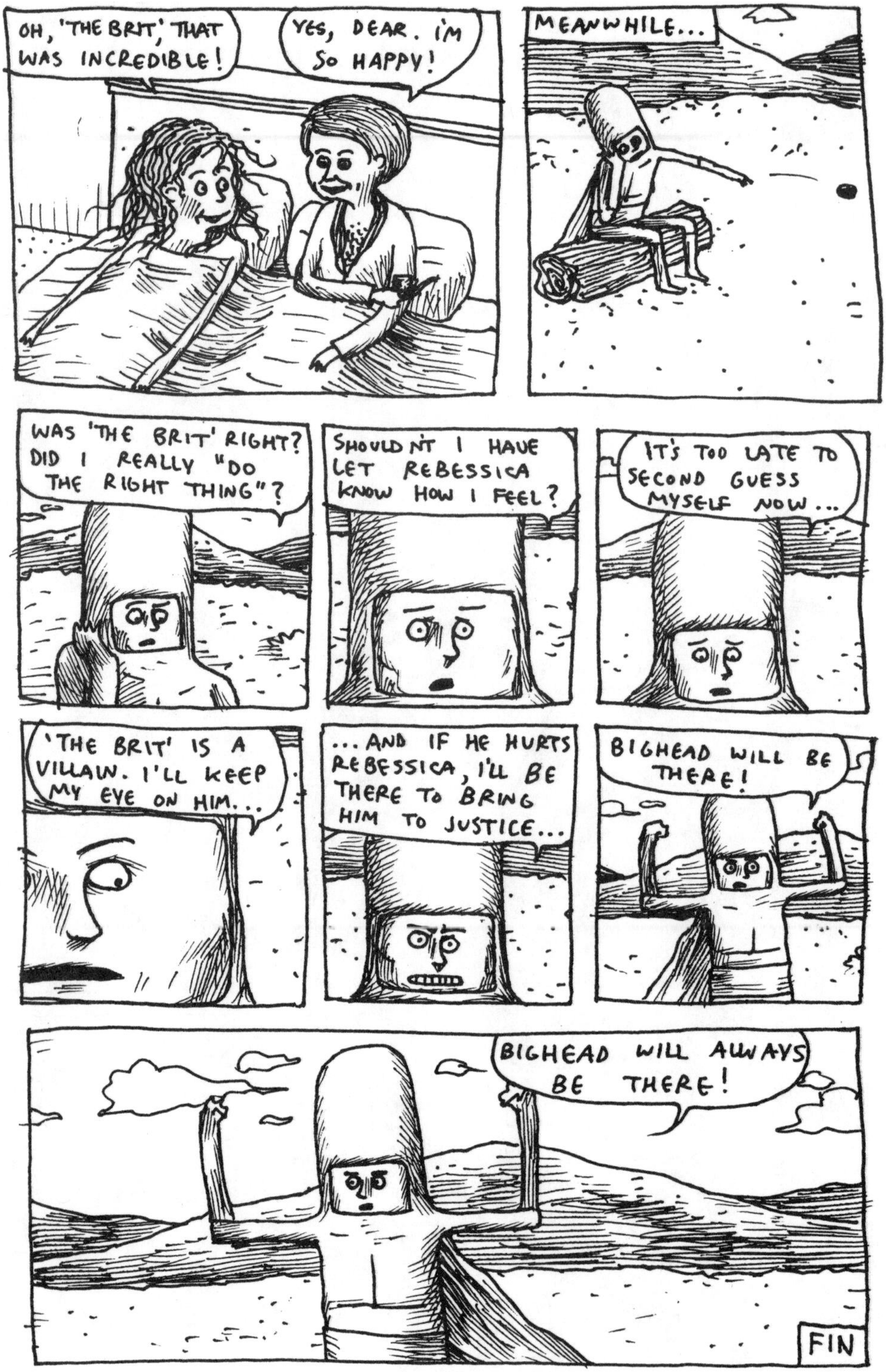
OH, 'THE BRIT,' THAT WAS INCREDIBLE!
YES, DEAR. I'M SO HAPPY!
MEANWHILE...
WAS 'THE BRIT' RIGHT? DID I REALLY "DO THE RIGHT THING"?
SHOULDN'T I HAVE LET REBESSICA KNOW HOW I FEEL?
IT'S TOO LATE TO SECOND GUESS MYSELF NOW...
'THE BRIT' IS A VILLAIN. I'LL KEEP MY EYE ON HIM...
...AND IF HE HURTS REBESSICA, I'LL BE THERE TO BRING HIM TO JUSTICE...
BIGHEAD WILL BE THERE!
BIGHEAD WILL ALWAYS BE THERE!
FIN

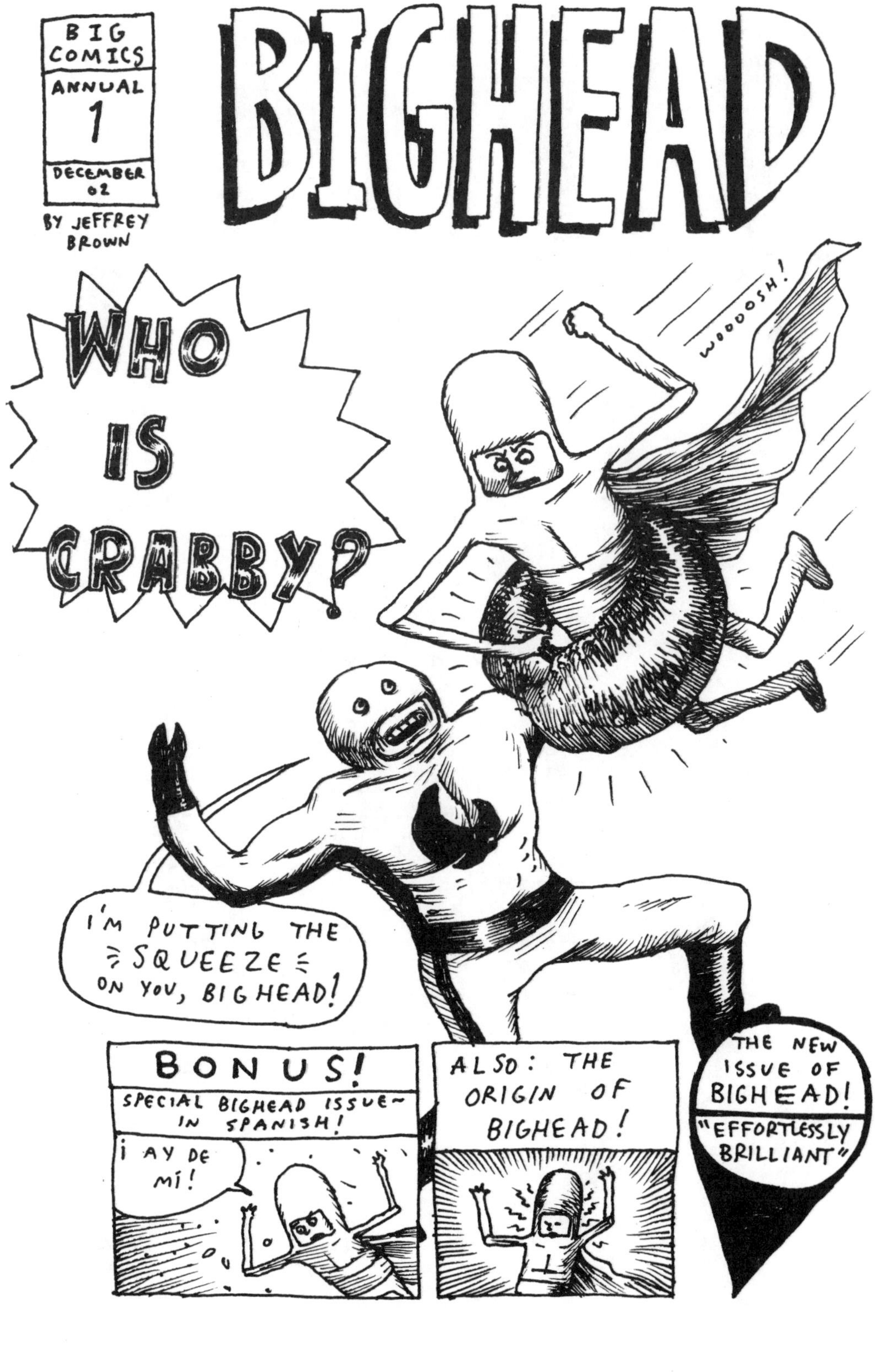
BIG COMICS
ANNUAL
1
DECEMBER 02
BIGHEAD
BY JEFFREY BROWN
WHO IS CRABBY?
WOOOOSH!
I'M PUTTING THE SQUEEZE ON YOU, BIGHEAD!
BONUS!
SPECIAL BIGHEAD ISSUE– IN SPANISH!
¡AY DE MÍ!
ALSO: THE ORIGIN OF BIGHEAD!
THE NEW ISSUE OF BIGHEAD!
"EFFORTLESSLY BRILLIANT"

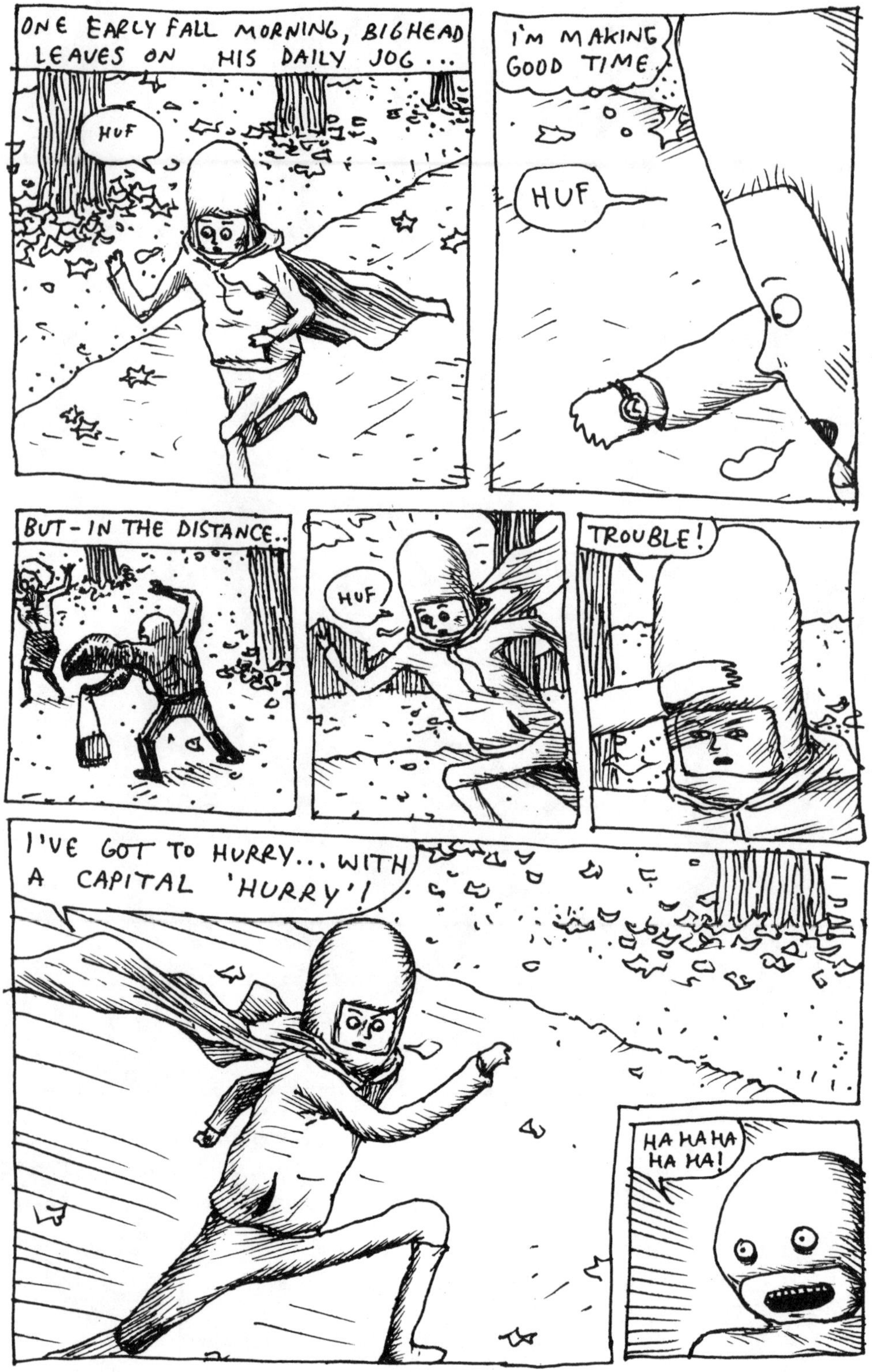
ONE EARLY FALL MORNING, BIGHEAD LEAVES ON HIS DAILY JOG...
HUF
I'M MAKING GOOD TIME.
HUF
BUT - IN THE DISTANCE..
HUF
TROUBLE!
I'VE GOT TO HURRY... WITH A CAPITAL 'HURRY'!
HA HA HA HA HA!

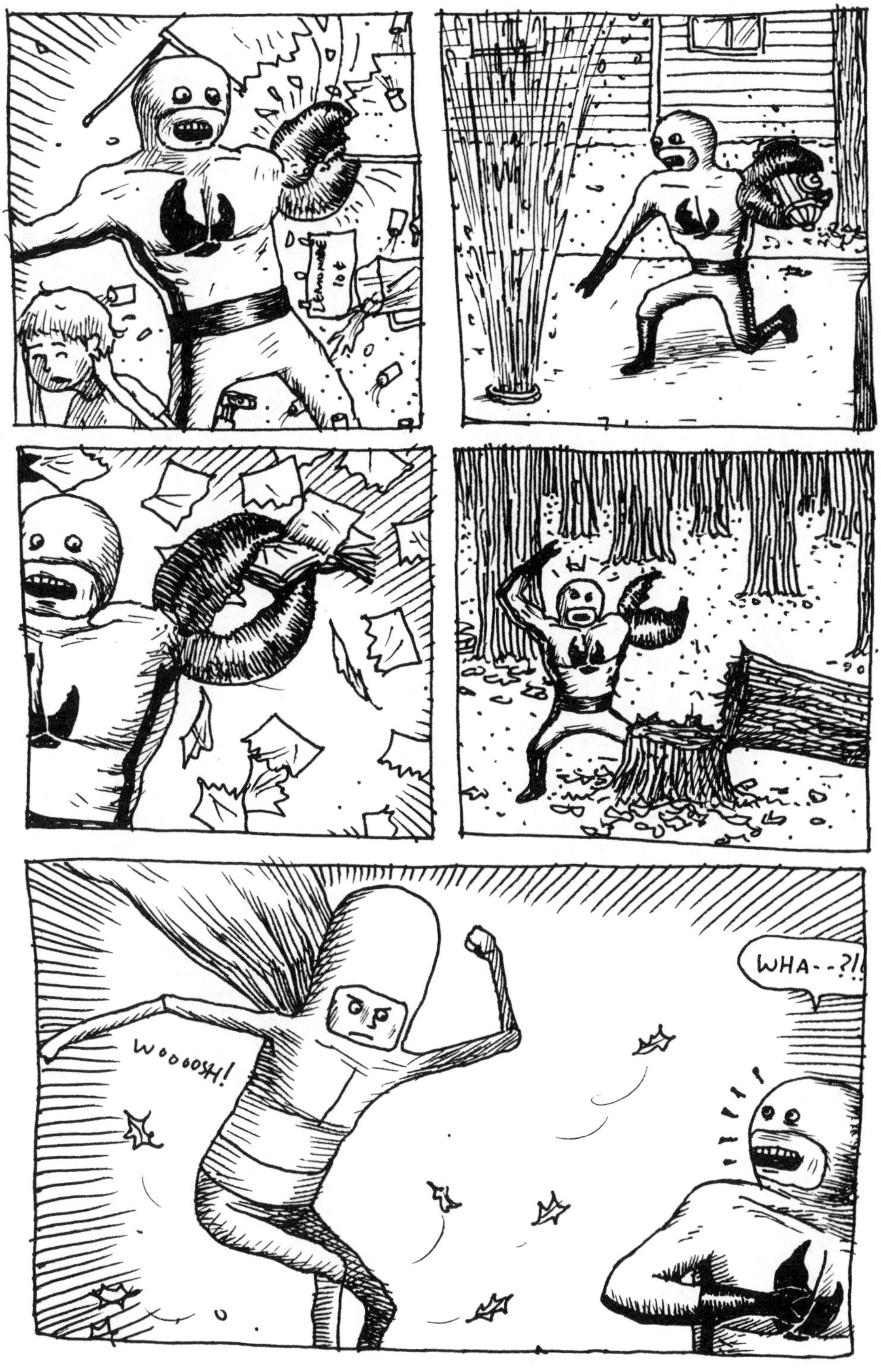
LEMONADE
10¢
WOOOOSH!
WHA--?!

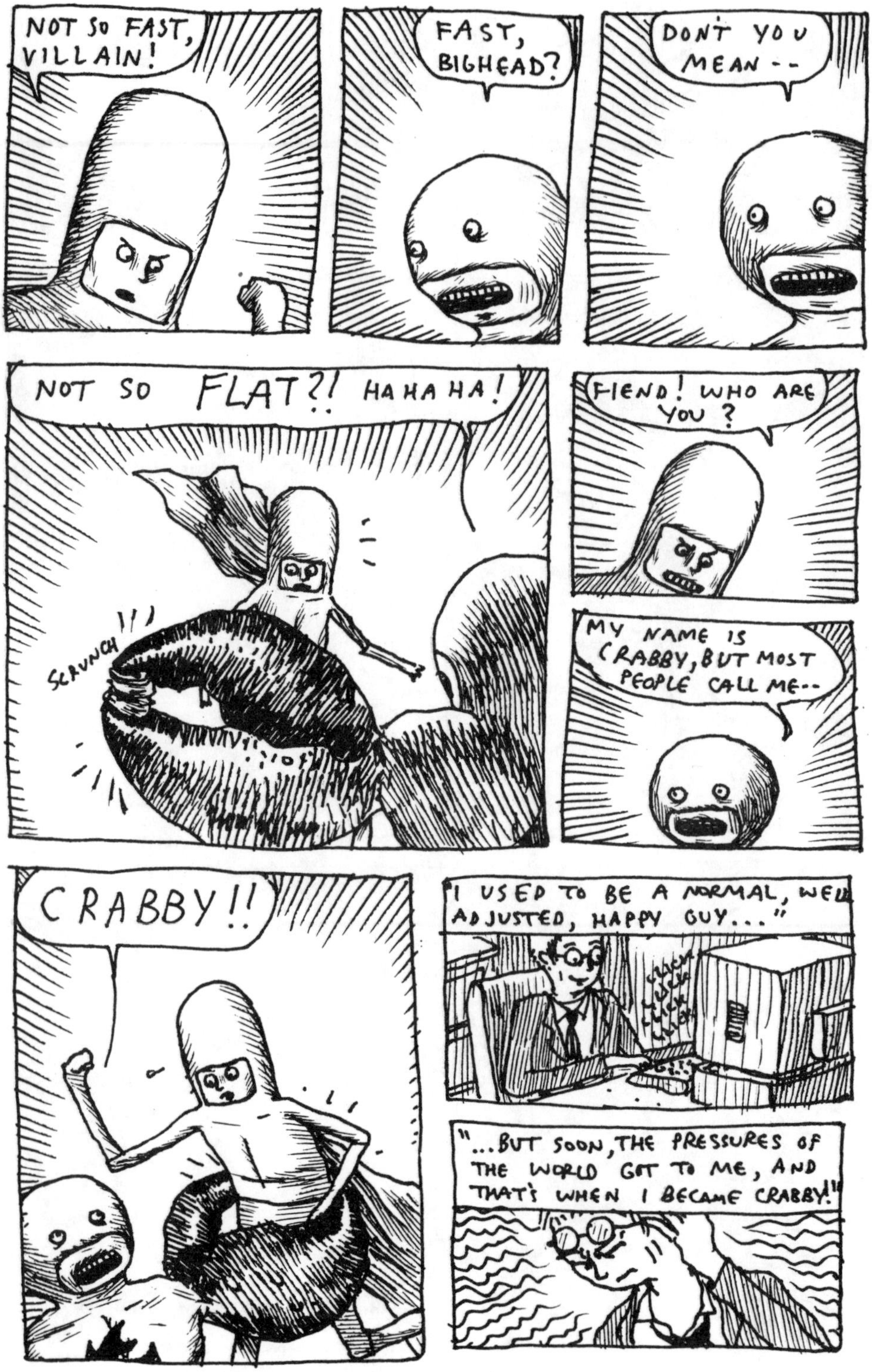
NOT SO FAST, VILLAIN!
FAST, BIGHEAD?
DON'T YOU MEAN --
NOT SO FLAT?! HAHAHA!
SCRUNCH
FIEND! WHO ARE YOU?
MY NAME IS CRABBY, BUT MOST PEOPLE CALL ME--
CRABBY!!
"I USED TO BE A NORMAL, WELL ADJUSTED, HAPPY GUY..."
"...BUT SOON, THE PRESSURES OF THE WORLD GOT TO ME, AND THAT'S WHEN I BECAME CRABBY!"

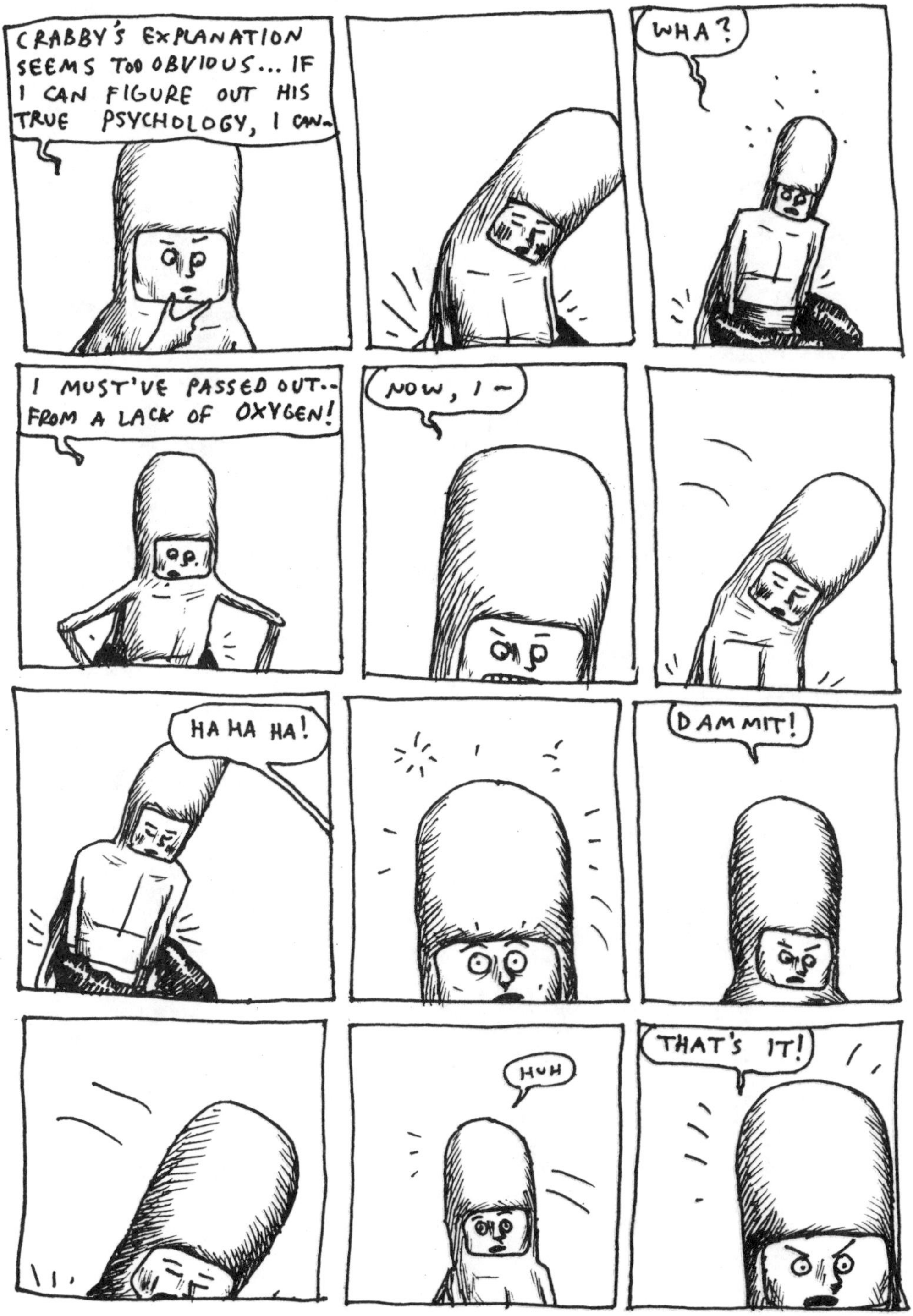
CRABBY'S EXPLANATION SEEMS TOO OBVIOUS... IF I CAN FIGURE OUT HIS TRUE PSYCHOLOGY, I CAN-
WHA?
I MUST'VE PASSED OUT.. FROM A LACK OF OXYGEN!
NOW, I-
HA HA HA!
DAMMIT!
HUH
THAT'S IT!

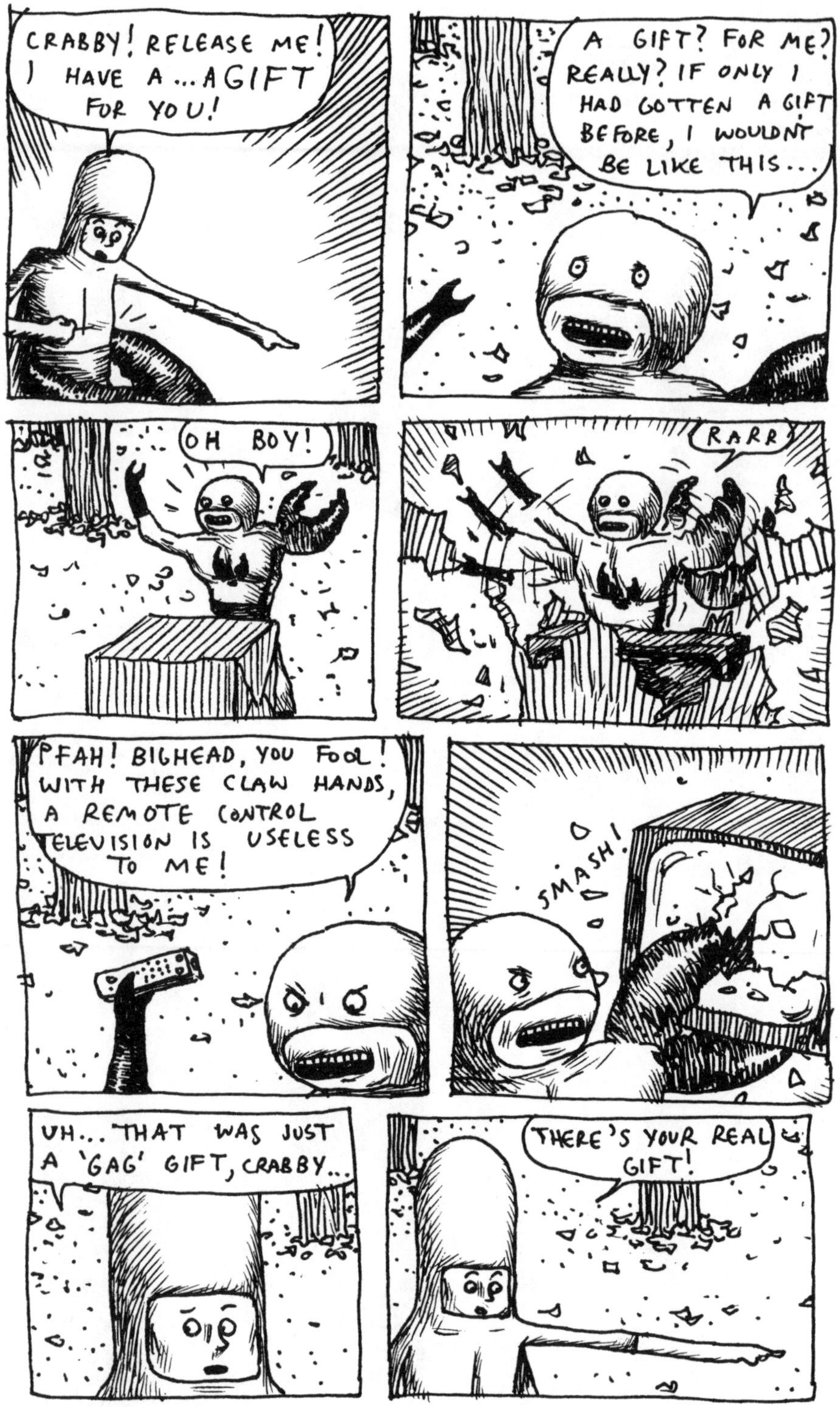
CRABBY! RELEASE ME! I HAVE A...A GIFT FOR YOU!
A GIFT? FOR ME? REALLY? IF ONLY I HAD GOTTEN A GIFT BEFORE, I WOULDNT BE LIKE THIS...
OH BOY!
RARR
PFAH! BIGHEAD, YOU FOOL! WITH THESE CLAW HANDS, A REMOTE CONTROL TELEVISION IS USELESS TO ME!
SMASH!
UH... THAT WAS JUST A 'GAG' GIFT, CRABBY...
THERE'S YOUR REAL GIFT!

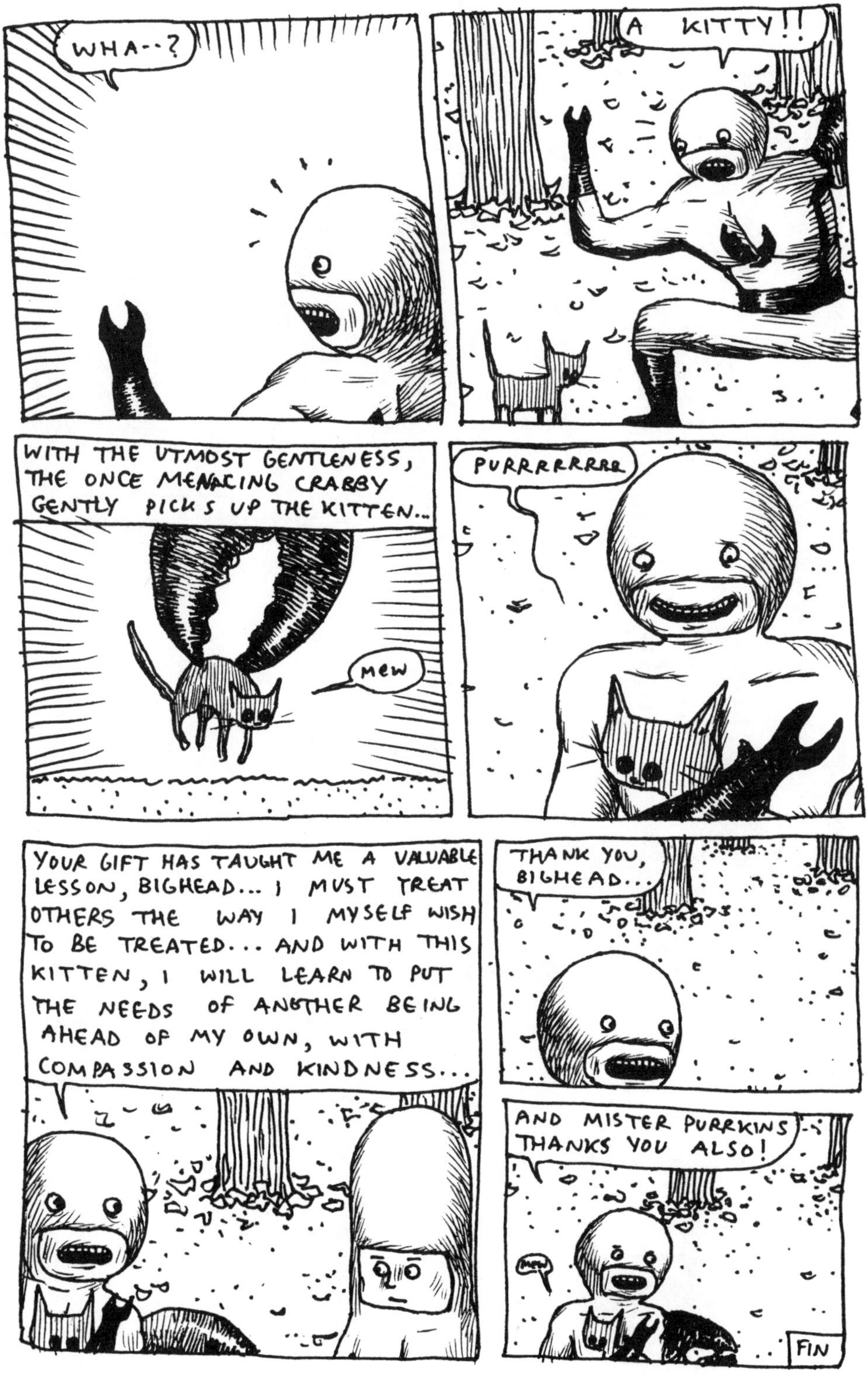

WHA--?
A KITTY!!
WITH THE UTMOST GENTLENESS, THE ONCE MENACING CRABBY GENTLY PICKS UP THE KITTEN...
MEW
PURRRRRRRR
YOUR GIFT HAS TAUGHT ME A VALUABLE LESSON, BIGHEAD... I MUST TREAT OTHERS THE WAY I MYSELF WISH TO BE TREATED... AND WITH THIS KITTEN, I WILL LEARN TO PUT THE NEEDS OF ANOTHER BEING AHEAD OF MY OWN, WITH COMPASSION AND KINDNESS...
THANK YOU, BIGHEAD...
AND MISTER PURRKINS THANKS YOU ALSO!
MEW
FIN

THE ORIGIN OF BIGHEAD

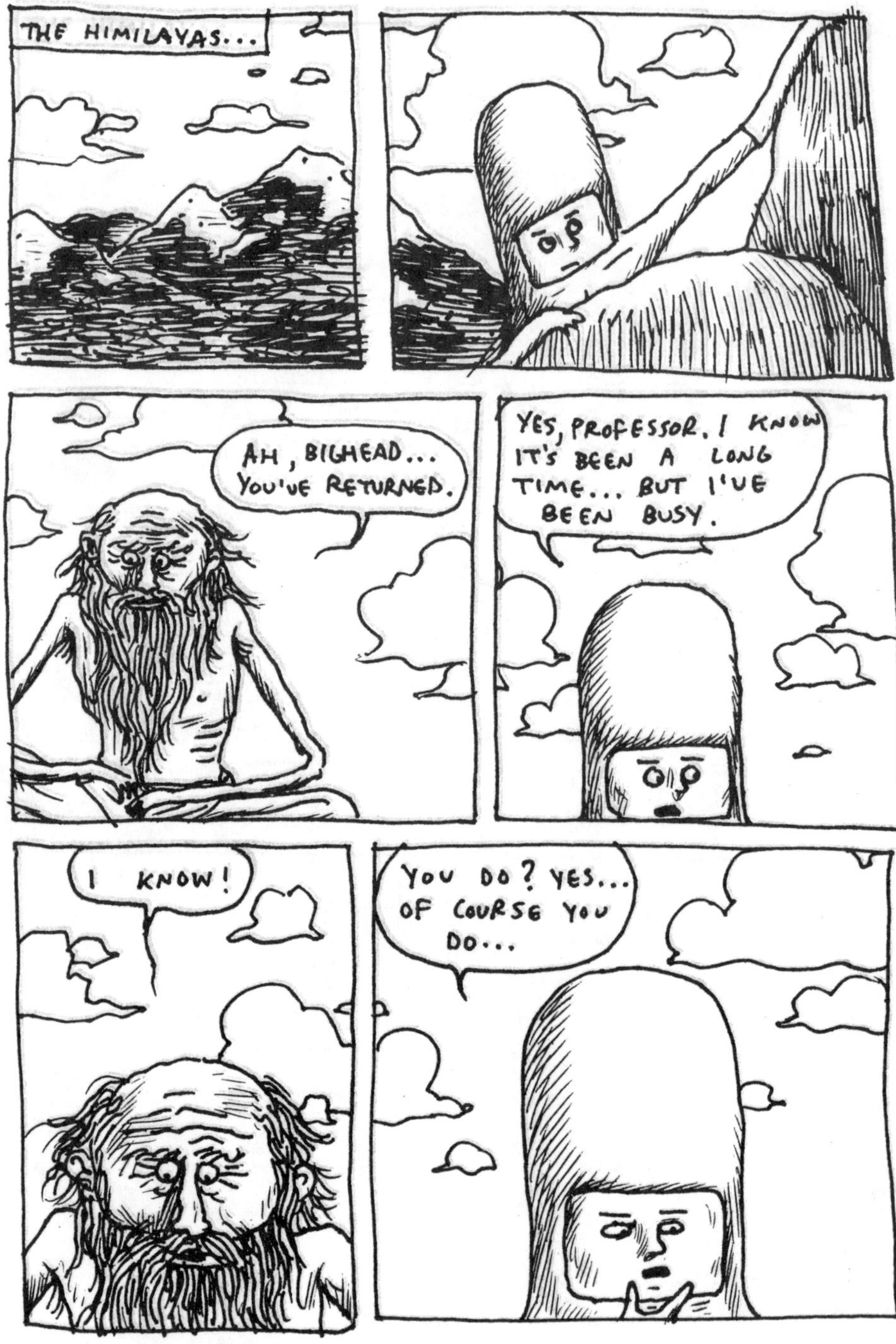
THE HIMILAYAS...
AH, BIGHEAD... YOU'VE RETURNED.
YES, PROFESSOR. I KNOW IT'S BEEN A LONG TIME... BUT I'VE BEEN BUSY.
I KNOW!
YOU DO? YES... OF COURSE YOU DO...

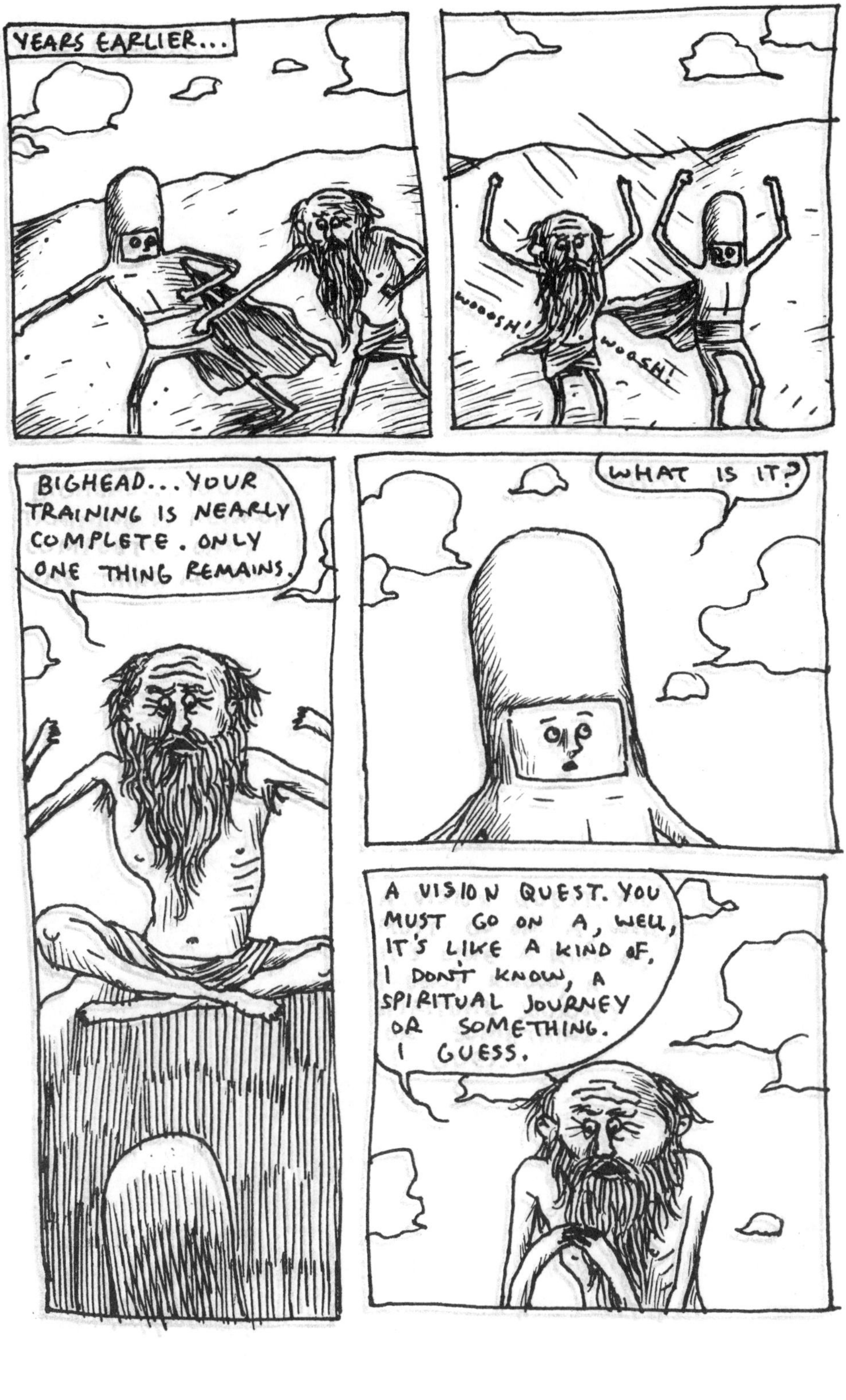
YEARS EARLIER...
WOOOSH!
WOOOSH!
BIGHEAD... YOUR TRAINING IS NEARLY COMPLETE. ONLY ONE THING REMAINS.
WHAT IS IT?
A VISION QUEST. YOU MUST GO ON A, WELL, IT'S LIKE A KIND OF, I DON'T KNOW, A SPIRITUAL JOURNEY OR SOMETHING. I GUESS.

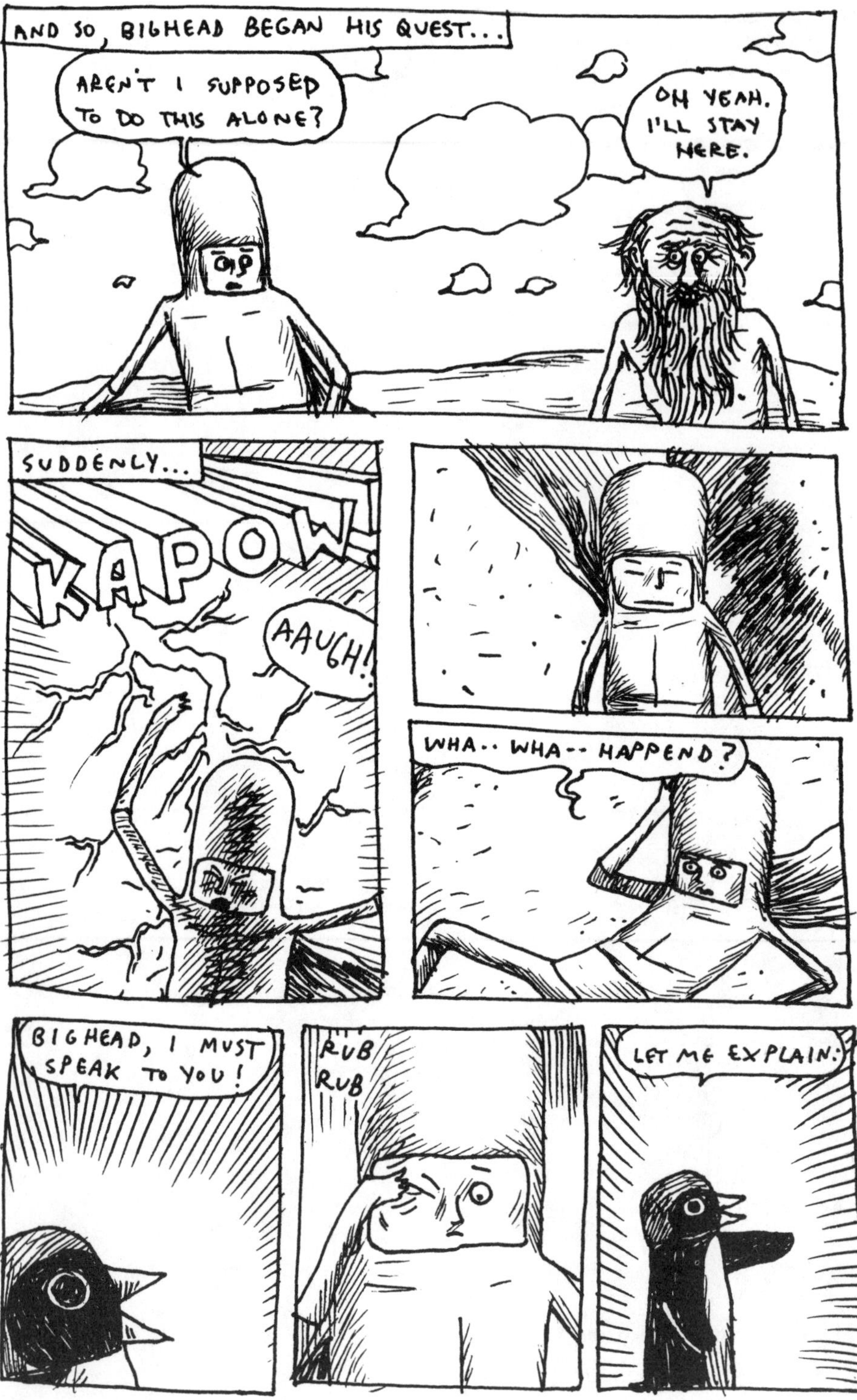
AND SO, BIGHEAD BEGAN HIS QUEST...
AREN'T I SUPPOSED TO DO THIS ALONE?
OH YEAH. I'LL STAY HERE.
SUDDENLY...
KAPOW!
AAUGH!
WHA.. WHA-- HAPPEND?
BIGHEAD, I MUST SPEAK TO YOU!
RUB RUB
LET ME EXPLAIN:

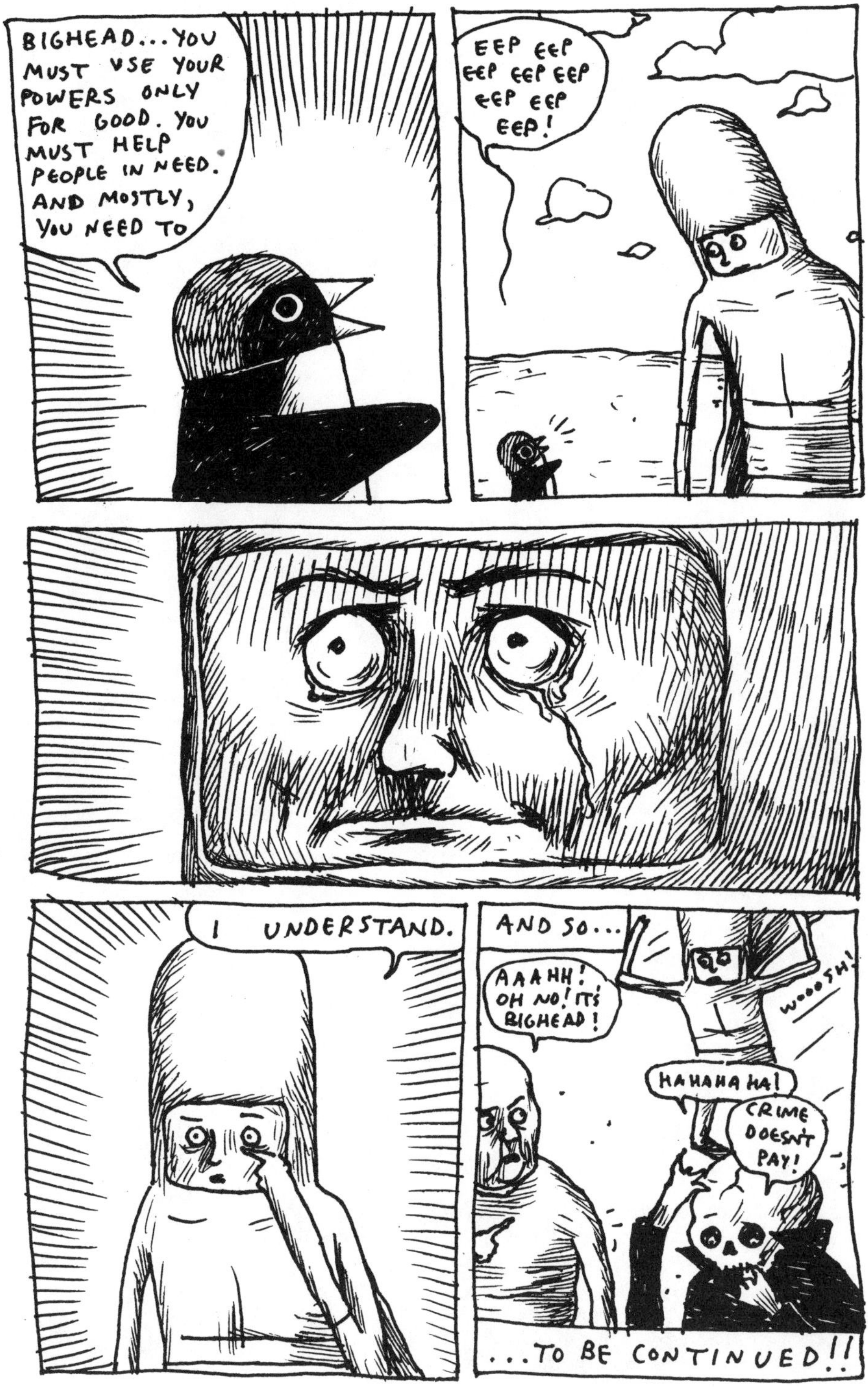
BIGHEAD... YOU MUST USE YOUR POWERS ONLY FOR GOOD. YOU MUST HELP PEOPLE IN NEED. AND MOSTLY, YOU NEED TO
EEP EEP EEP EEP EEP EEP EEP EEP!
I UNDERSTAND.
AND SO...
AAAHH! OH NO! IT'S BIGHEAD!
WOOOSH!
HAHAHAHA!
CRIME DOESN'T PAY!
...TO BE CONTINUED!!

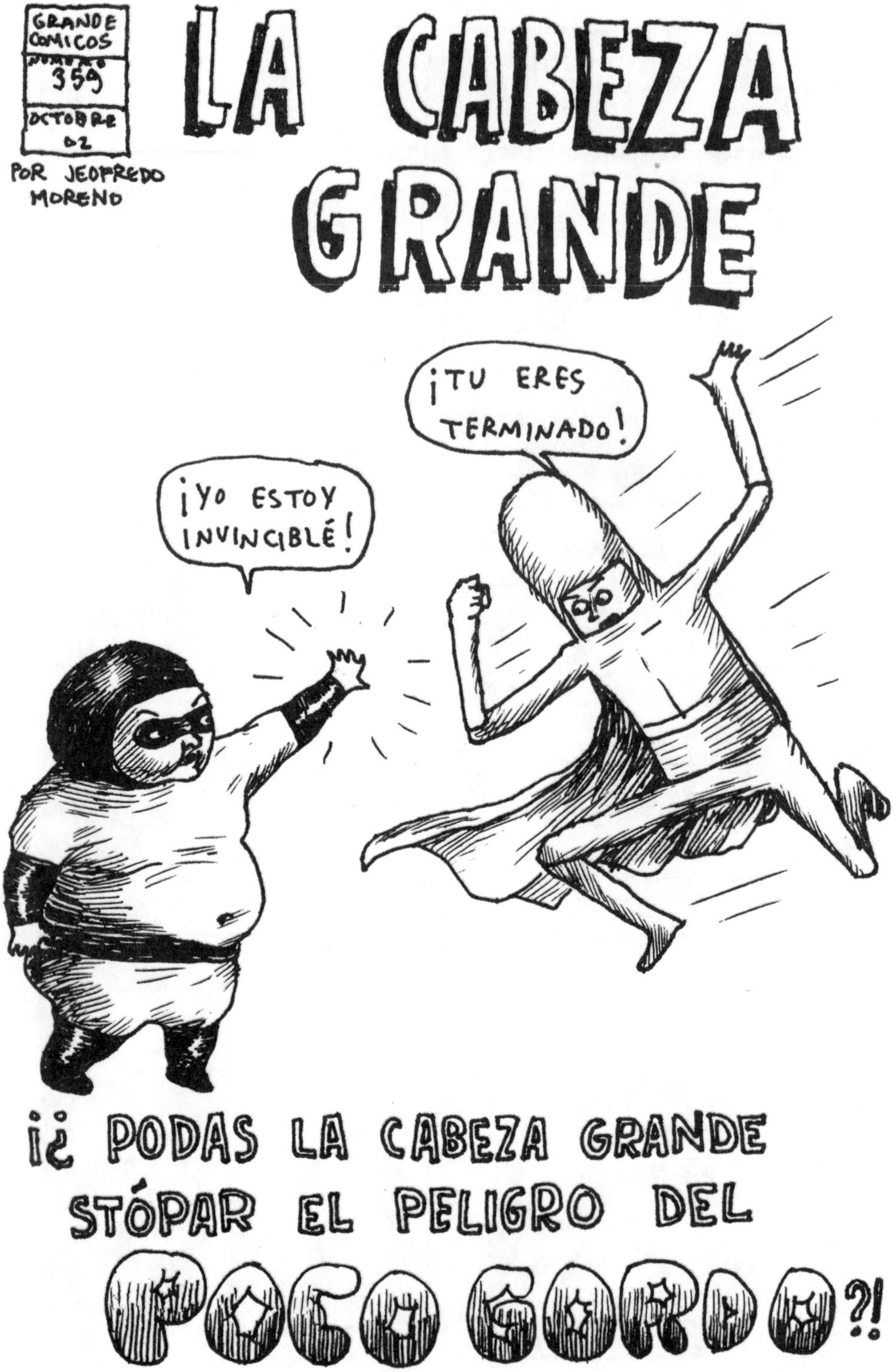
GRANDE COMICOS
359
OCTOBRE 02
POR JEOFREDO MORENO
LA CABEZA GRANDE
¡TU ERES TERMINADO!
¡YO ESTOY INVINCIBLÉ!
¿¡ PODAS LA CABEZA GRANDE STÓPAR EL PELIGRO DEL POCO GORDO?!

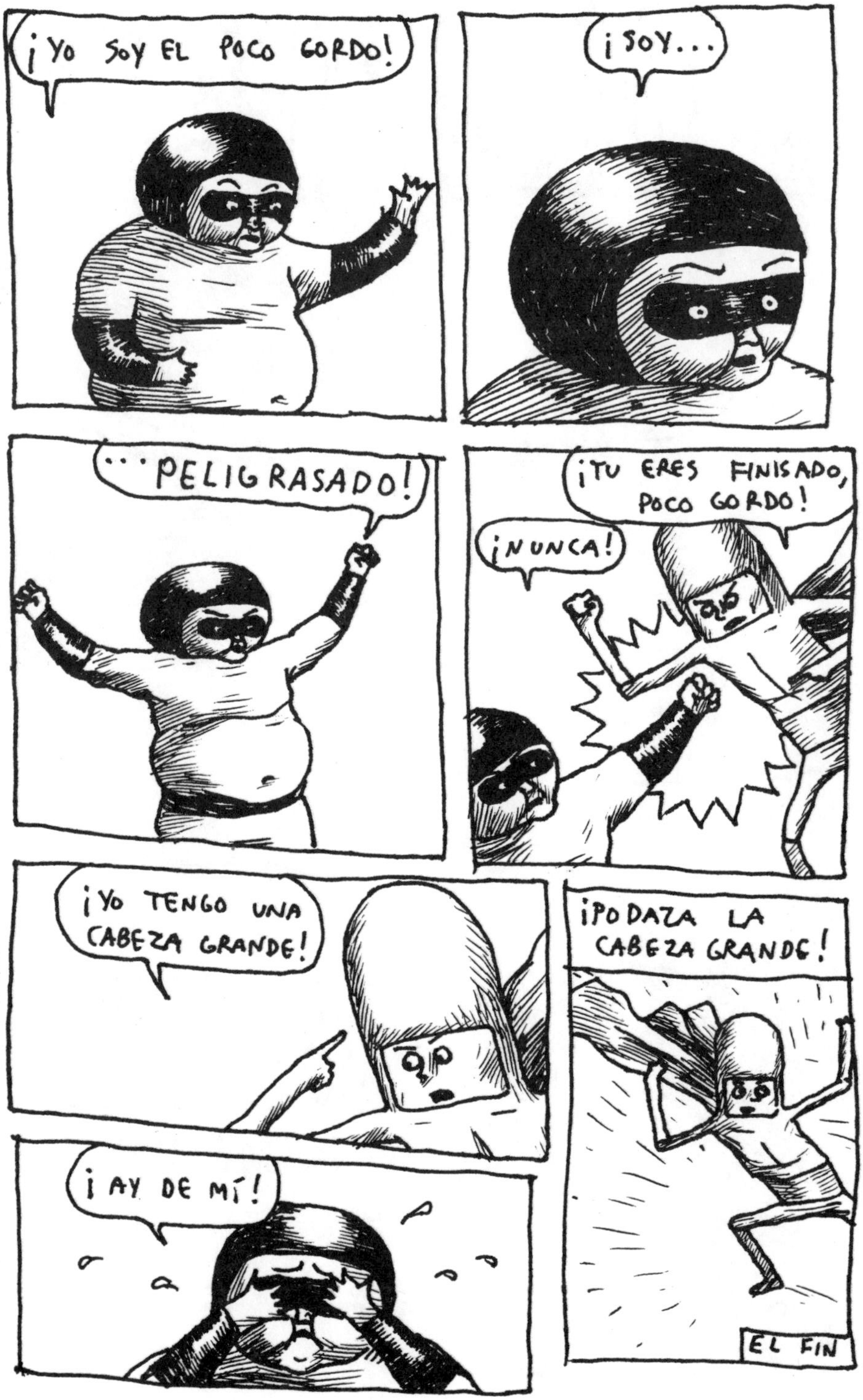
¡YO SOY EL POCO GORDO!
¡SOY...
...PELIGRASADO!
¡TU ERES FINISADO, POCO GORDO!
¡NUNCA!
¡YO TENGO UNA CABEZA GRANDE!
¡PODAZA LA CABEZA GRANDE!
¡AY DE MÍ!
EL FIN

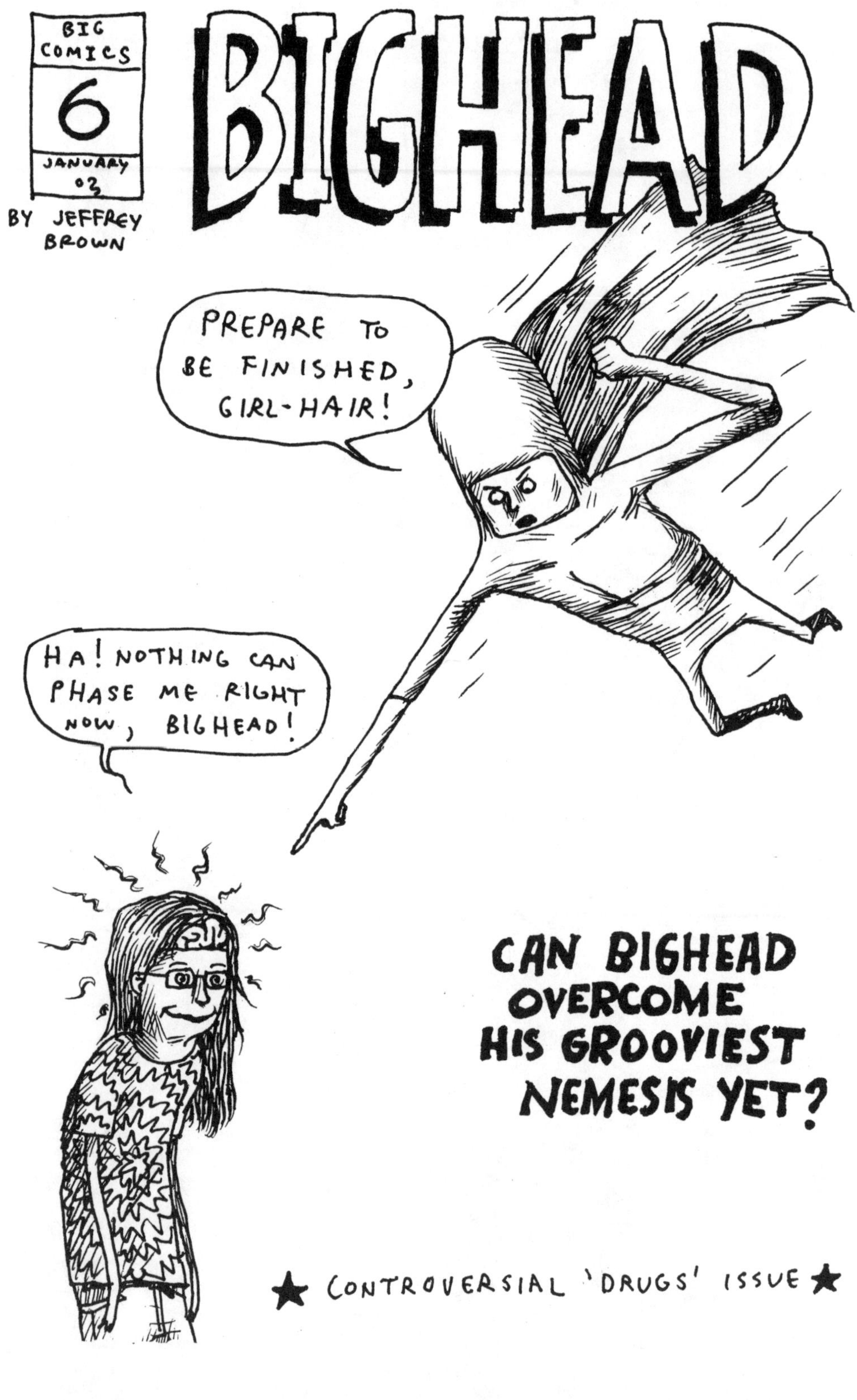
BIG COMICS
6
JANUARY 03
BIGHEAD
BY JEFFREY BROWN
PREPARE TO BE FINISHED, GIRL-HAIR!
HA! NOTHING CAN PHASE ME RIGHT NOW, BIGHEAD!
CAN BIGHEAD OVERCOME HIS GROOVIEST NEMESIS YET?
★ CONTROVERSIAL 'DRUGS' ISSUE ★

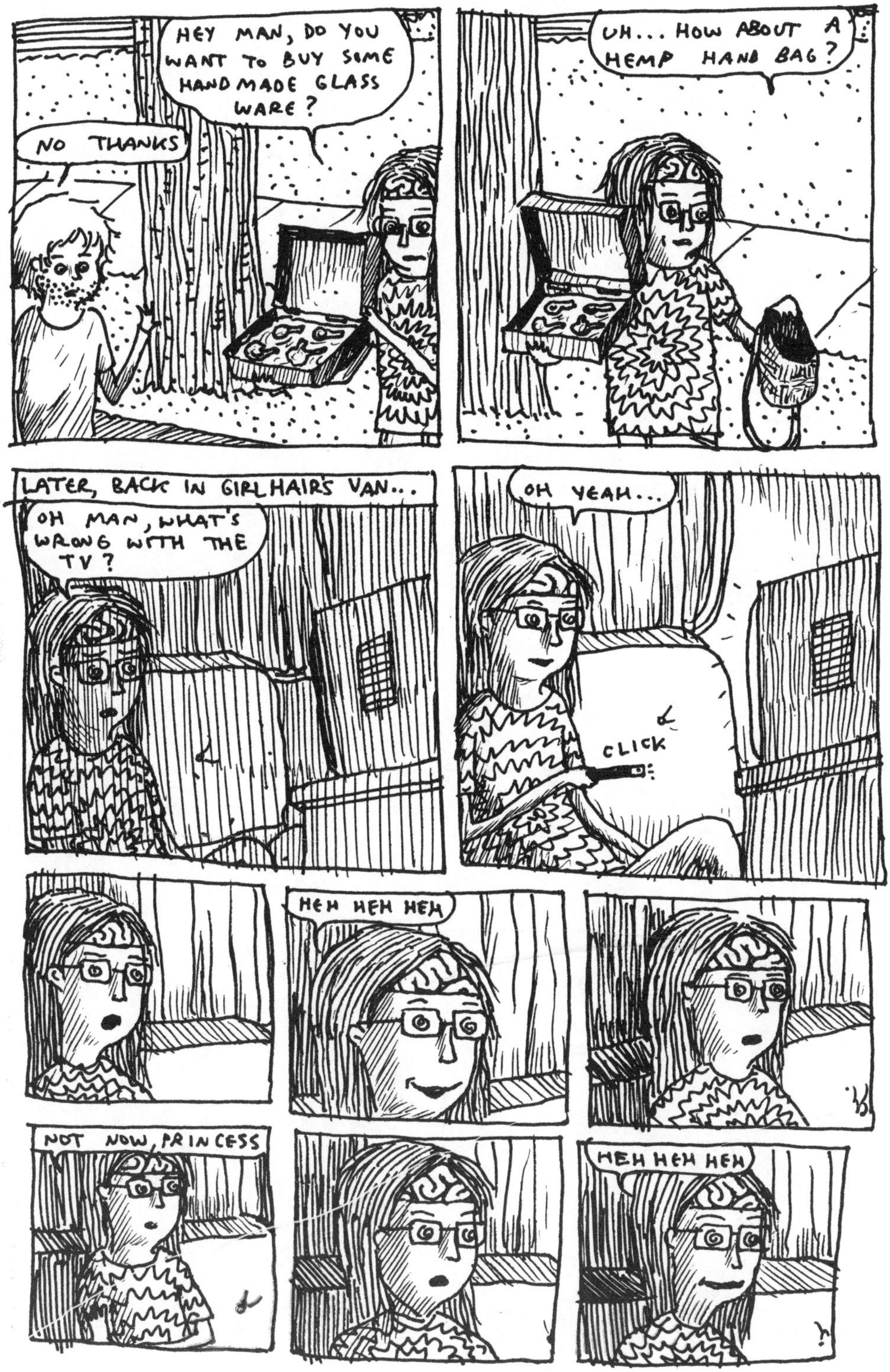
HEY MAN, DO YOU WANT TO BUY SOME HAND MADE GLASS WARE?
NO THANKS
UH... HOW ABOUT A HEMP HAND BAG?
LATER, BACK IN GIRLHAIR'S VAN...
OH MAN, WHAT'S WRONG WITH THE TV?
OH YEAH...
CLICK
HEH HEH HEH
NOT NOW, PRINCESS
HEH HEH HEH

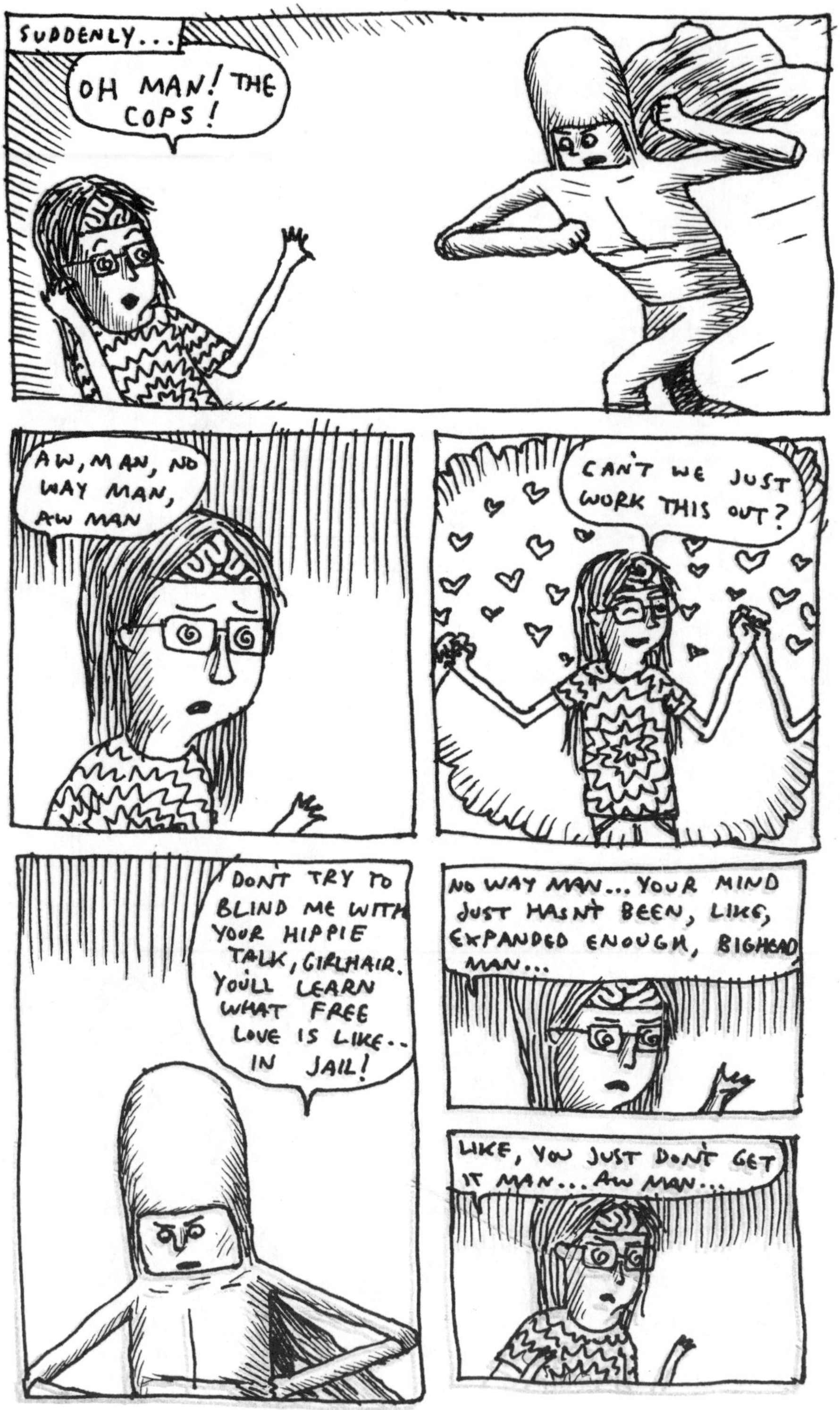
SUDDENLY...
OH MAN! THE COPS!
AW, MAN, NO WAY MAN, AW MAN
CAN'T WE JUST WORK THIS OUT?
DON'T TRY TO BLIND ME WITH YOUR HIPPIE TALK, GIRLHAIR. YOU'LL LEARN WHAT FREE LOVE IS LIKE.. IN JAIL!
NO WAY MAN... YOUR MIND JUST HASN'T BEEN, LIKE, EXPANDED ENOUGH, BIGHEAD MAN...
LIKE, YOU JUST DON'T GET IT MAN... AW MAN...

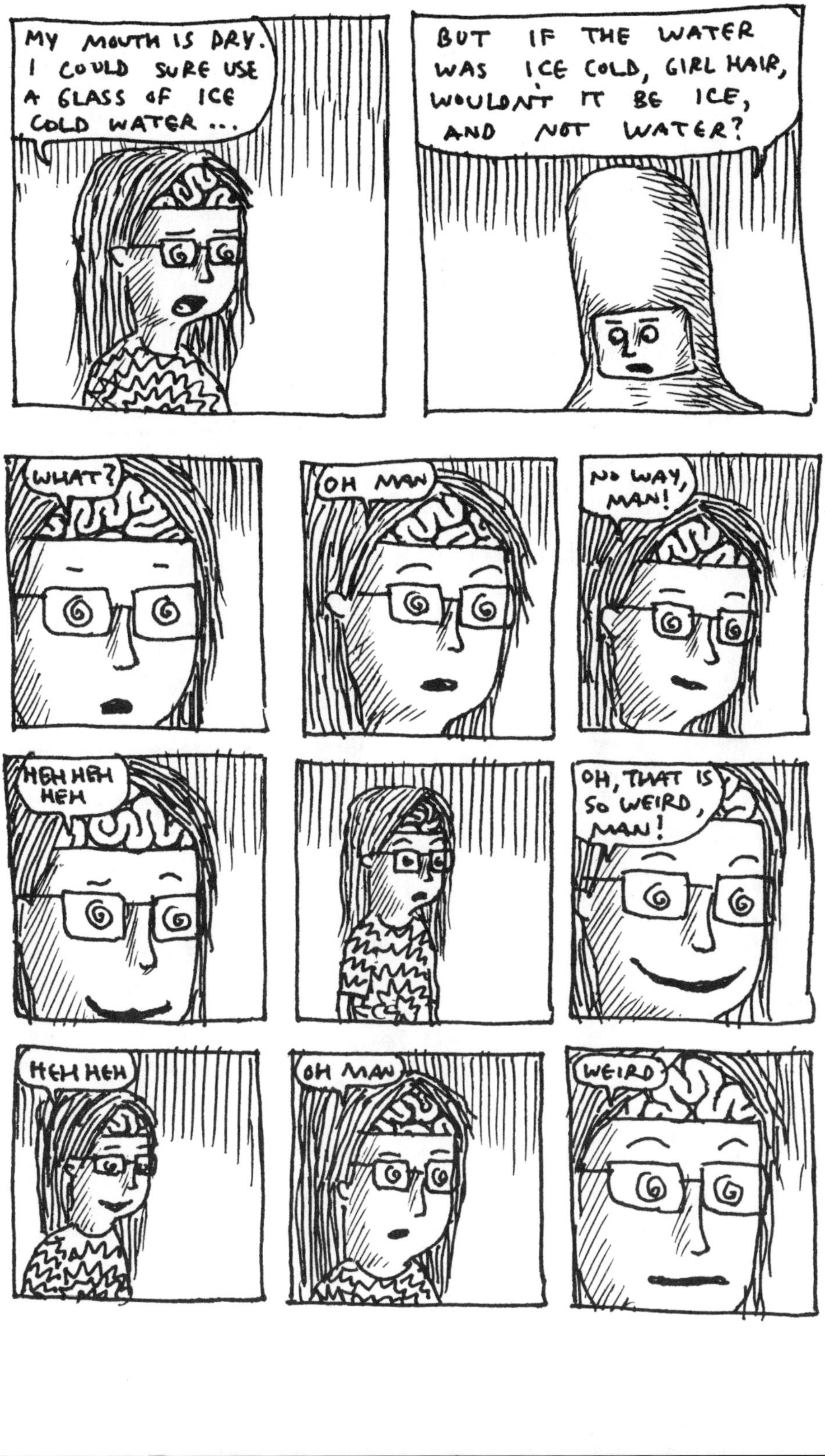
MY MOUTH IS DRY. I COULD SURE USE A GLASS OF ICE COLD WATER...
BUT IF THE WATER WAS ICE COLD, GIRL HAIR, WOULDN'T IT BE ICE, AND NOT WATER?
WHAT?
OH MAN
NO WAY, MAN!
HEH HEH HEH
OH, THAT IS SO WEIRD, MAN!
HEH HEH
OH MAN
WEIRD

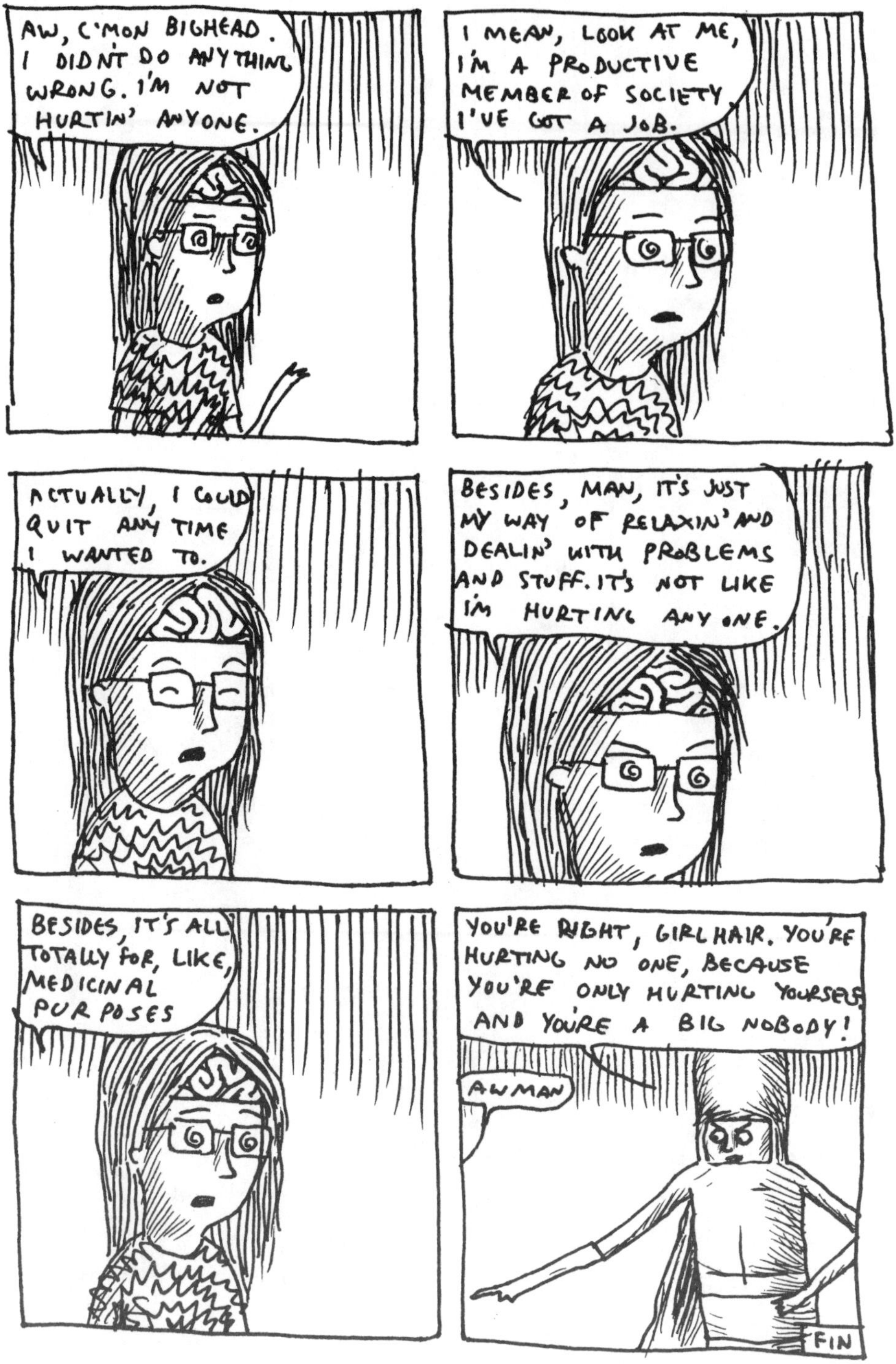
AW, C'MON BIGHEAD. I DIDN'T DO ANYTHING WRONG. I'M NOT HURTIN' ANYONE.
I MEAN, LOOK AT ME, I'M A PRODUCTIVE MEMBER OF SOCIETY. I'VE GOT A JOB.
ACTUALLY, I COULD QUIT ANY TIME I WANTED TO.
BESIDES, MAN, IT'S JUST MY WAY OF RELAXIN' AND DEALIN' WITH PROBLEMS AND STUFF. IT'S NOT LIKE I'M HURTING ANYONE.
BESIDES, IT'S ALL TOTALLY FOR, LIKE, MEDICINAL PURPOSES
YOU'RE RIGHT, GIRLHAIR. YOU'RE HURTING NO ONE, BECAUSE YOU'RE ONLY HURTING YOURSELF AND YOU'RE A BIG NOBODY!
AW MAN
FIN

GALLERY!

YOU'RE GOING TO PAY, RYBORG!
I TOLD YOU I'D HAVE THE MONEY NEXT WEEK, BIGHEAD!

BIGHEAD
FAN CLUB

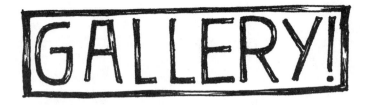

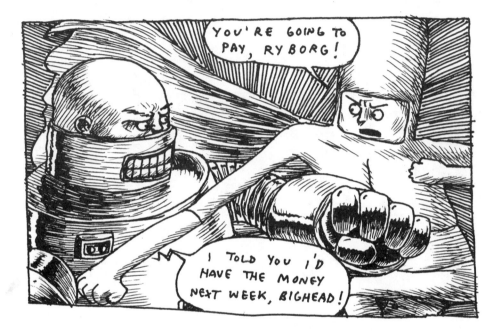

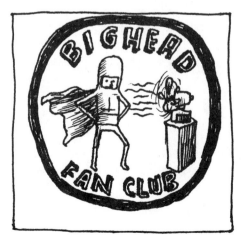

THIS PAGE

TOP: UNUSED POSTER ILLUSTRATION CONCEPT DESIGN SKETCH

BOTTOM: UNUSED BIGHEAD FAN CLUB PATCH DESIGN

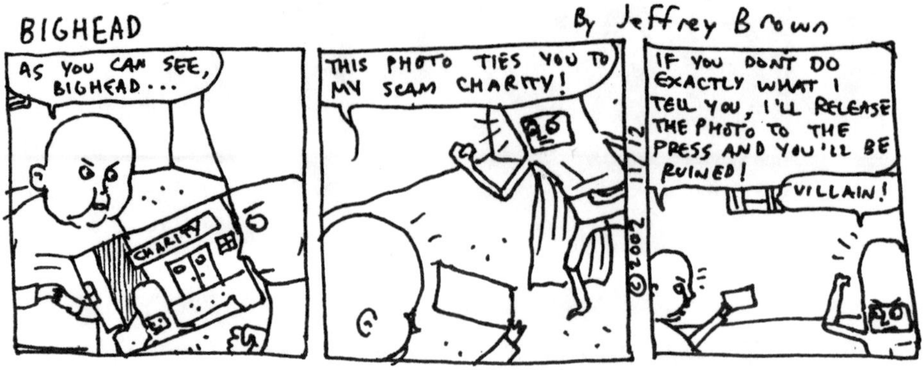
BIGHEAD
By Jeffrey Brown
AS YOU CAN SEE, BIGHEAD...
CHARITY
THIS PHOTO TIES YOU TO MY SCAM CHARITY!
© 2002 11/12
IF YOU DONT DO EXACTLY WHAT I TELL YOU, I'LL RELEASE THE PHOTO TO THE PRESS AND YOU'LL BE RUINED!
VILLAIN!

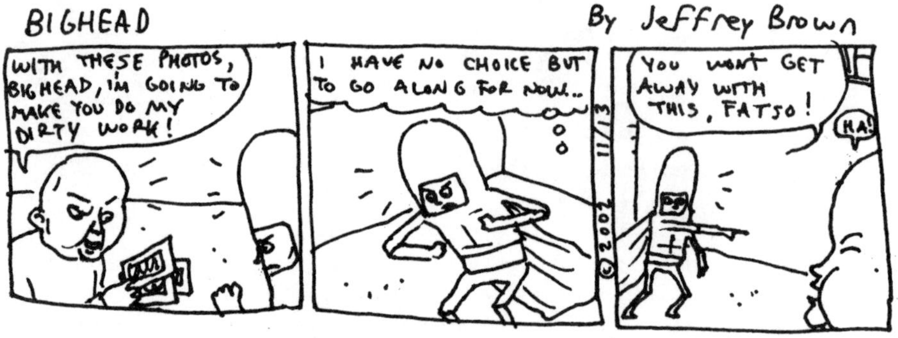
BIGHEAD
By Jeffrey Brown
WITH THESE PHOTOS, BIGHEAD, I'M GOING TO MAKE YOU DO MY DIRTY WORK!
I HAVE NO CHOICE BUT TO GO ALONG FOR NOW...
© 2002 11/13
YOU WON'T GET AWAY WITH THIS, FATSO!
HA!

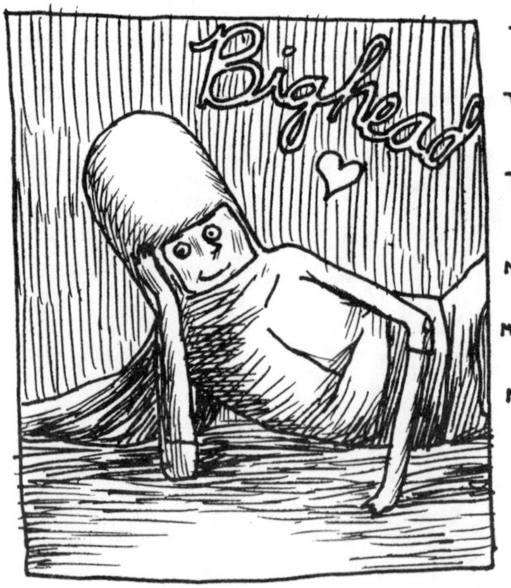
Bighead

THIS PAGE:

TOP LEFT: PANEL 1 OF PROPOSED BIGHEAD NEWSPAPER STRIP

TOP MIDDLE: PANEL 2 OF PROPOSED BIGHEAD NEWSPAPER STRIP

TOP RIGHT: PANELL 3 OF PROPOSED BIGHEAD NEWSPAPER STRIP

MIDDLE LEFT: PANEL 1 OF PROPOSED BIGHEAD NEWSPAPER STRIP

MIDDLE MIDDLE: PANEL 2 OF PROPOSED BIGHEAD NEWSPAPER STRIP

MIDDLE RIGHT: PANEL 3 OF PROPOSED BIGHEAD NEWSPAPER STRIP

BOTTOM: UNUSED BIGHEAD SPOT ILLUSTRATION

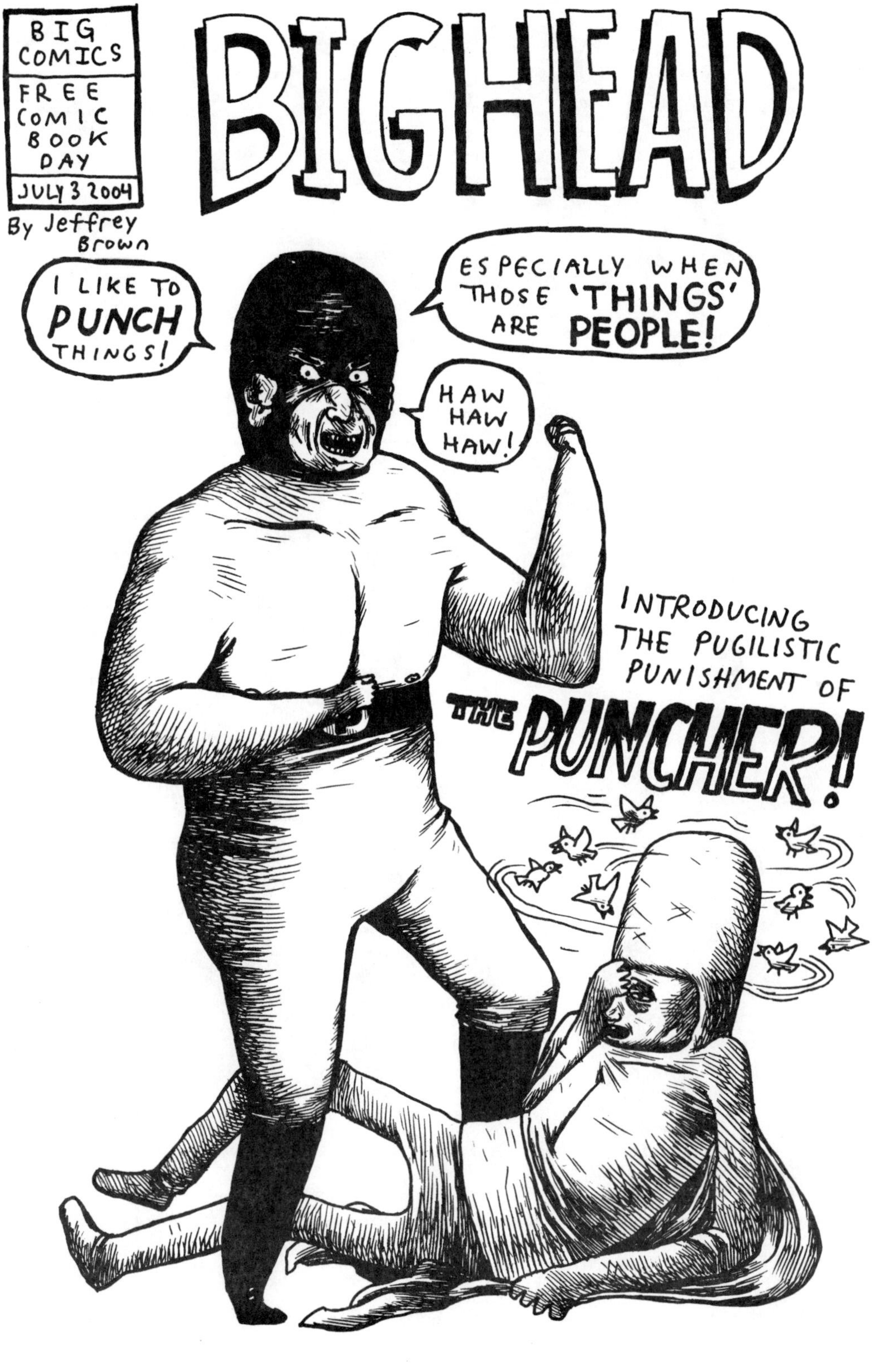
BIG COMICS
FREE COMIC BOOK DAY
JULY 3 2004
BIGHEAD
By Jeffrey Brown
I LIKE TO PUNCH THINGS!
ESPECIALLY WHEN THOSE 'THINGS' ARE PEOPLE!
HAW HAW HAW!
INTRODUCING THE PUGILISTIC PUNISHMENT OF
THE PUNCHER!

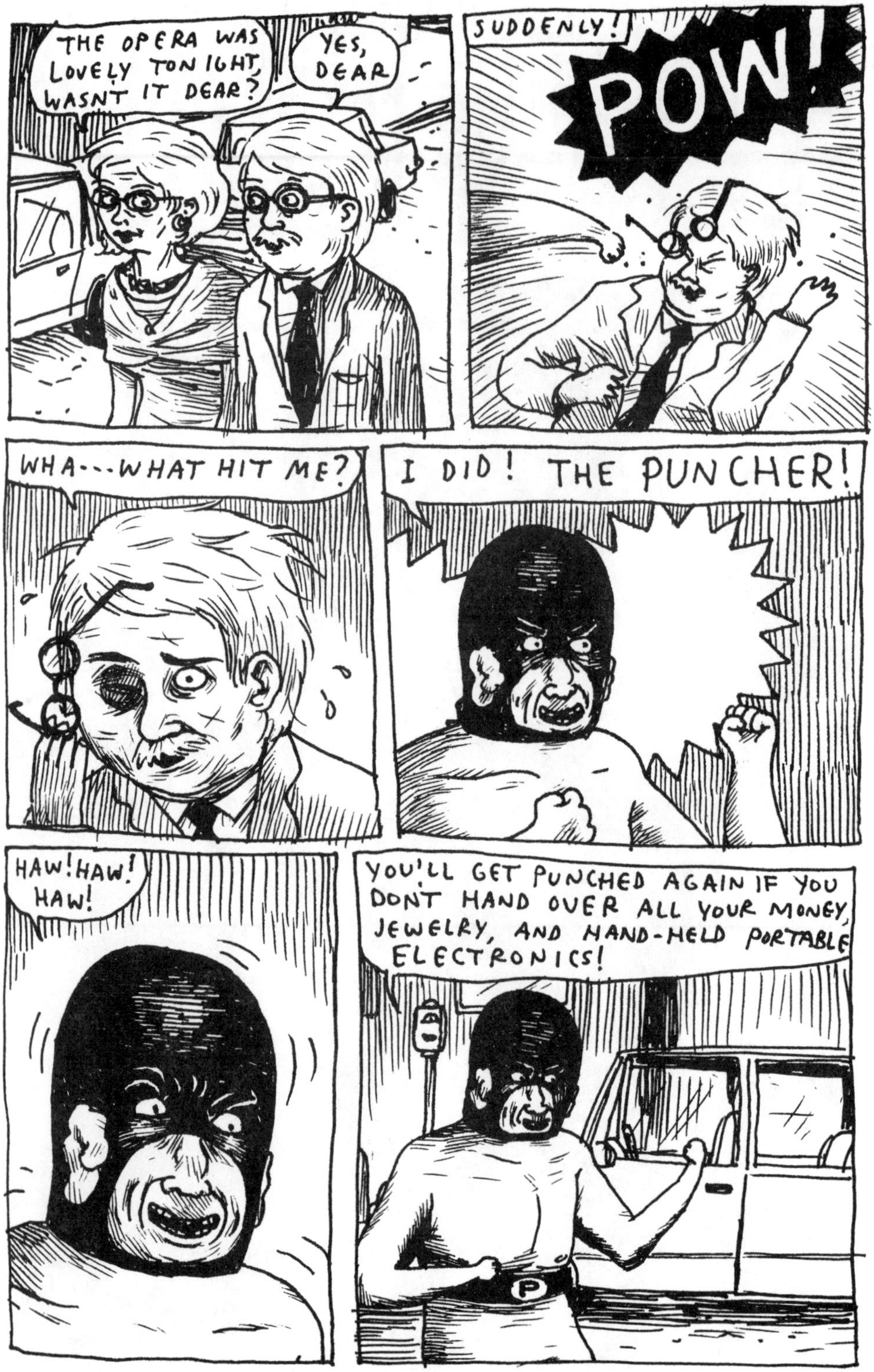
THE OPERA WAS LOVELY TONIGHT, WASN'T IT DEAR?
YES, DEAR
SUDDENLY!
POW!
WHA---WHAT HIT ME?
I DID! THE PUNCHER!
HAW! HAW! HAW!
YOU'LL GET PUNCHED AGAIN IF YOU DON'T HAND OVER ALL YOUR MONEY, JEWELRY, AND HAND-HELD PORTABLE ELECTRONICS!

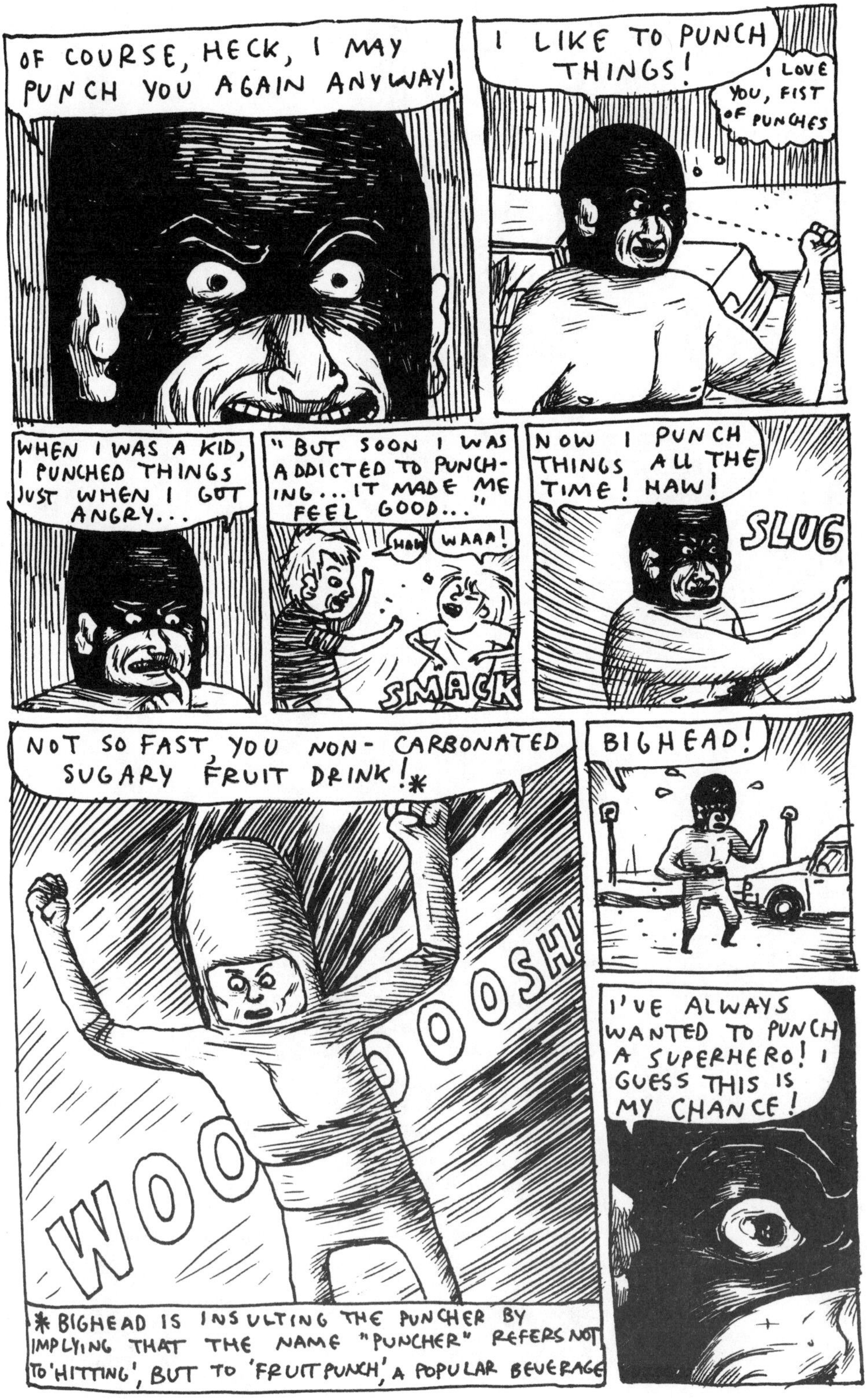

OF COURSE, HECK, I MAY PUNCH YOU AGAIN ANYWAY!
I LIKE TO PUNCH THINGS!
I LOVE YOU, FIST OF PUNCHES
WHEN I WAS A KID, I PUNCHED THINGS JUST WHEN I GOT ANGRY...
"BUT SOON I WAS ADDICTED TO PUNCHING... IT MADE ME FEEL GOOD..."
HAW
WAAA!
SMACK
NOW I PUNCH THINGS ALL THE TIME! HAW!
SLUG
NOT SO FAST, YOU NON-CARBONATED SUGARY FRUIT DRINK!*
WOOOOOOSH!
BIGHEAD!
I'VE ALWAYS WANTED TO PUNCH A SUPERHERO! I GUESS THIS IS MY CHANCE!
* BIGHEAD IS INSULTING THE PUNCHER BY IMPLYING THAT THE NAME "PUNCHER" REFERS NOT TO 'HITTING', BUT TO 'FRUIT PUNCH', A POPULAR BEVERAGE

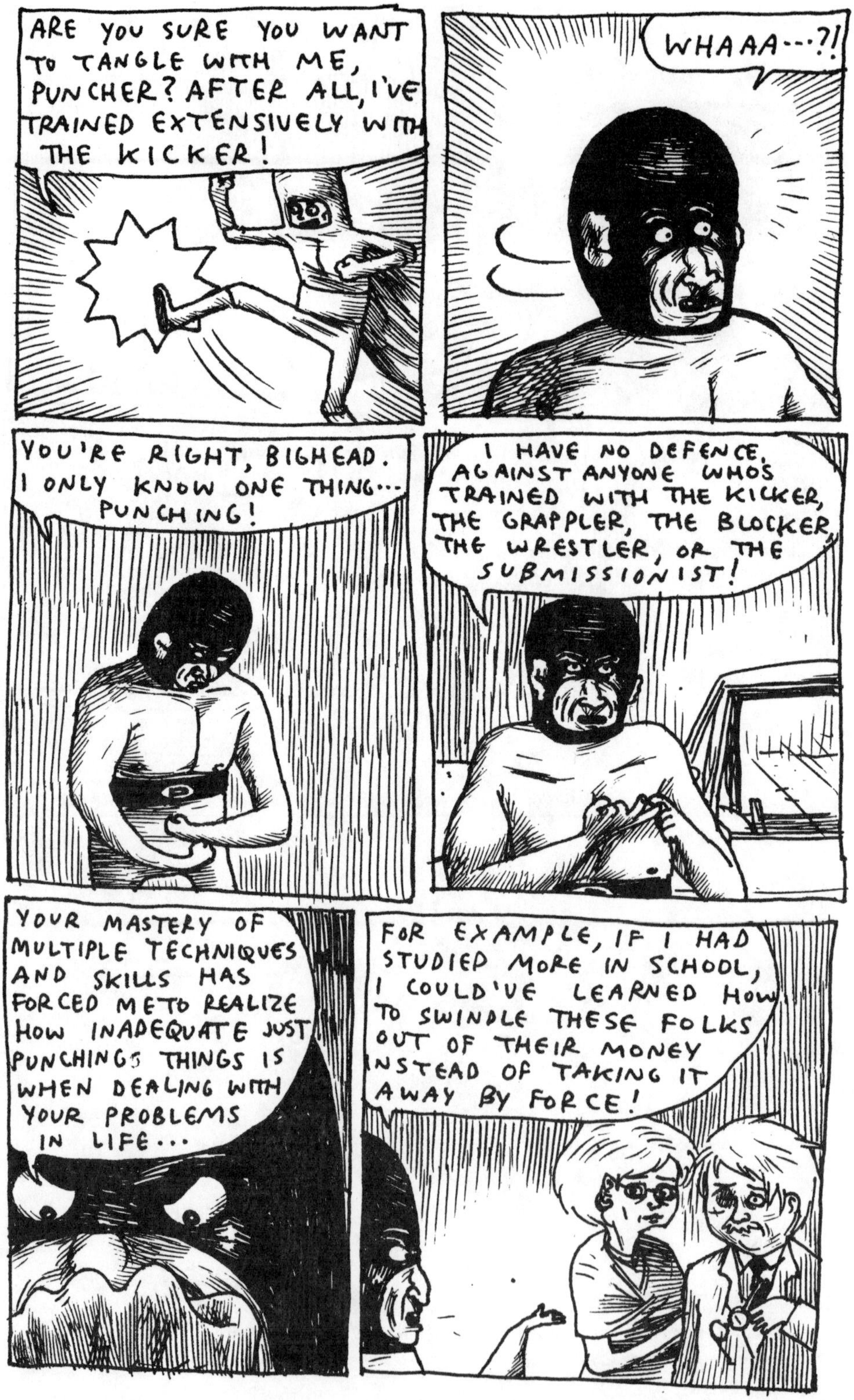
ARE YOU SURE YOU WANT TO TANGLE WITH ME, PUNCHER? AFTER ALL, I'VE TRAINED EXTENSIVELY WITH THE KICKER!
WHAAA...?!
YOU'RE RIGHT, BIGHEAD. I ONLY KNOW ONE THING... PUNCHING!
I HAVE NO DEFENCE AGAINST ANYONE WHO'S TRAINED WITH THE KICKER, THE GRAPPLER, THE BLOCKER, THE WRESTLER, OR THE SUBMISSIONIST!
YOUR MASTERY OF MULTIPLE TECHNIQUES AND SKILLS HAS FORCED ME TO REALIZE HOW INADEQUATE JUST PUNCHINGS THINGS IS WHEN DEALING WITH YOUR PROBLEMS IN LIFE...
FOR EXAMPLE, IF I HAD STUDIED MORE IN SCHOOL, I COULD'VE LEARNED HOW TO SWINDLE THESE FOLKS OUT OF THEIR MONEY INSTEAD OF TAKING IT AWAY BY FORCE!

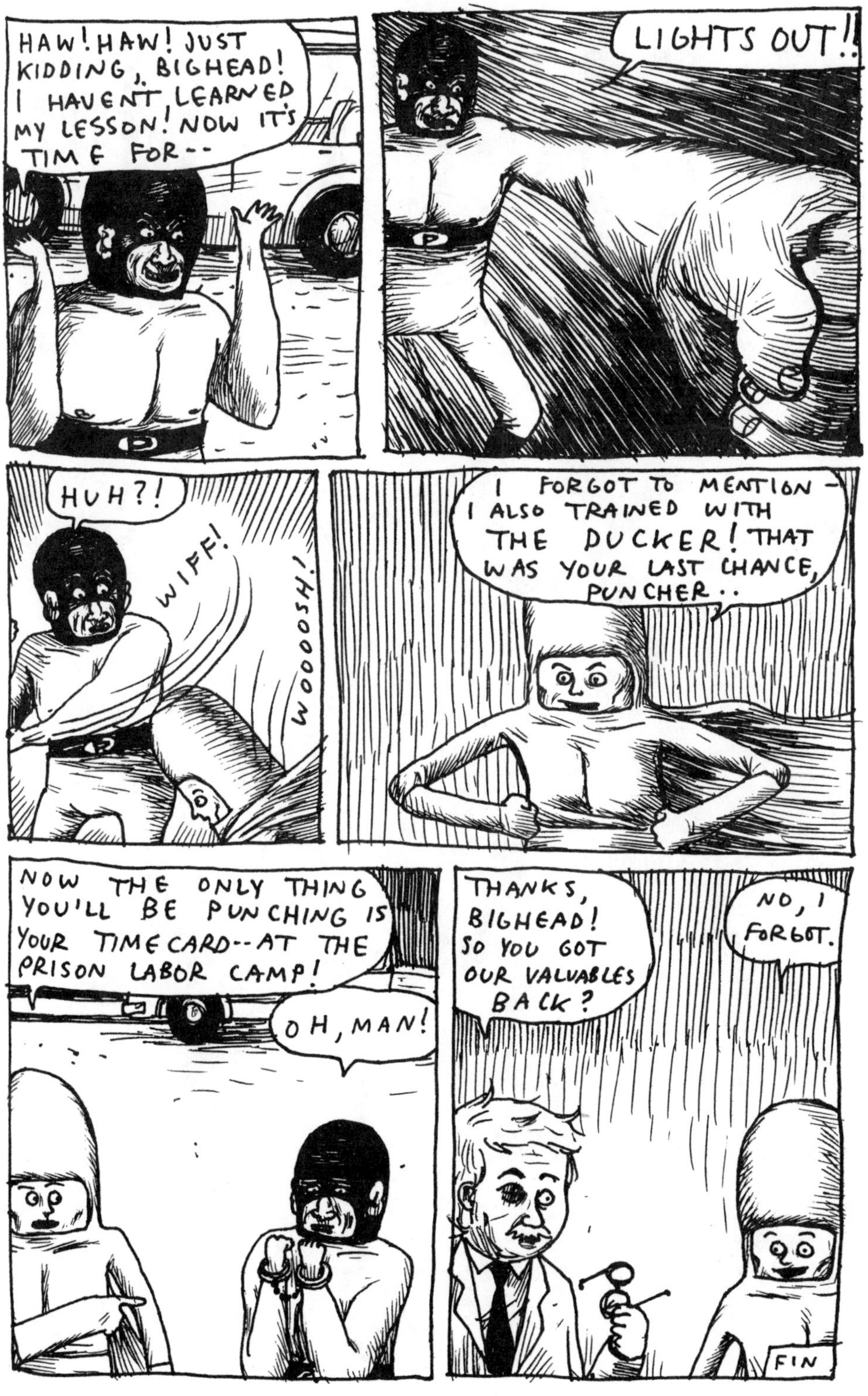
HAW! HAW! JUST KIDDING, BIGHEAD! I HAVEN'T LEARNED MY LESSON! NOW IT'S TIME FOR--
LIGHTS OUT!!
HUH?!
WIFF!
WOOOOOSH!
I FORGOT TO MENTION - I ALSO TRAINED WITH THE DUCKER! THAT WAS YOUR LAST CHANCE, PUNCHER..
NOW THE ONLY THING YOU'LL BE PUNCHING IS YOUR TIMECARD--AT THE PRISON LABOR CAMP!
OH, MAN!
THANKS, BIGHEAD! SO YOU GOT OUR VALUABLES BACK?
NO, I FORGOT.
FIN

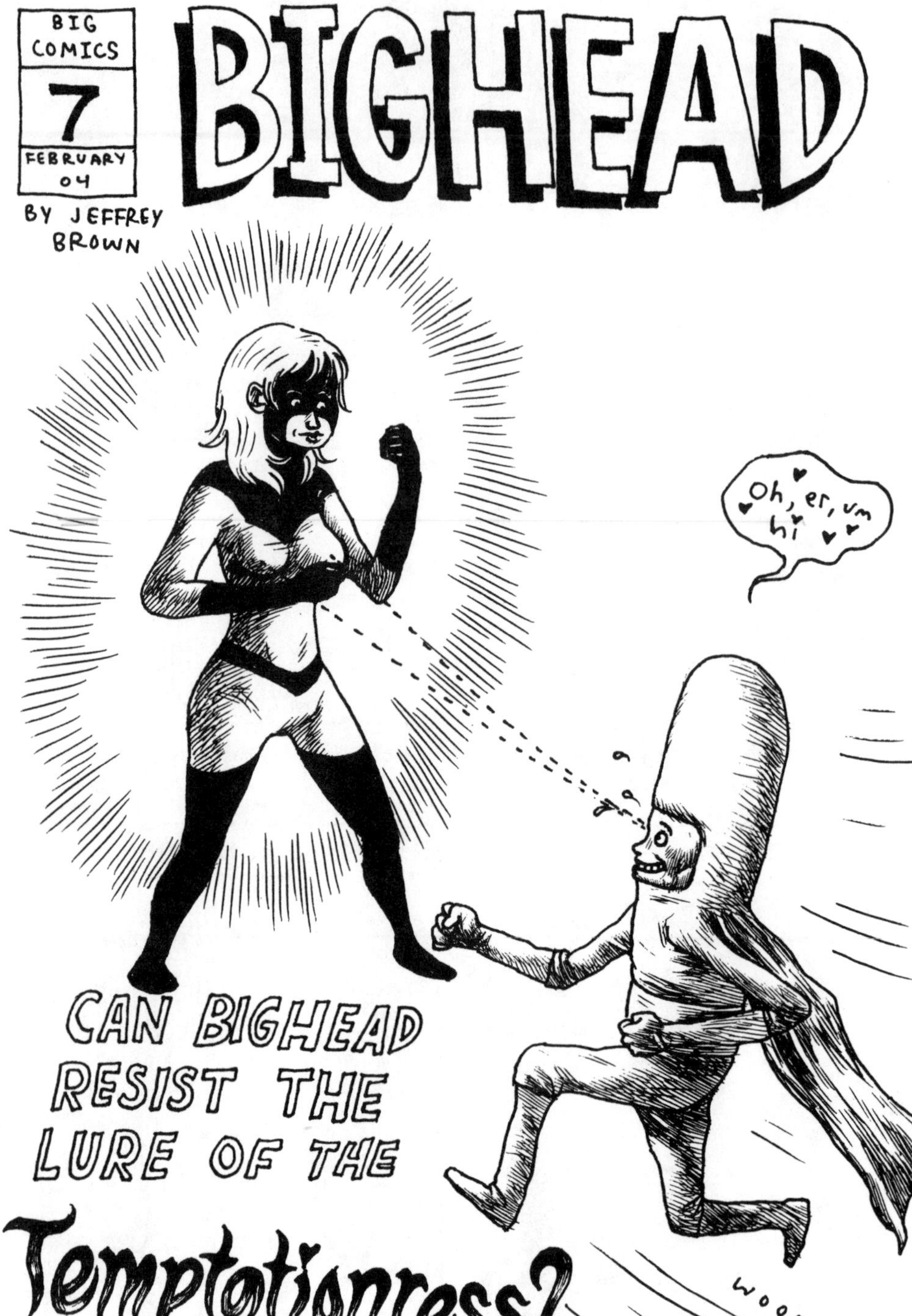

BIG COMICS
7
FEBRUARY 04
BIGHEAD
BY JEFFREY BROWN
Oh, er, um hi
CAN BIGHEAD RESIST THE LURE OF THE
Temptotionress?
WOOOOOOSH!

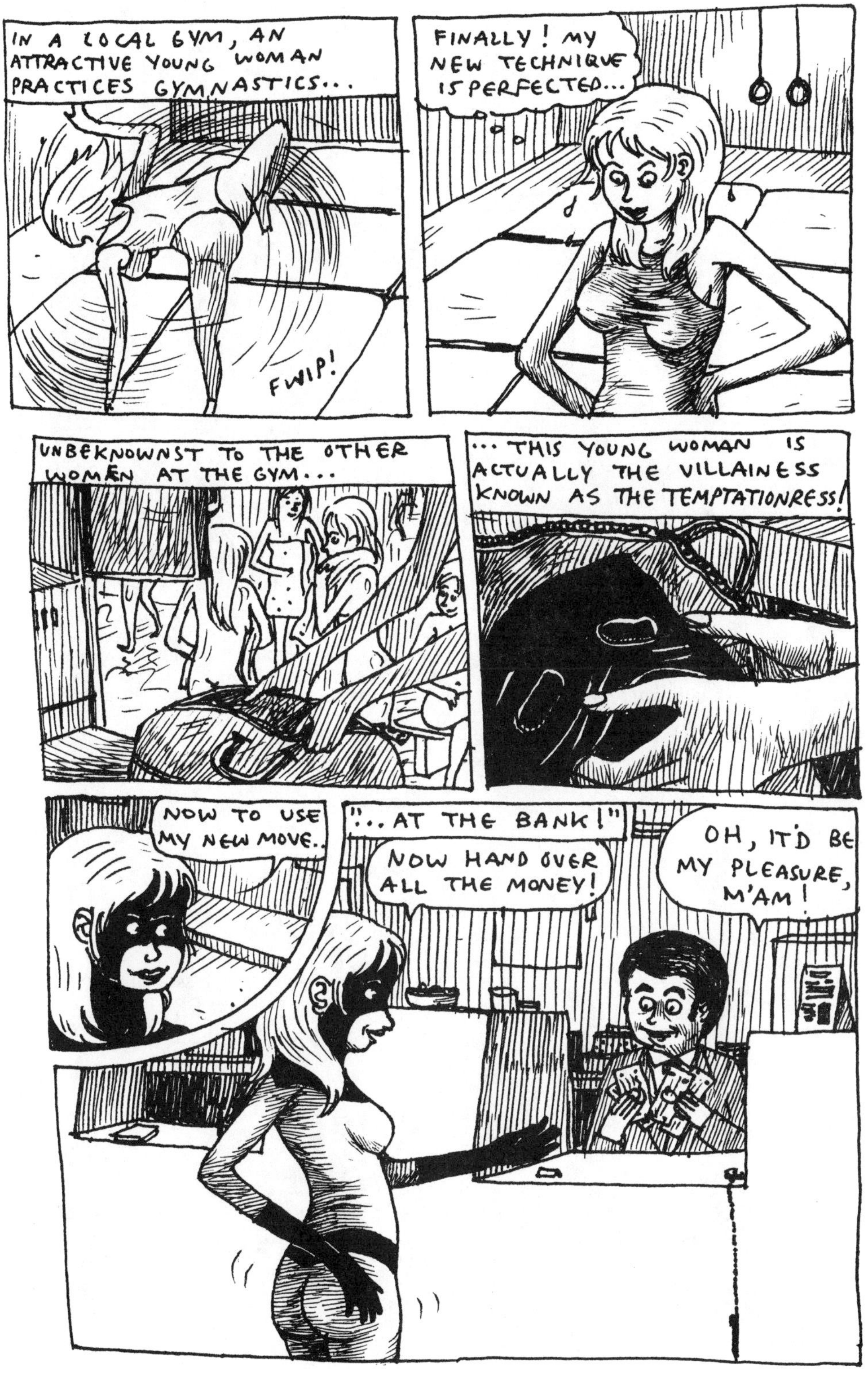
IN A LOCAL GYM, AN ATTRACTIVE YOUNG WOMAN PRACTICES GYMNASTICS...
FWIP!
FINALLY! MY NEW TECHNIQUE IS PERFECTED...
UNBEKNOWNST TO THE OTHER WOMEN AT THE GYM...
... THIS YOUNG WOMAN IS ACTUALLY THE VILLAINESS KNOWN AS THE TEMPTATIONRESS!
NOW TO USE MY NEW MOVE..
"..AT THE BANK!"
NOW HAND OVER ALL THE MONEY!
OH, IT'D BE MY PLEASURE, M'AM!

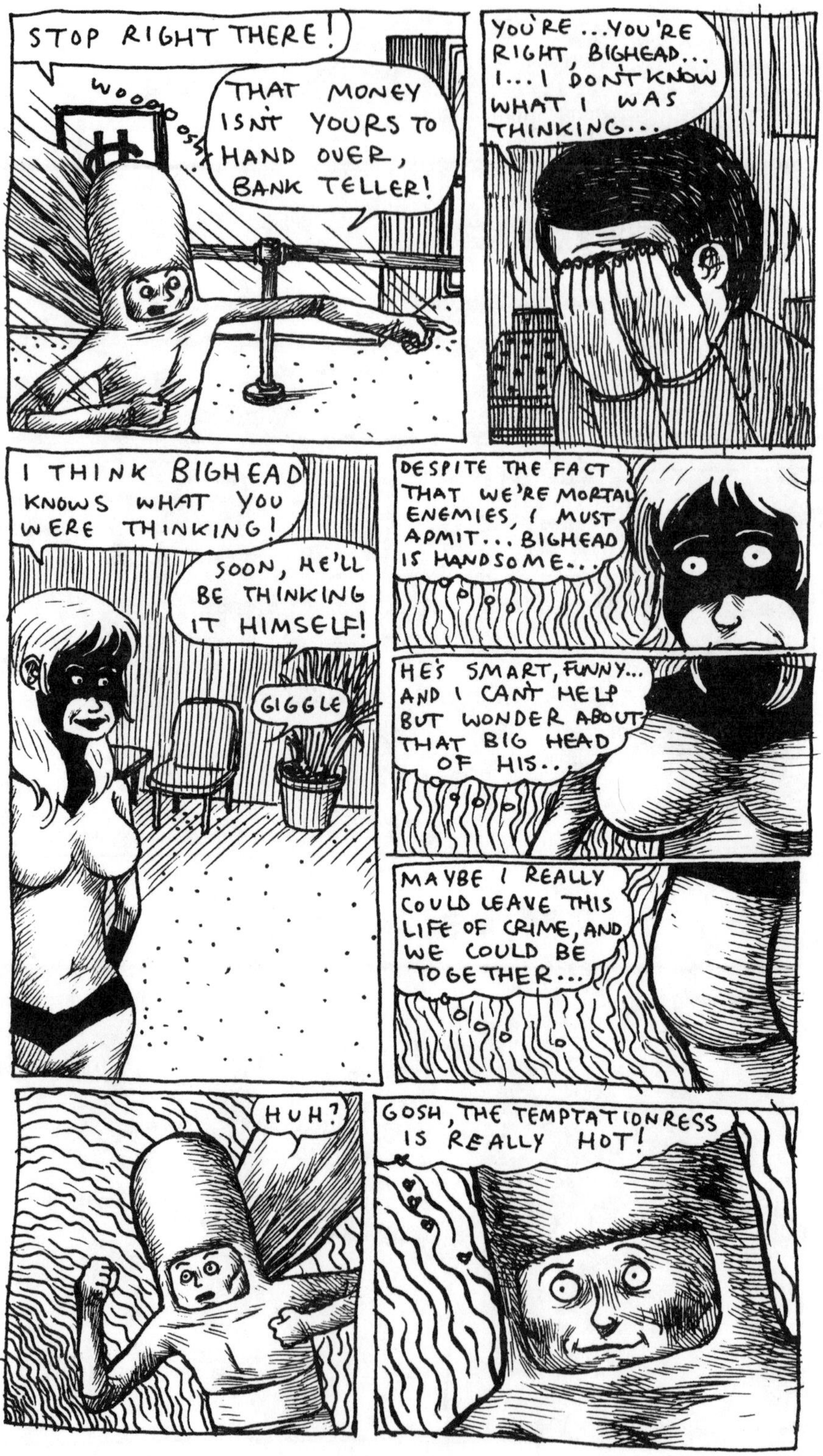
STOP RIGHT THERE!
WOOOOOOSH
THAT MONEY ISN'T YOURS TO HAND OVER, BANK TELLER!
YOU'RE ...YOU'RE RIGHT, BIGHEAD... I... I DON'T KNOW WHAT I WAS THINKING...
I THINK BIGHEAD KNOWS WHAT YOU WERE THINKING!
SOON, HE'LL BE THINKING IT HIMSELF!
GIGGLE
DESPITE THE FACT THAT WE'RE MORTAL ENEMIES, I MUST ADMIT... BIGHEAD IS HANDSOME...
HE'S SMART, FUNNY... AND I CAN'T HELP BUT WONDER ABOUT THAT BIG HEAD OF HIS...
MAYBE I REALLY COULD LEAVE THIS LIFE OF CRIME, AND WE COULD BE TOGETHER...
HUH?
GOSH, THE TEMPTATIONRESS IS REALLY HOT!

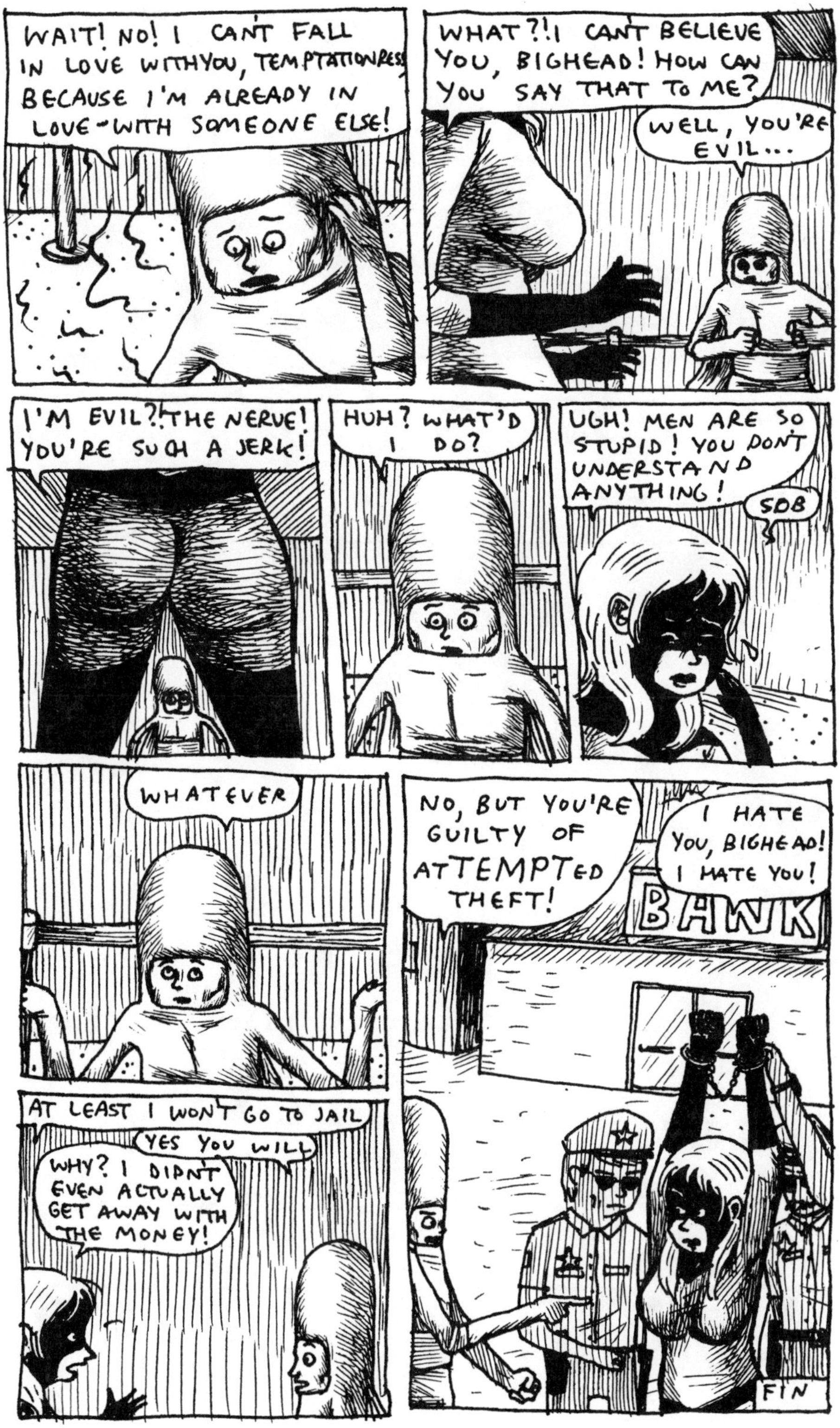
WAIT! NO! I CAN'T FALL IN LOVE WITH YOU, TEMPTATIONRESS BECAUSE I'M ALREADY IN LOVE-WITH SOMEONE ELSE!
WHAT?! I CAN'T BELIEVE YOU, BIGHEAD! HOW CAN YOU SAY THAT TO ME?
WELL, YOU'RE EVIL...
I'M EVIL?! THE NERVE! YOU'RE SUCH A JERK!
HUH? WHAT'D I DO?
UGH! MEN ARE SO STUPID! YOU DON'T UNDERSTAND ANYTHING!
SOB
WHATEVER
NO, BUT YOU'RE GUILTY OF ATTEMPTED THEFT!
I HATE YOU, BIGHEAD! I HATE YOU!
BANK
AT LEAST I WON'T GO TO JAIL
YES YOU WILL
WHY? I DIDN'T EVEN ACTUALLY GET AWAY WITH THE MONEY!
FIN

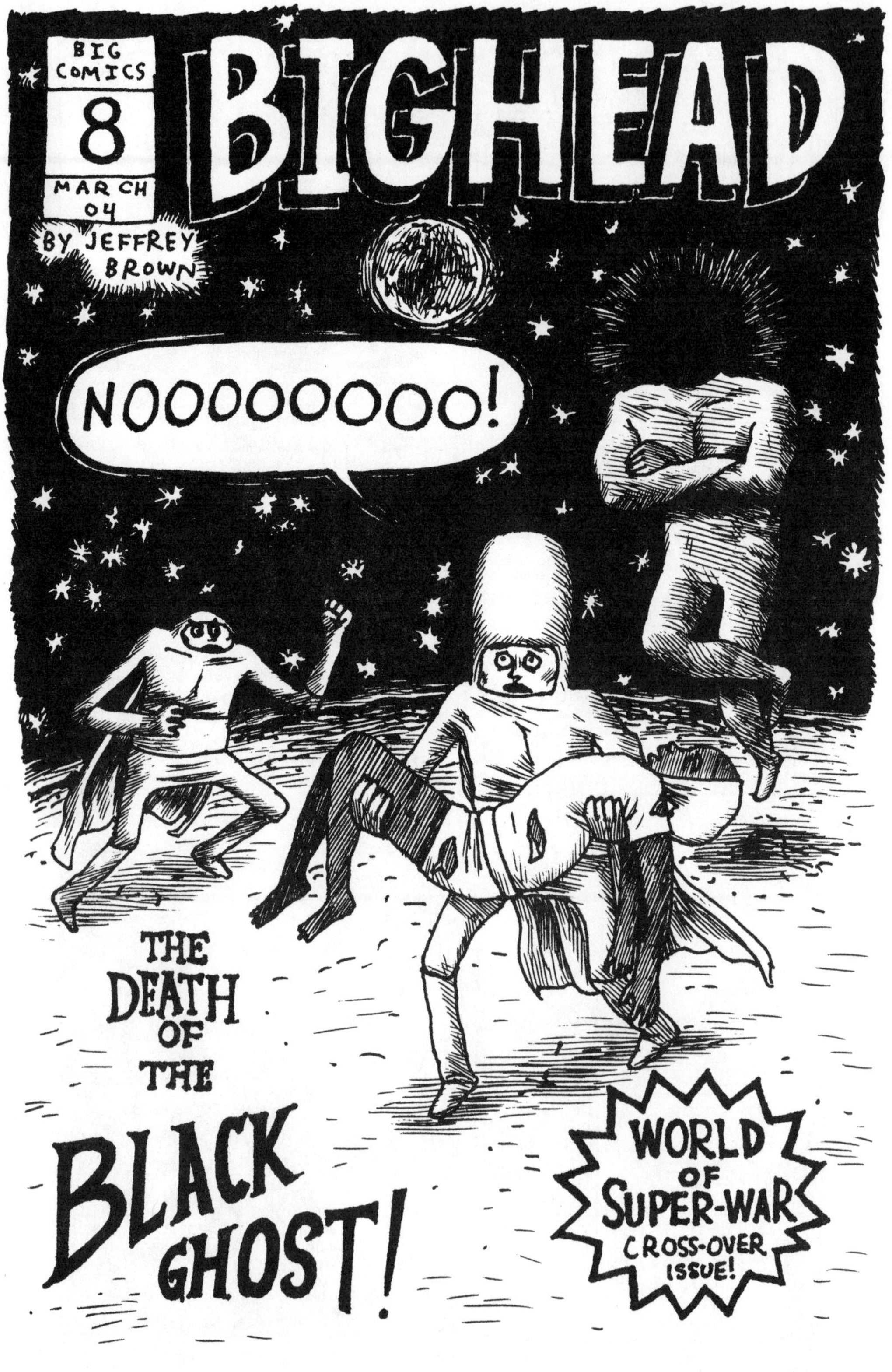
BIG COMICS
8
MARCH 04
BIGHEAD
BY JEFFREY BROWN
NOOOOOOOO!
THE DEATH OF THE BLACK GHOST!
WORLD OF SUPER-WAR CROSS-OVER ISSUE!

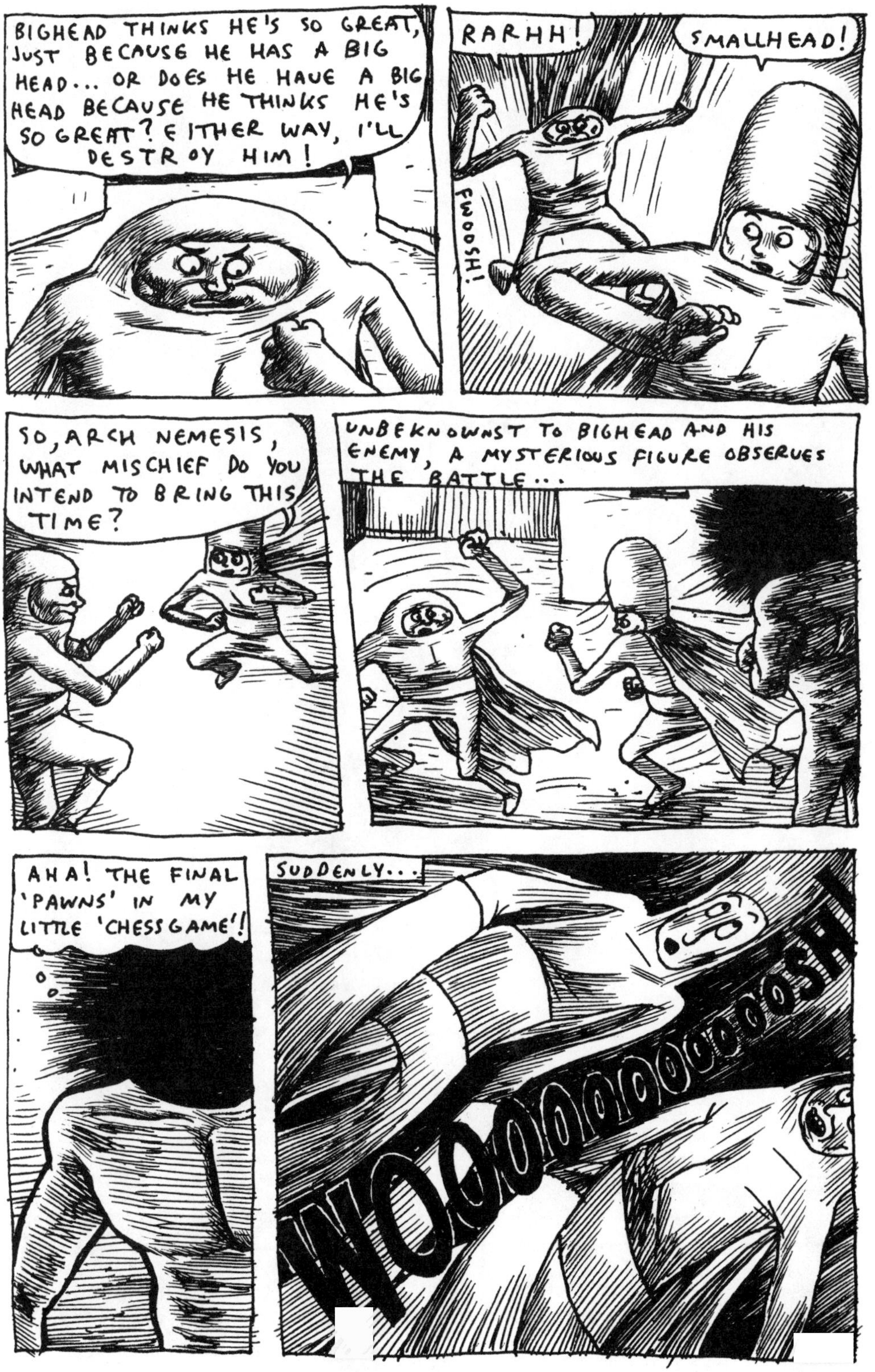
BIGHEAD THINKS HE'S SO GREAT, JUST BECAUSE HE HAS A BIG HEAD... OR DOES HE HAVE A BIG HEAD BECAUSE HE THINKS HE'S SO GREAT? EITHER WAY, I'LL DESTROY HIM!
RARHH!
SMALLHEAD!
FWOOSH!
SO, ARCH NEMESIS, WHAT MISCHIEF DO YOU INTEND TO BRING THIS TIME?
UNBEKNOWNST TO BIGHEAD AND HIS ENEMY, A MYSTERIOUS FIGURE OBSERVES THE BATTLE...
AHA! THE FINAL 'PAWNS' IN MY LITTLE 'CHESSGAME'!
SUDDENLY...
WOOOOOOOOOOOOSH!

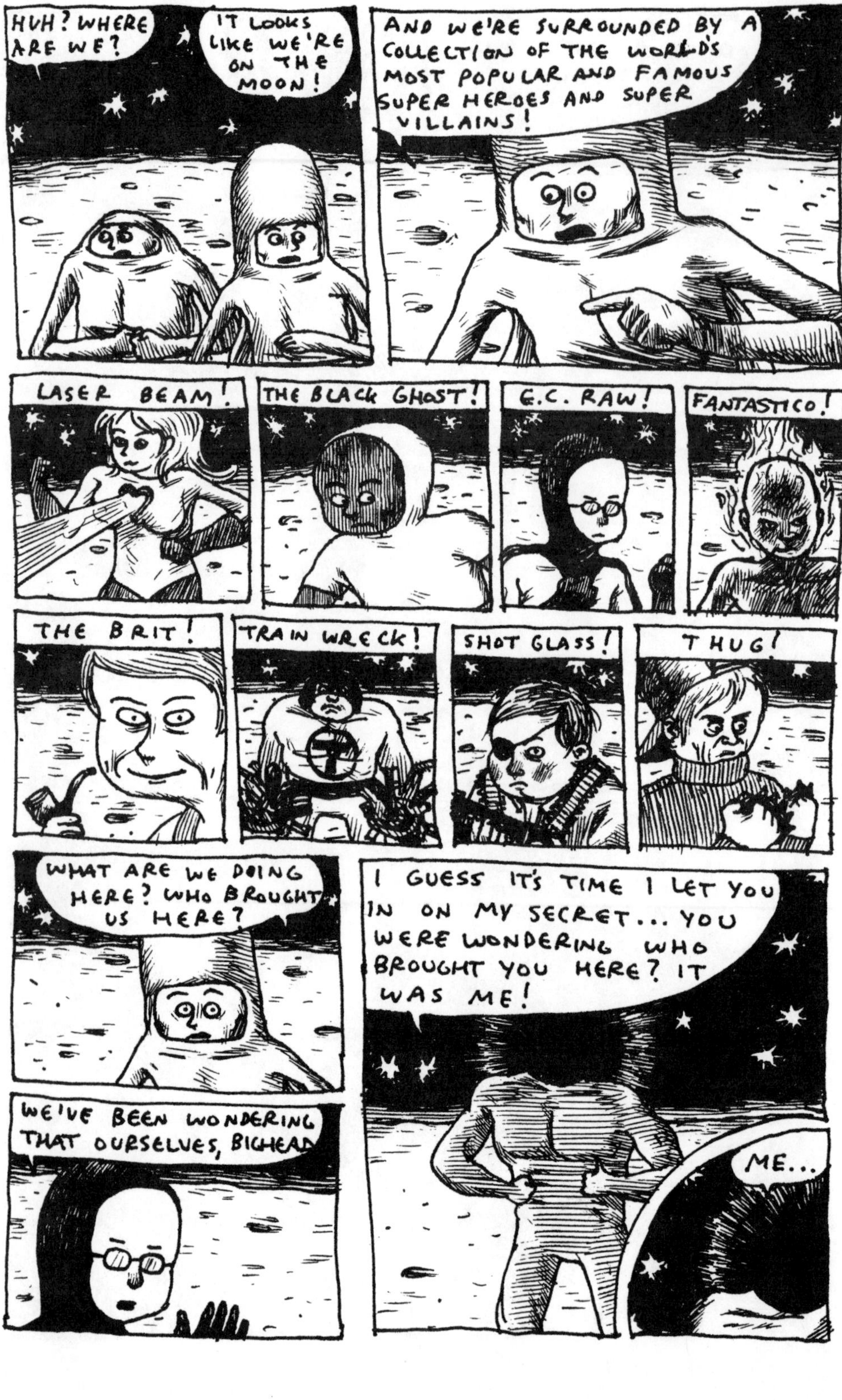
HUH? WHERE ARE WE?
IT LOOKS LIKE WE'RE ON THE MOON!
AND WE'RE SURROUNDED BY A COLLECTION OF THE WORLD'S MOST POPULAR AND FAMOUS SUPER HEROES AND SUPER VILLAINS!
LASER BEAM!
THE BLACK GHOST!
E.C. RAW!
FANTASTICO!
THE BRIT!
TRAIN WRECK!
SHOT GLASS!
THUG!
WHAT ARE WE DOING HERE? WHO BROUGHT US HERE?
WE'VE BEEN WONDERING THAT OURSELVES, BIGHEAD
I GUESS IT'S TIME I LET YOU IN ON MY SECRET... YOU WERE WONDERING WHO BROUGHT YOU HERE? IT WAS ME!
ME...

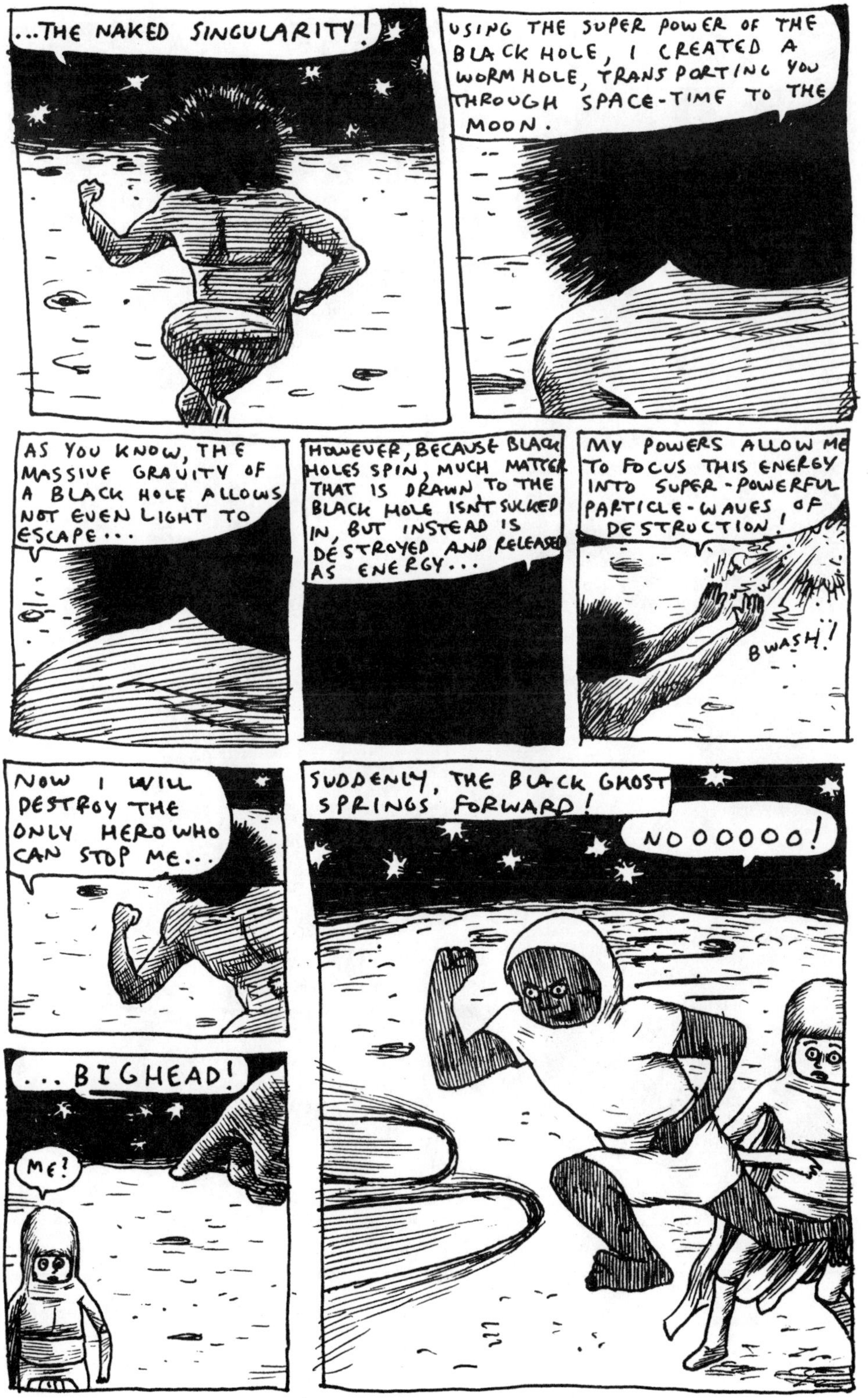
...THE NAKED SINGULARITY!
USING THE SUPER POWER OF THE BLACK HOLE, I CREATED A WORMHOLE, TRANSPORTING YOU THROUGH SPACE-TIME TO THE MOON.
AS YOU KNOW, THE MASSIVE GRAVITY OF A BLACK HOLE ALLOWS NOT EVEN LIGHT TO ESCAPE...
HOWEVER, BECAUSE BLACK HOLES SPIN, MUCH MATTER THAT IS DRAWN TO THE BLACK HOLE ISN'T SUCKED IN, BUT INSTEAD IS DESTROYED AND RELEASED AS ENERGY...
MY POWERS ALLOW ME TO FOCUS THIS ENERGY INTO SUPER-POWERFUL PARTICLE-WAVES OF DESTRUCTION!
BWASH!
NOW I WILL DESTROY THE ONLY HERO WHO CAN STOP ME...
...BIGHEAD!
ME?
SUDDENLY, THE BLACK GHOST SPRINGS FORWARD!
NOOOOOO!

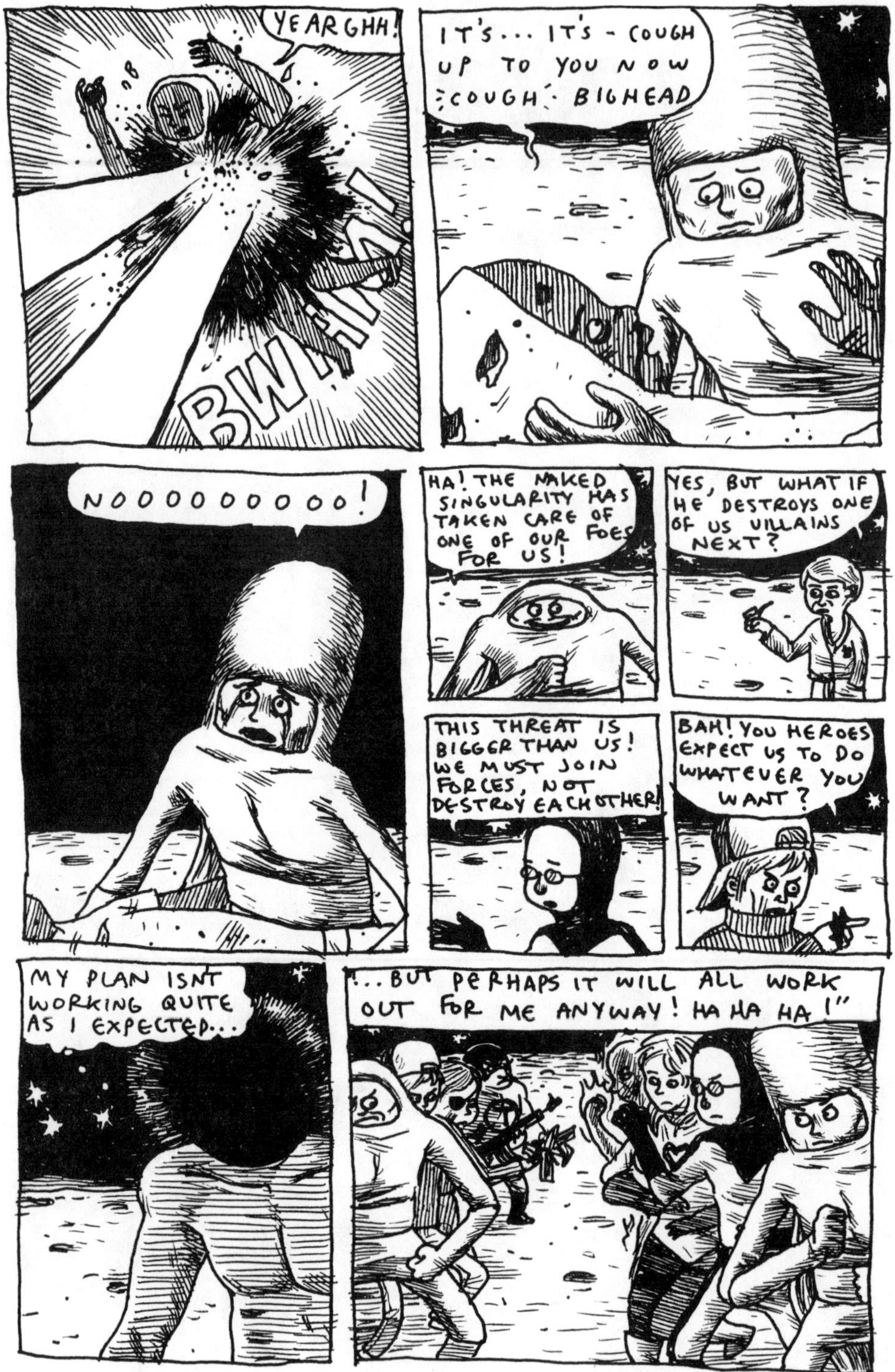
YEARGHH!
BWHAM!
IT'S... IT'S - COUGH UP TO YOU NOW :COUGH: BIGHEAD
NOOOOOOOOOO!
HA! THE NAKED SINGULARITY HAS TAKEN CARE OF ONE OF OUR FOES FOR US!
YES, BUT WHAT IF HE DESTROYS ONE OF US VILLAINS NEXT?
THIS THREAT IS BIGGER THAN US! WE MUST JOIN FORCES, NOT DESTROY EACHOTHER!
BAH! YOU HEROES EXPECT US TO DO WHATEVER YOU WANT?
MY PLAN ISNT WORKING QUITE AS I EXPECTED...
"...BUT PERHAPS IT WILL ALL WORK OUT FOR ME ANYWAY! HA HA HA!"

CONTINUED IN WORLD OF SUPER-WAR ISSUE #7!

BIG COMICS
9
APRIL 04

BIGHEAD

BY JEFFREY BROWN

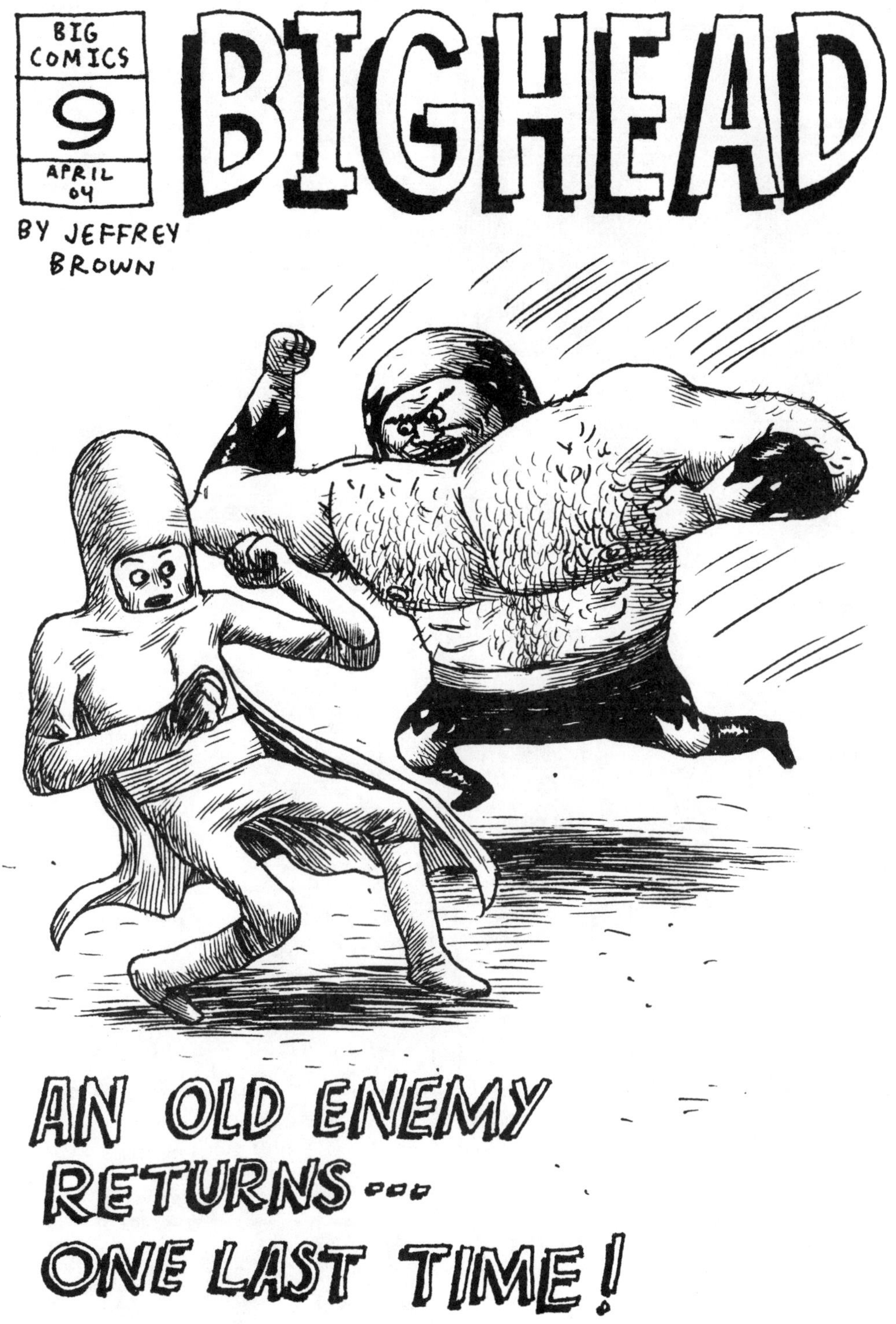

AN OLD ENEMY RETURNS... ONE LAST TIME!

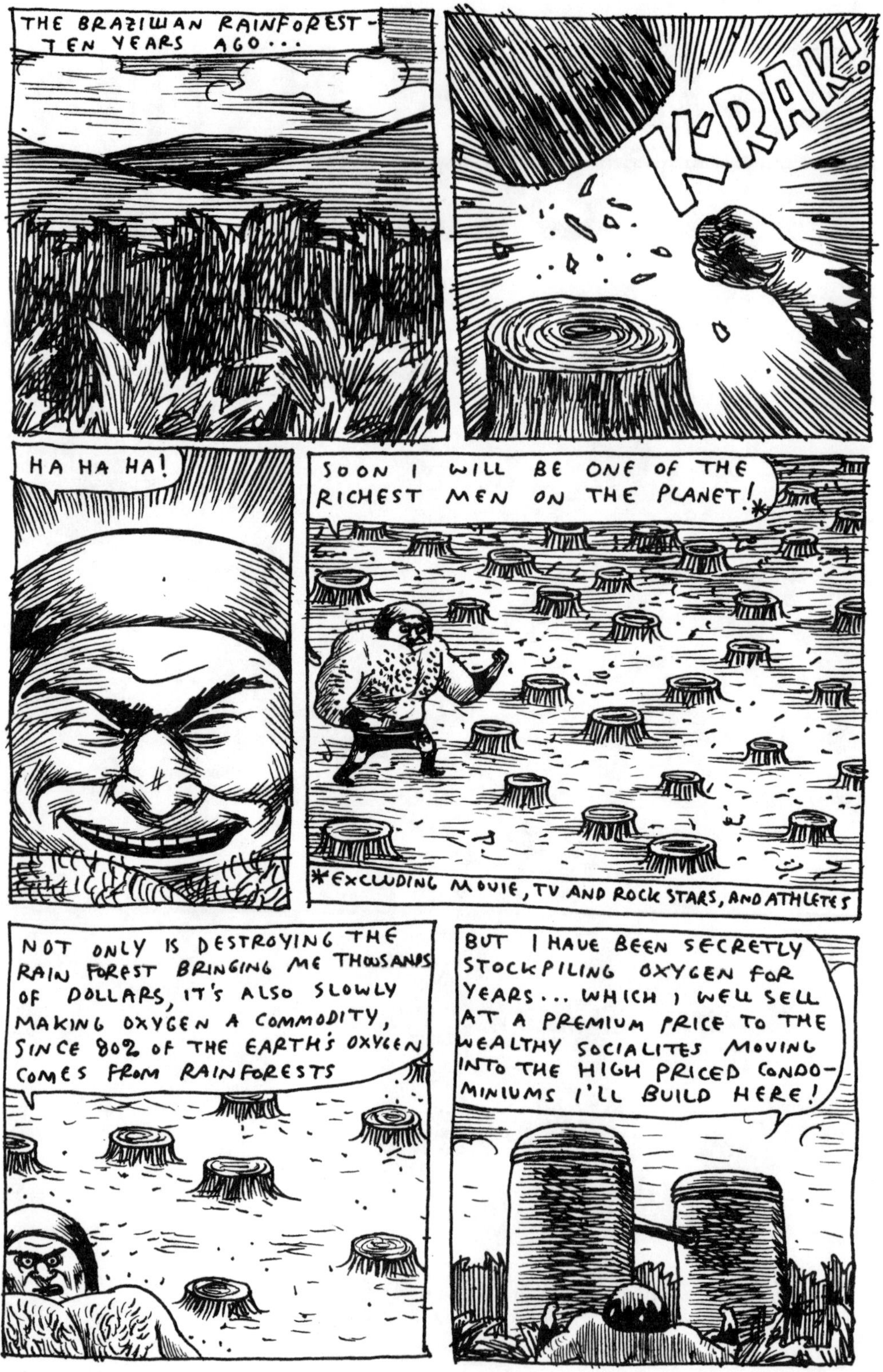
THE BRAZILIAN RAINFOREST - TEN YEARS AGO...
K'RAK!
HA HA HA!
SOON I WILL BE ONE OF THE RICHEST MEN ON THE PLANET!*
*EXCLUDING MOVIE, TV AND ROCK STARS, AND ATHLETES
NOT ONLY IS DESTROYING THE RAIN FOREST BRINGING ME THOUSANDS OF DOLLARS, IT'S ALSO SLOWLY MAKING OXYGEN A COMMODITY, SINCE 80% OF THE EARTH'S OXYGEN COMES FROM RAINFORESTS
BUT I HAVE BEEN SECRETLY STOCKPILING OXYGEN FOR YEARS... WHICH I WILL SELL AT A PREMIUM PRICE TO THE WEALTHY SOCIALITES MOVING INTO THE HIGH PRICED CONDOMINIUMS I'LL BUILD HERE!

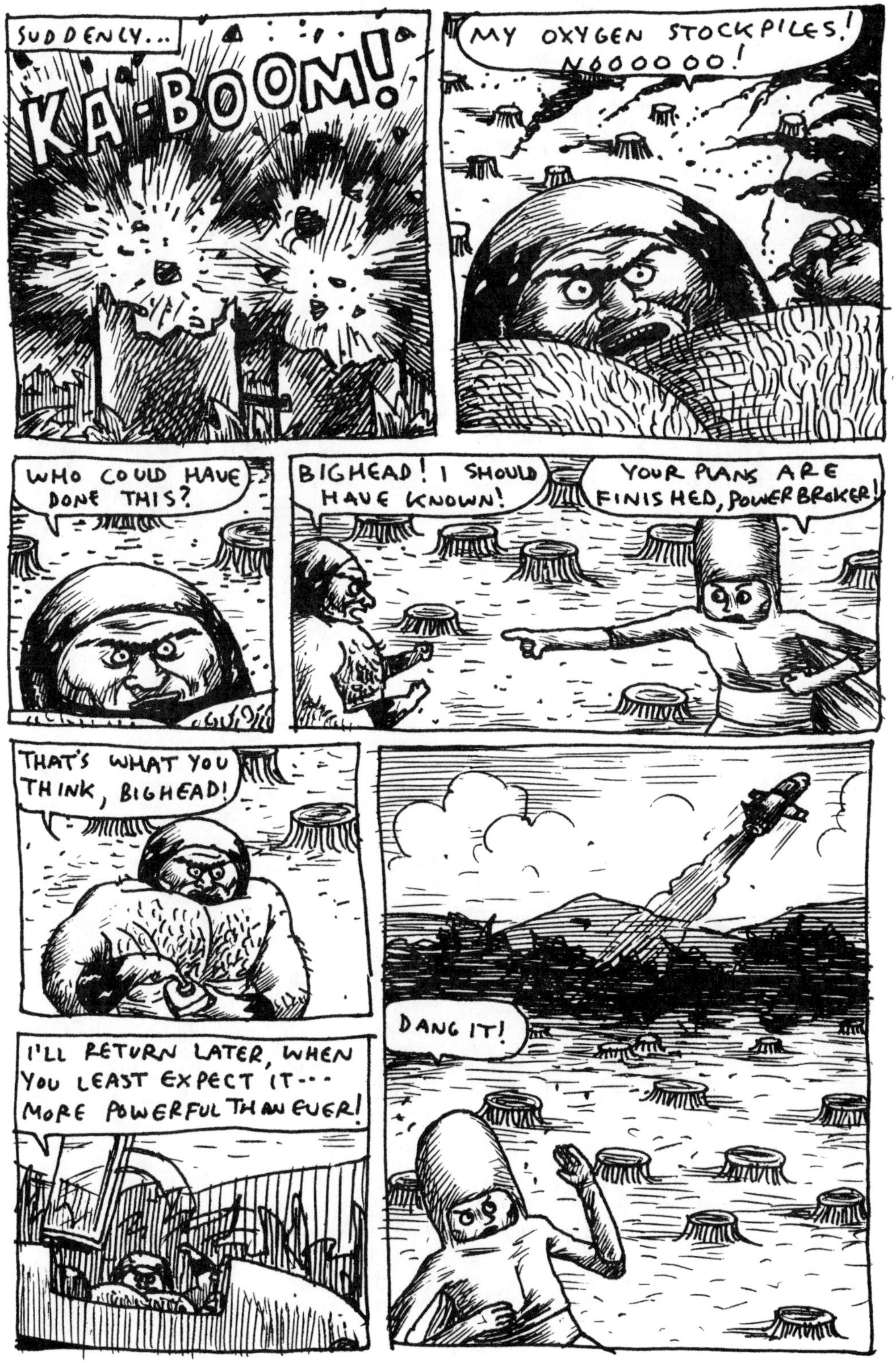
SUDDENLY...
KA-BOOM!
MY OXYGEN STOCKPILES! NOOOOOOO!
WHO COULD HAVE DONE THIS?
BIGHEAD! I SHOULD HAVE KNOWN!
YOUR PLANS ARE FINISHED, POWERBROKER!
THAT'S WHAT YOU THINK, BIGHEAD!
I'LL RETURN LATER, WHEN YOU LEAST EXPECT IT--- MORE POWERFUL THAN EVER!
DANG IT!

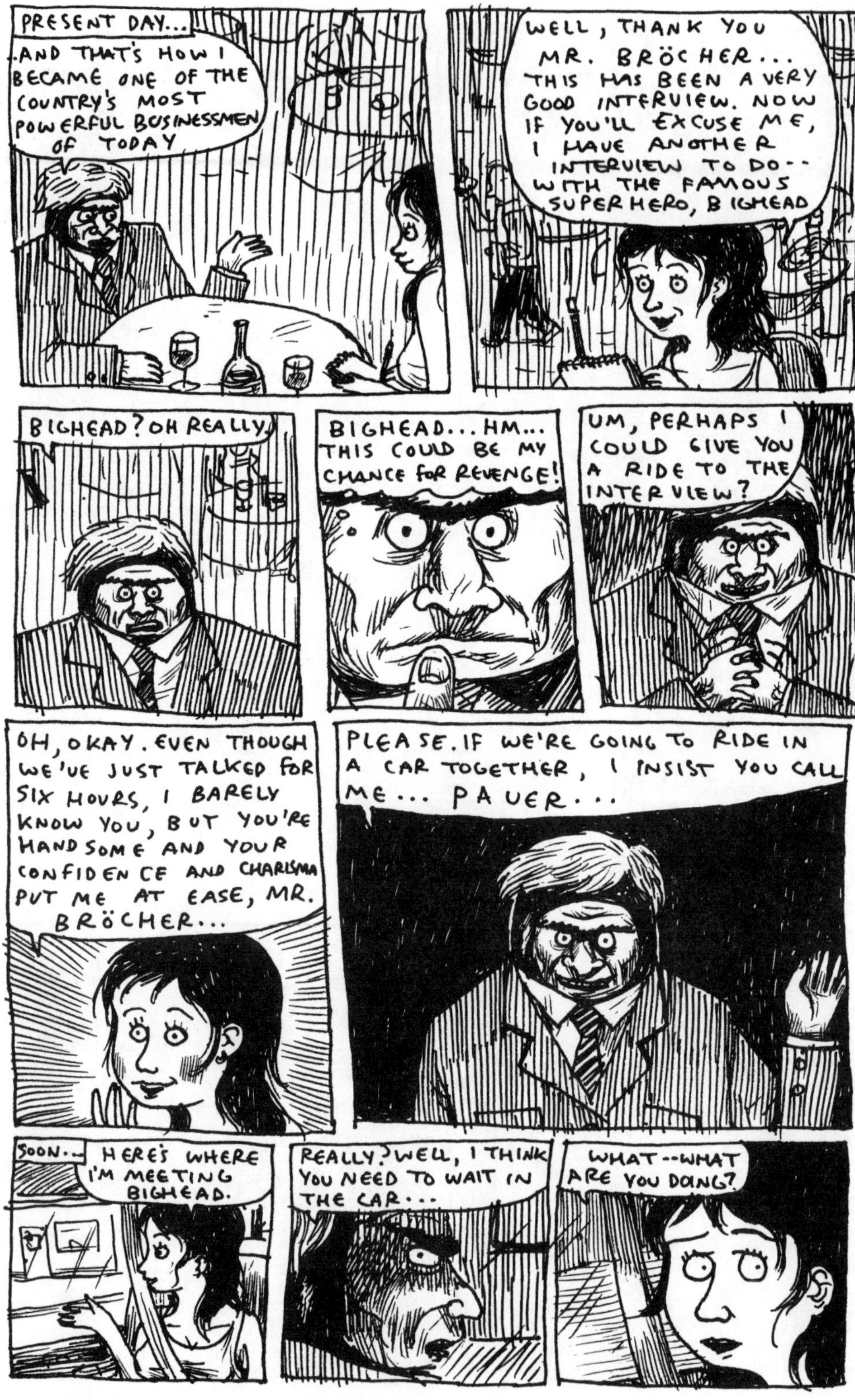
PRESENT DAY...
..AND THAT'S HOW I BECAME ONE OF THE COUNTRY'S MOST POWERFUL BUSINESSMEN OF TODAY
WELL, THANK YOU MR. BRÖCHER... THIS HAS BEEN A VERY GOOD INTERVIEW. NOW IF YOU'LL EXCUSE ME, I HAVE ANOTHER INTERVIEW TO DO-- WITH THE FAMOUS SUPERHERO, BIGHEAD
BIGHEAD? OH REALLY.
BIGHEAD...HM... THIS COULD BE MY CHANCE FOR REVENGE!
UM, PERHAPS I COULD GIVE YOU A RIDE TO THE INTERVIEW?
OH, OKAY. EVEN THOUGH WE'VE JUST TALKED FOR SIX HOURS, I BARELY KNOW YOU, BUT YOU'RE HANDSOME AND YOUR CONFIDENCE AND CHARISMA PUT ME AT EASE, MR. BRÖCHER...
PLEASE. IF WE'RE GOING TO RIDE IN A CAR TOGETHER, I INSIST YOU CALL ME... PAUER...
SOON...
HERE'S WHERE I'M MEETING BIGHEAD.
REALLY? WELL, I THINK YOU NEED TO WAIT IN THE CAR...
WHAT--WHAT ARE YOU DOING?

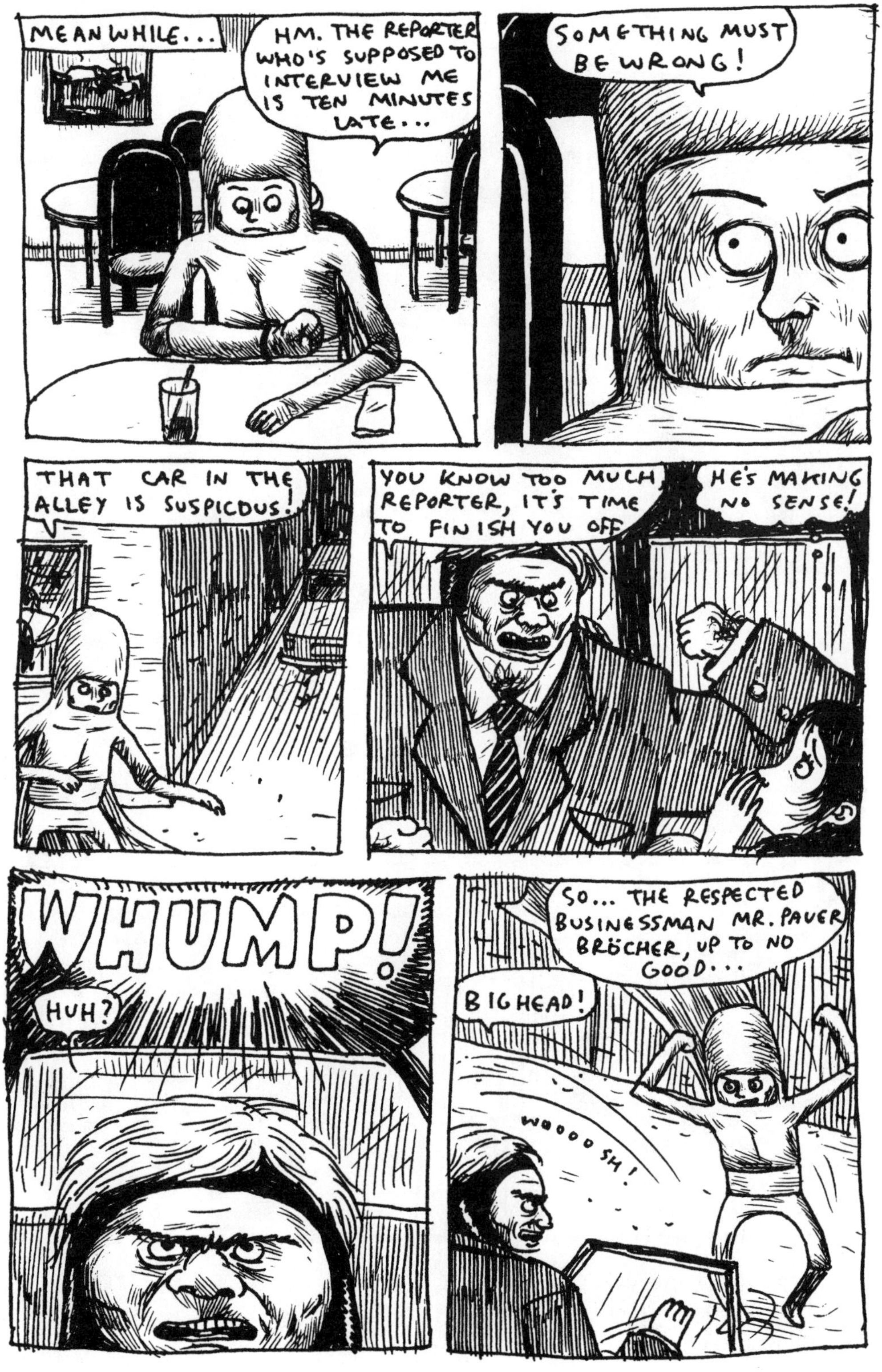
MEANWHILE...
HM. THE REPORTER WHO'S SUPPOSED TO INTERVIEW ME IS TEN MINUTES LATE...
SOMETHING MUST BE WRONG!
THAT CAR IN THE ALLEY IS SUSPICIOUS!
YOU KNOW TOO MUCH, REPORTER, IT'S TIME TO FINISH YOU OFF
HE'S MAKING NO SENSE!
WHUMP!
HUH?
SO... THE RESPECTED BUSINESSMAN MR. PAUER BRÖCHER, UP TO NO GOOD...
BIGHEAD!
WOOOOSH!

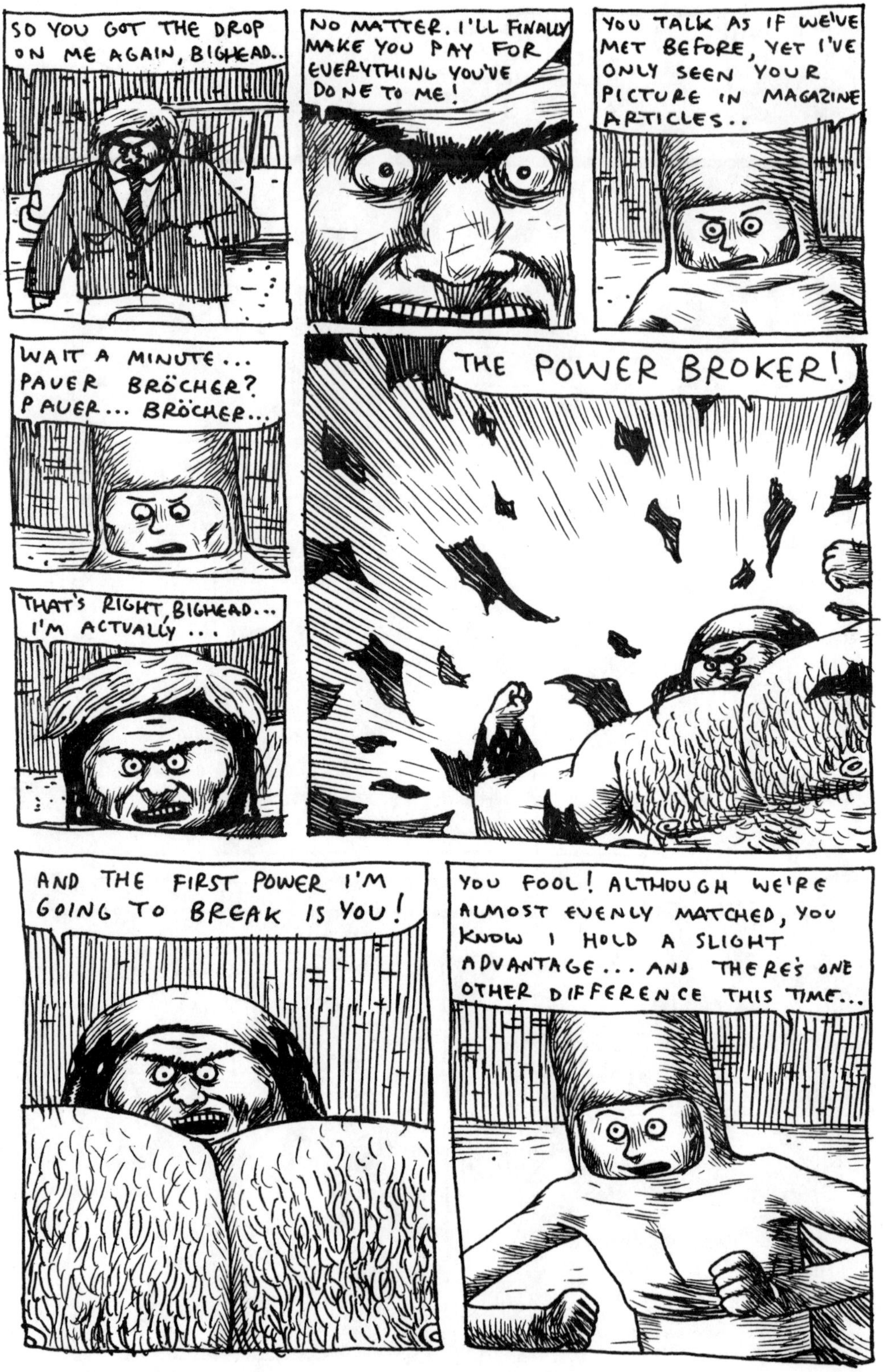
SO YOU GOT THE DROP ON ME AGAIN, BIGHEAD..
NO MATTER. I'LL FINALLY MAKE YOU PAY FOR EVERYTHING YOU'VE DONE TO ME!
YOU TALK AS IF WE'VE MET BEFORE, YET I'VE ONLY SEEN YOUR PICTURE IN MAGAZINE ARTICLES..
WAIT A MINUTE... PAUER BRÖCHER? PAUER... BRÖCHER...
THAT'S RIGHT, BIGHEAD... I'M ACTUALLY...
THE POWER BROKER!
AND THE FIRST POWER I'M GOING TO BREAK IS YOU!
YOU FOOL! ALTHOUGH WE'RE ALMOST EVENLY MATCHED, YOU KNOW I HOLD A SLIGHT ADVANTAGE... AND THERE'S ONE OTHER DIFFERENCE THIS TIME...

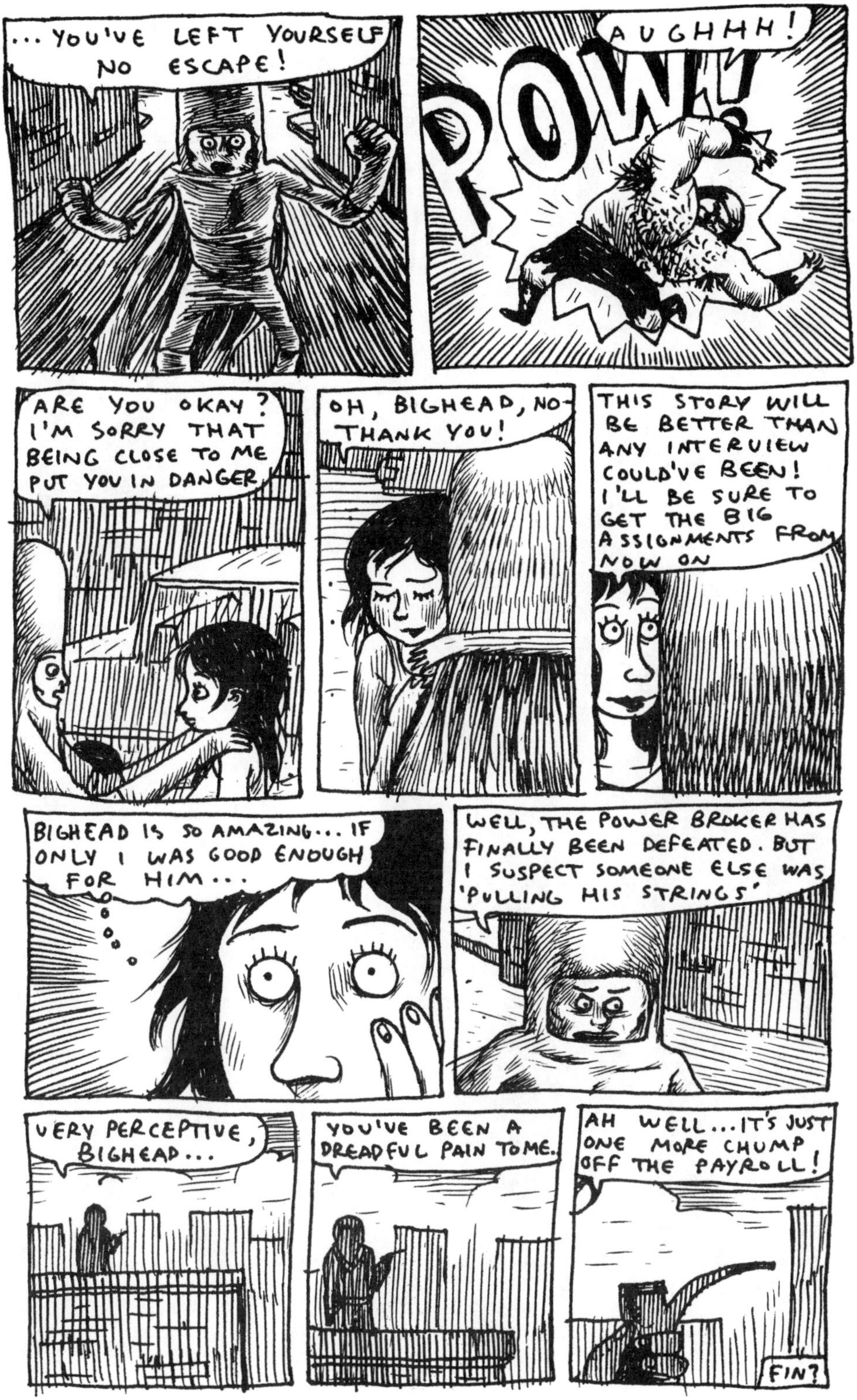
...YOU'VE LEFT YOURSELF NO ESCAPE!
AUGHHH!
POW!
ARE YOU OKAY? I'M SORRY THAT BEING CLOSE TO ME PUT YOU IN DANGER
OH, BIGHEAD, NO- THANK YOU!
THIS STORY WILL BE BETTER THAN ANY INTERVIEW COULD'VE BEEN! I'LL BE SURE TO GET THE BIG ASSIGNMENTS FROM NOW ON
BIGHEAD IS SO AMAZING... IF ONLY I WAS GOOD ENOUGH FOR HIM...
WELL, THE POWER BROKER HAS FINALLY BEEN DEFEATED. BUT I SUSPECT SOMEONE ELSE WAS 'PULLING HIS STRINGS'
VERY PERCEPTIVE, BIGHEAD...
YOU'VE BEEN A DREADFUL PAIN TO ME.
AH WELL... IT'S JUST ONE MORE CHUMP OFF THE PAYROLL!
FIN?

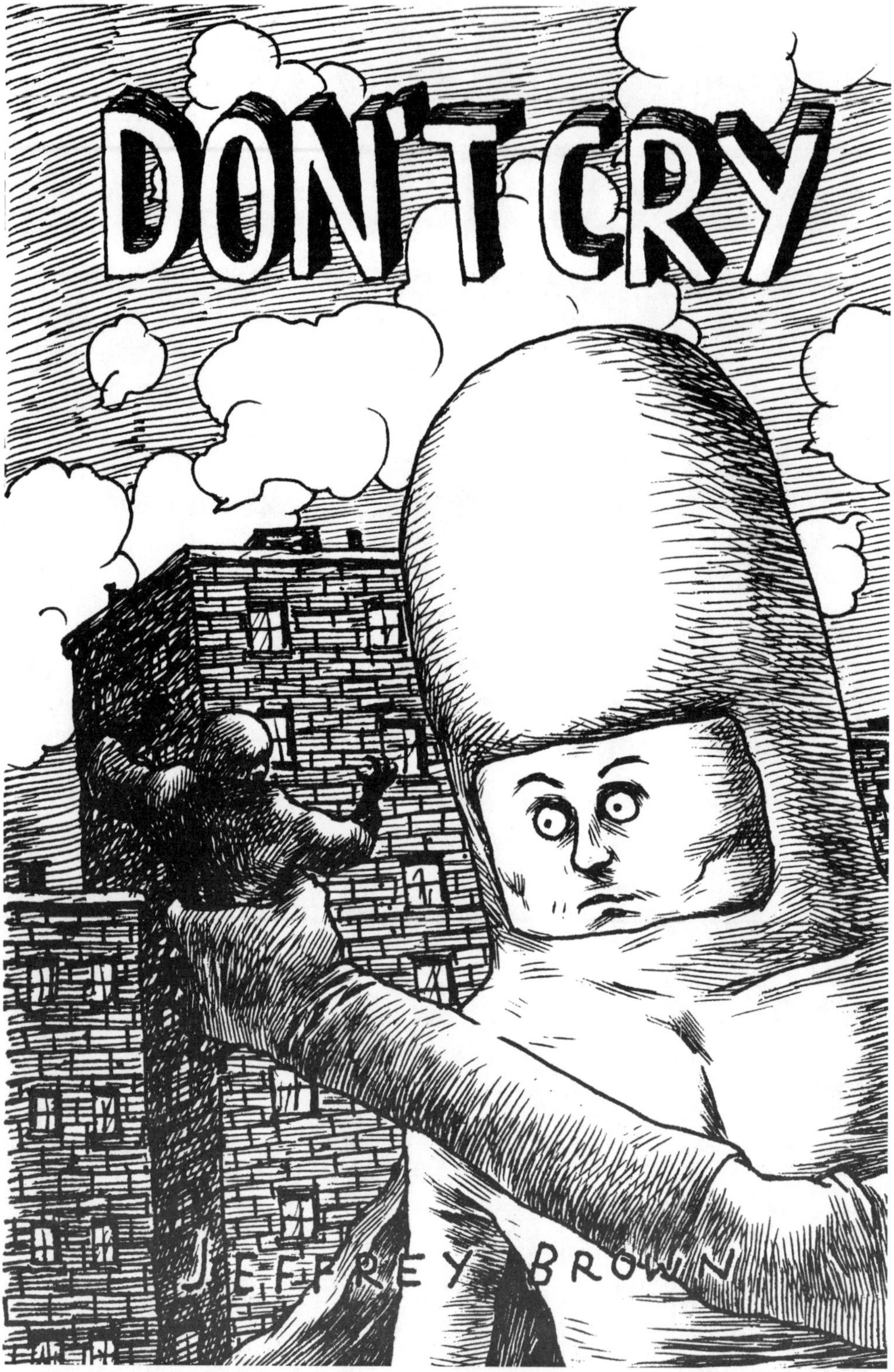
DON'T CRY
JEFFREY BROWN

ONE

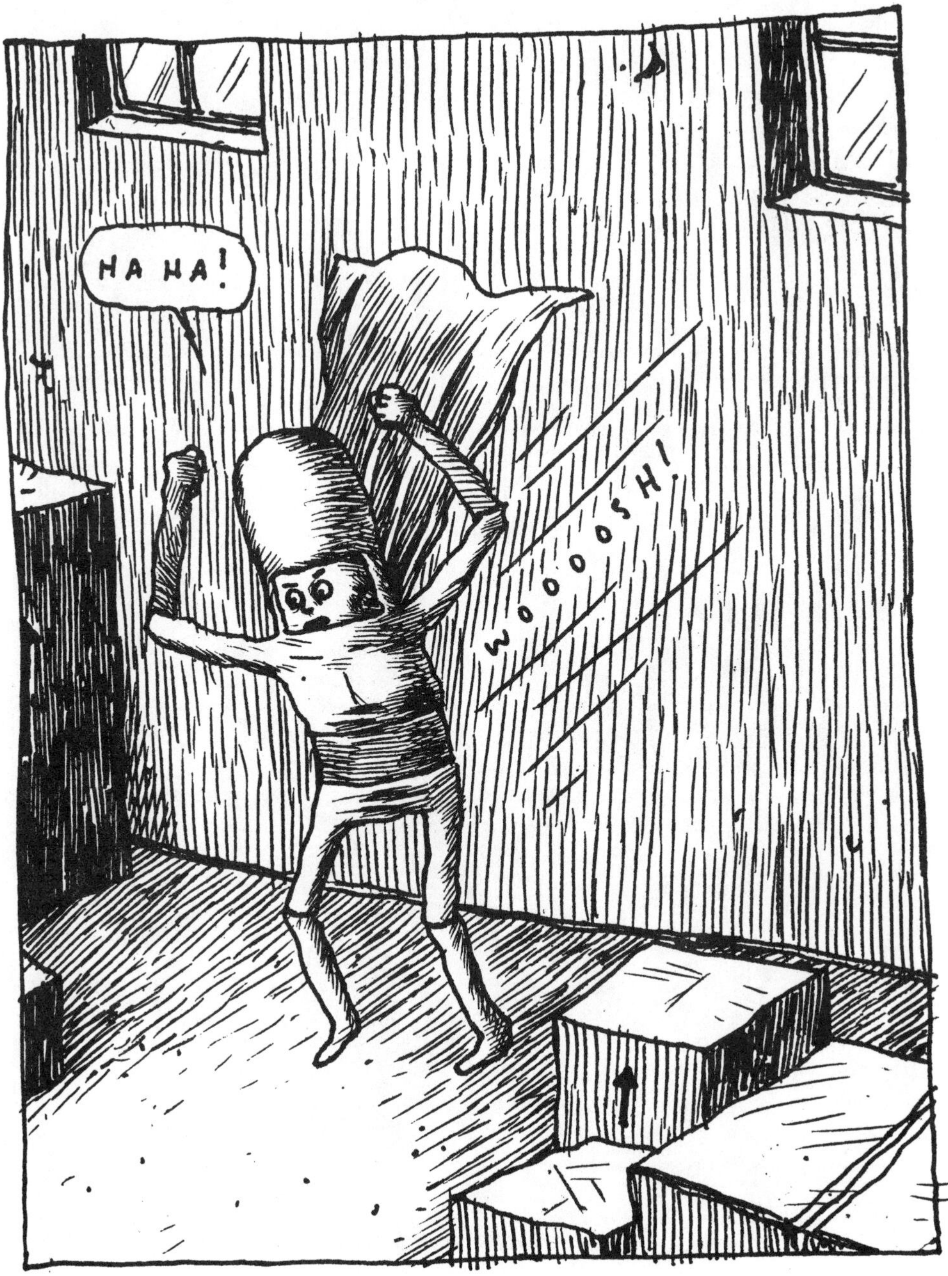
HA HA!
WOOOOSH!

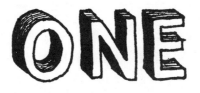

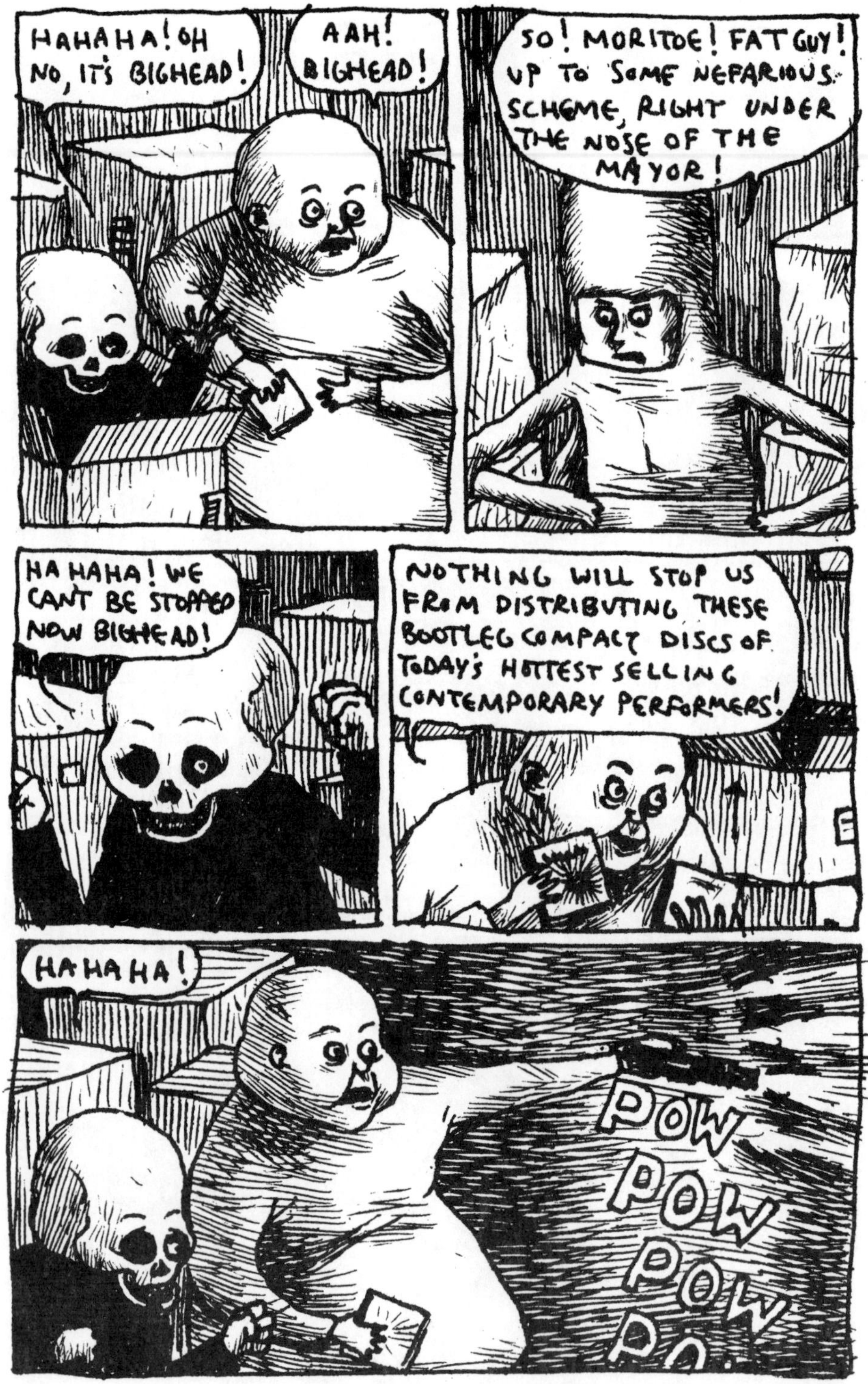
HAHAHA! OH NO, IT'S BIGHEAD!
AAH! BIGHEAD!
SO! MORITOE! FAT GUY! UP TO SOME NEFARIOUS SCHEME, RIGHT UNDER THE NOSE OF THE MAYOR!
HA HAHA! WE CANT BE STOPPED NOW BIGHEAD!
NOTHING WILL STOP US FROM DISTRIBUTING THESE BOOTLEG COMPACT DISCS OF TODAY'S HOTTEST SELLING CONTEMPORARY PERFORMERS!
HAHAHA!
POW
POW
POW

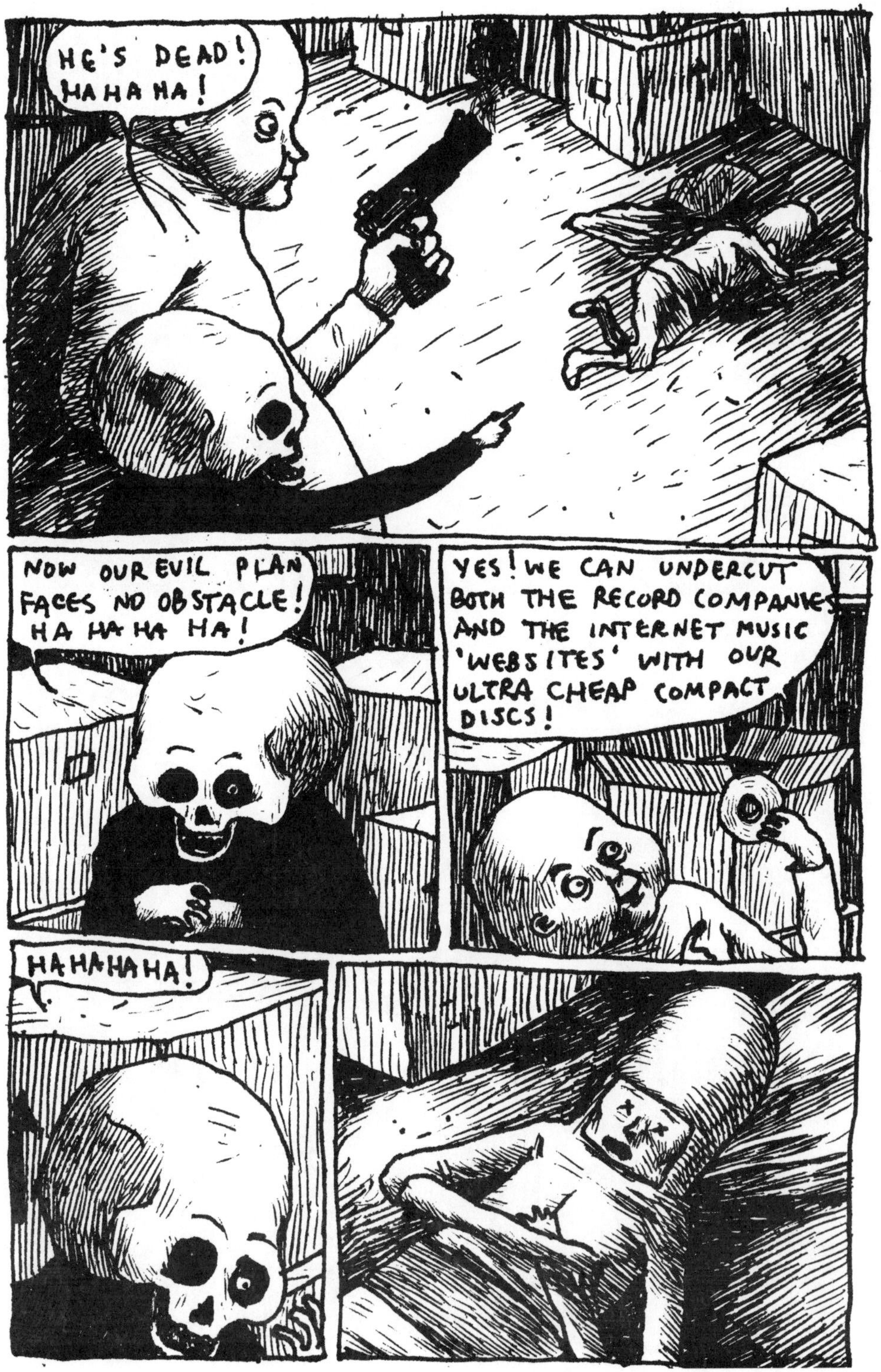
HE'S DEAD! HA HA HA!
NOW OUR EVIL PLAN FACES NO OBSTACLE! HA HA HA HA!
YES! WE CAN UNDERCUT BOTH THE RECORD COMPANIES AND THE INTERNET MUSIC 'WEBSITES' WITH OUR ULTRA CHEAP COMPACT DISCS!
HAHAHAHA!

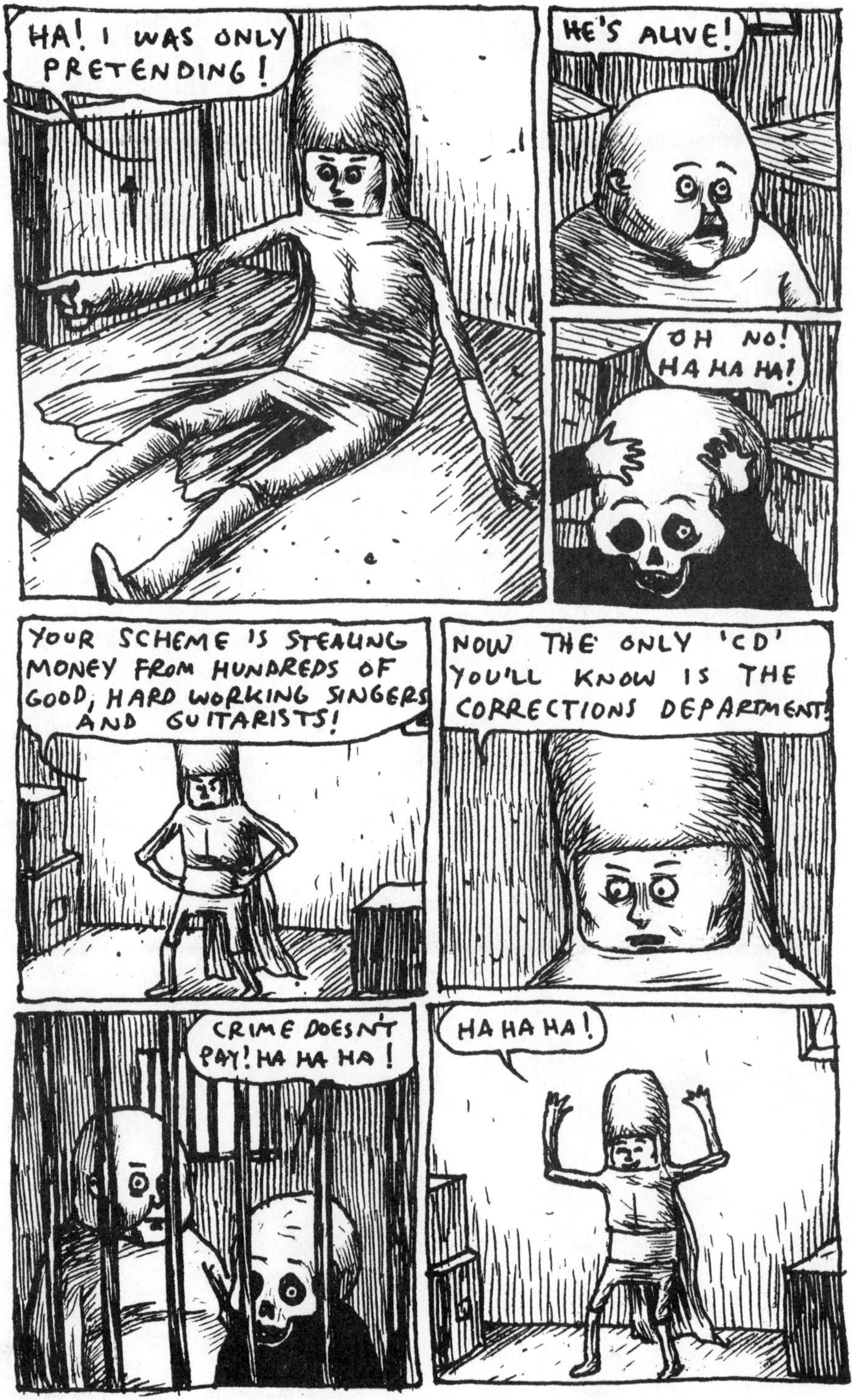
HA! I WAS ONLY PRETENDING!
HE'S ALIVE!
OH NO! HA HA HA!
YOUR SCHEME IS STEALING MONEY FROM HUNDREDS OF GOOD, HARD WORKING SINGERS AND GUITARISTS!
NOW THE ONLY 'CD' YOU'LL KNOW IS THE CORRECTIONS DEPARTMENT!
CRIME DOESN'T PAY! HA HA HA!
HA HA HA!

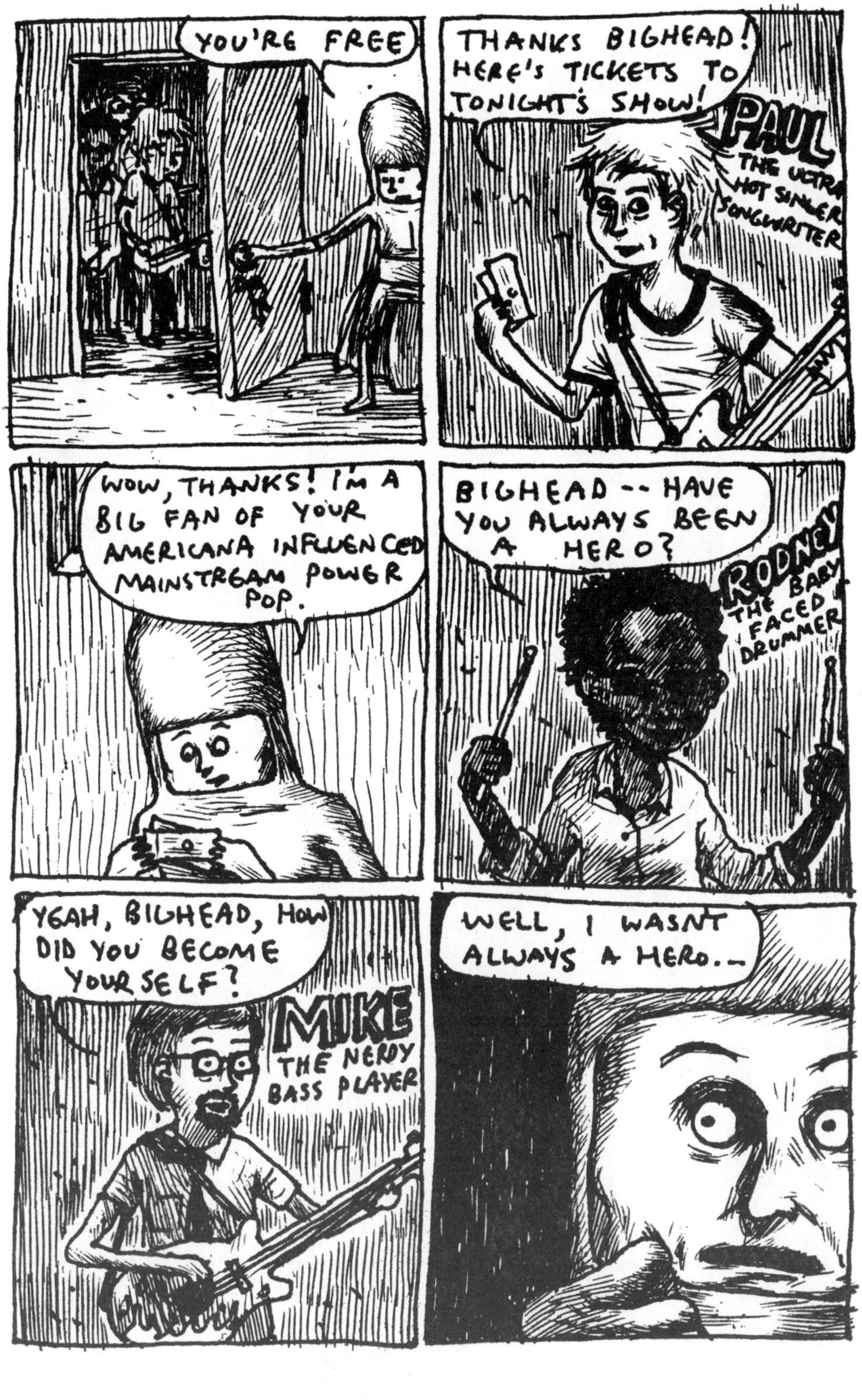
YOU'RE FREE
THANKS BIGHEAD! HERE'S TICKETS TO TONIGHT'S SHOW!
PAUL
THE ULTRA HOT SINGER SONGWRITER
WOW, THANKS! I'M A BIG FAN OF YOUR AMERICANA INFLUENCED MAINSTREAM POWER POP.
BIGHEAD -- HAVE YOU ALWAYS BEEN A HERO?
RODNEY
THE BABY FACED DRUMMER
YEAH, BIGHEAD, HOW DID YOU BECOME YOURSELF?
MIKE
THE NERDY BASS PLAYER
WELL, I WASNT ALWAYS A HERO...

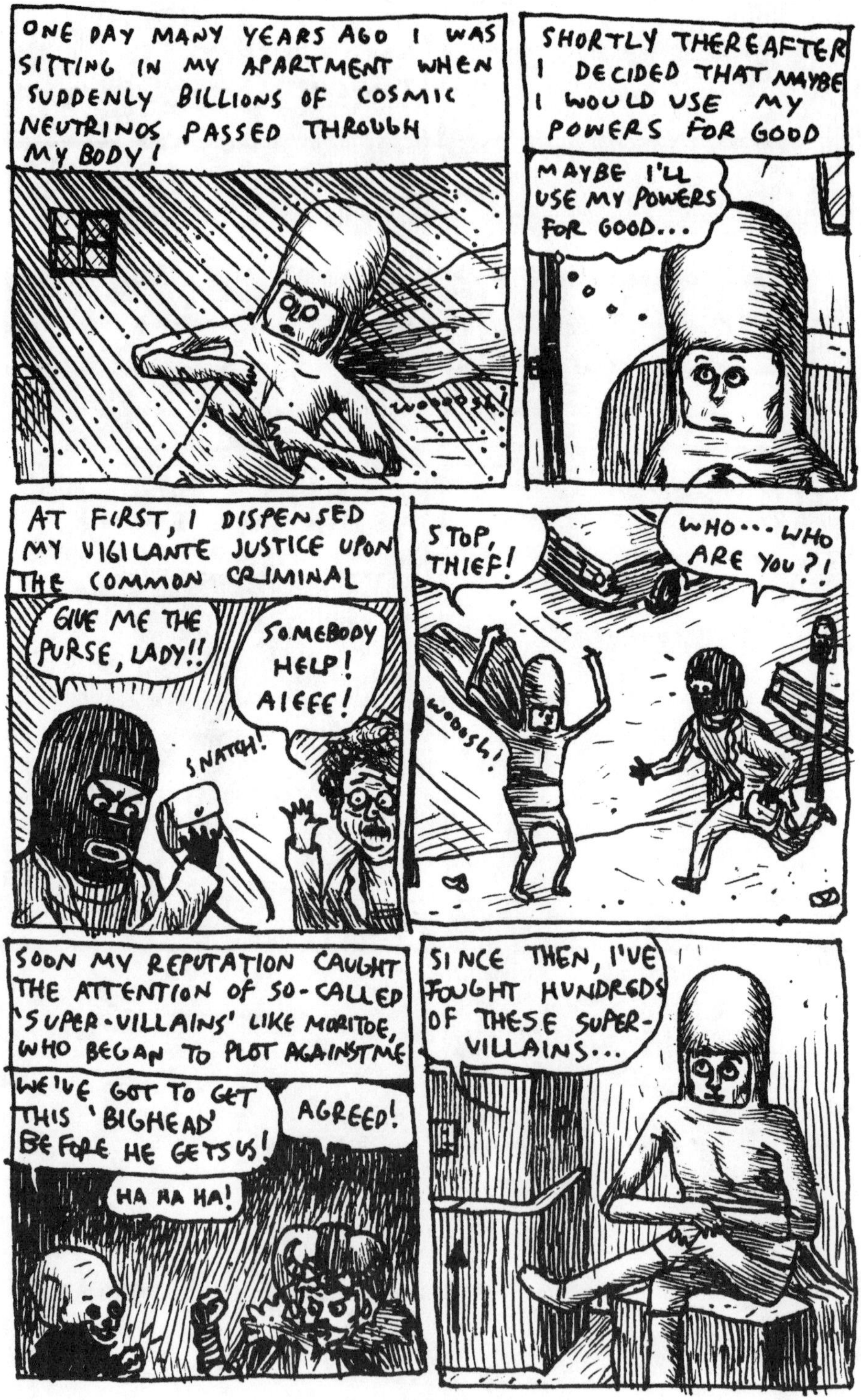
ONE DAY MANY YEARS AGO I WAS SITTING IN MY APARTMENT WHEN SUDDENLY BILLIONS OF COSMIC NEUTRINOS PASSED THROUGH MY BODY!
WOOOSH!
SHORTLY THEREAFTER I DECIDED THAT MAYBE I WOULD USE MY POWERS FOR GOOD
MAYBE I'LL USE MY POWERS FOR GOOD...
AT FIRST, I DISPENSED MY VIGILANTE JUSTICE UPON THE COMMON CRIMINAL
GIVE ME THE PURSE, LADY!!
SOMEBODY HELP! AIEEE!
SNATCH!
STOP, THIEF!
WHO... WHO ARE YOU?!
WOOOSH!
SOON MY REPUTATION CAUGHT THE ATTENTION OF SO-CALLED 'SUPER-VILLAINS' LIKE MORITOE, WHO BEGAN TO PLOT AGAINST ME
WE'VE GOT TO GET THIS 'BIGHEAD' BEFORE HE GETS US!
AGREED!
HA HA HA!
SINCE THEN, I'VE FOUGHT HUNDREDS OF THESE SUPER-VILLAINS...

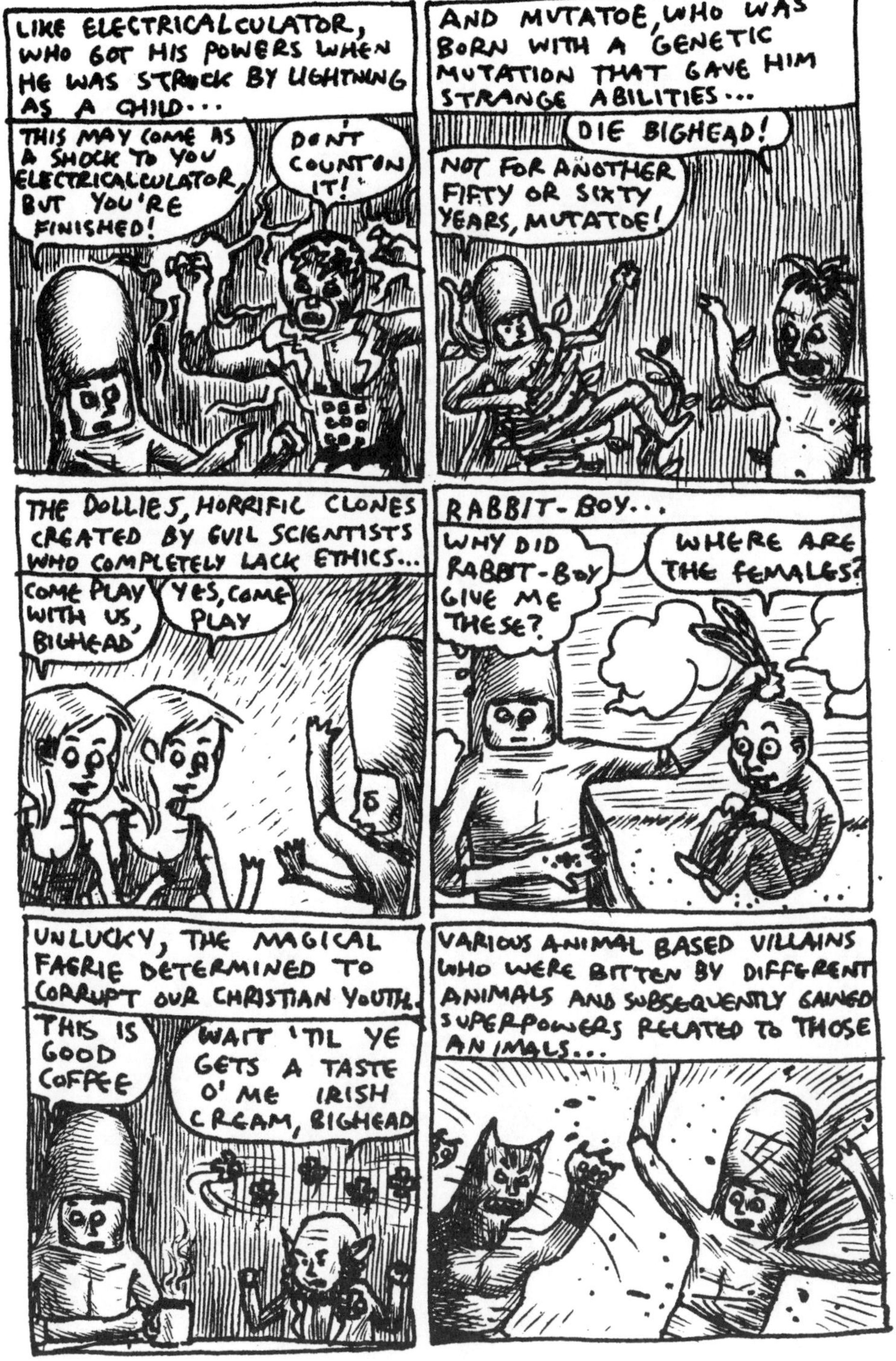
LIKE ELECTRICALCULATOR, WHO GOT HIS POWERS WHEN HE WAS STRUCK BY LIGHTNING AS A CHILD...
THIS MAY COME AS A SHOCK TO YOU ELECTRICALCULATOR, BUT YOU'RE FINISHED!
DON'T COUNT ON IT!
AND MUTATOE, WHO WAS BORN WITH A GENETIC MUTATION THAT GAVE HIM STRANGE ABILITIES...
DIE BIGHEAD!
NOT FOR ANOTHER FIFTY OR SIXTY YEARS, MUTATOE!
THE DOLLIES, HORRIFIC CLONES CREATED BY EVIL SCIENTISTS WHO COMPLETELY LACK ETHICS...
COME PLAY WITH US, BIGHEAD
YES, COME PLAY
RABBIT-BOY...
WHY DID RABBIT-BOY GIVE ME THESE?
WHERE ARE THE FEMALES?
UNLUCKY, THE MAGICAL FAERIE DETERMINED TO CORRUPT OUR CHRISTIAN YOUTH.
THIS IS GOOD COFFEE
WAIT 'TIL YE GETS A TASTE O' ME IRISH CREAM, BIGHEAD
VARIOUS ANIMAL BASED VILLAINS WHO WERE BITTEN BY DIFFERENT ANIMALS AND SUBSEQUENTLY GAINED SUPERPOWERS RELATED TO THOSE ANIMALS...

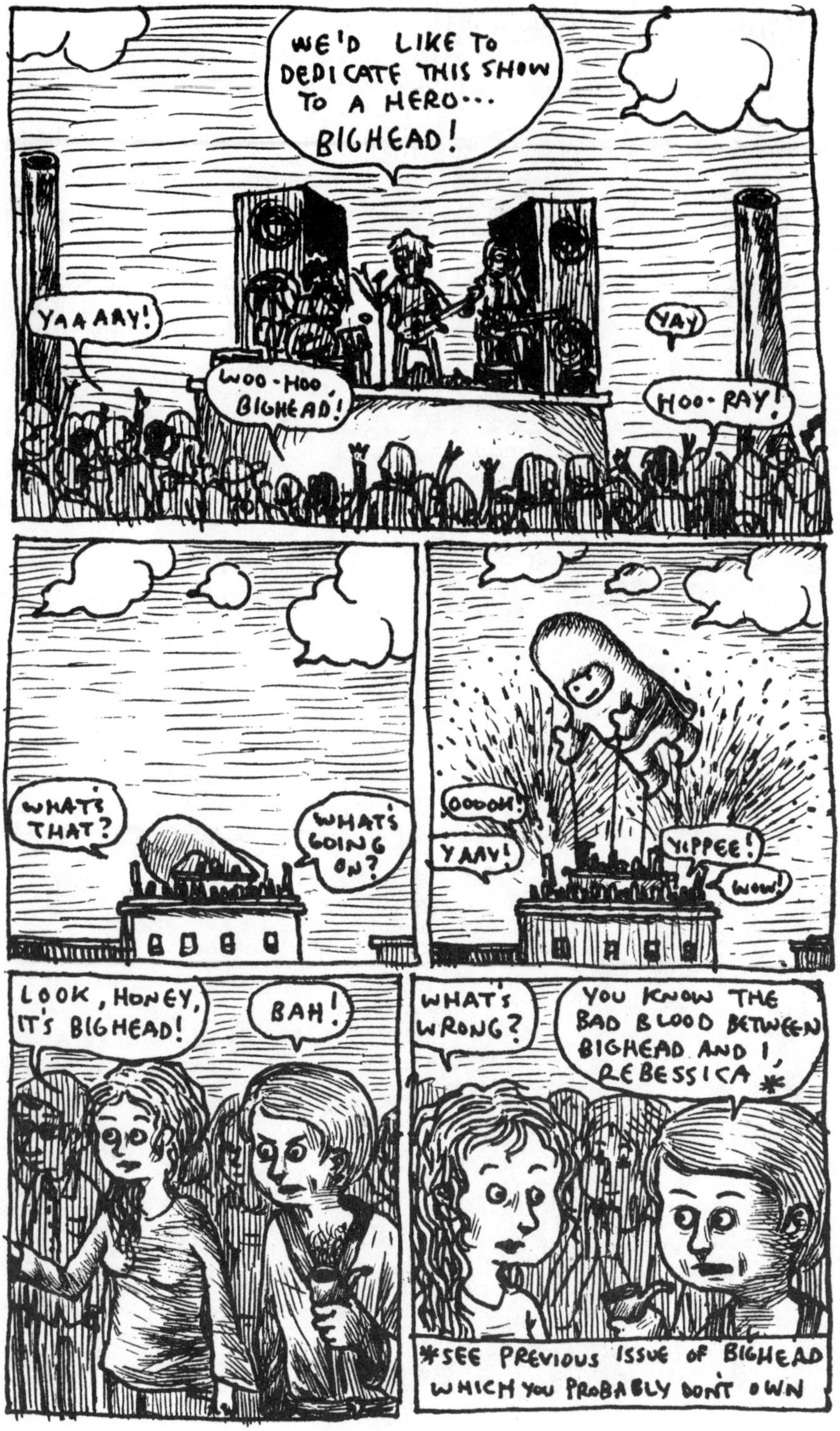
WE'D LIKE TO DEDICATE THIS SHOW TO A HERO... BIGHEAD!
YAAARY!
WOO-HOO, BIGHEAD!
YAY
HOO-RAY!
WHAT'S THAT?
WHAT'S GOING ON?
OOOOH!
YAAY!
YIPPEE!
WOW!
LOOK, HONEY, IT'S BIGHEAD!
BAH!
WHAT'S WRONG?
YOU KNOW THE BAD BLOOD BETWEEN BIGHEAD AND I, REBESSICA *
*SEE PREVIOUS ISSUE OF BIGHEAD WHICH YOU PROBABLY DON'T OWN

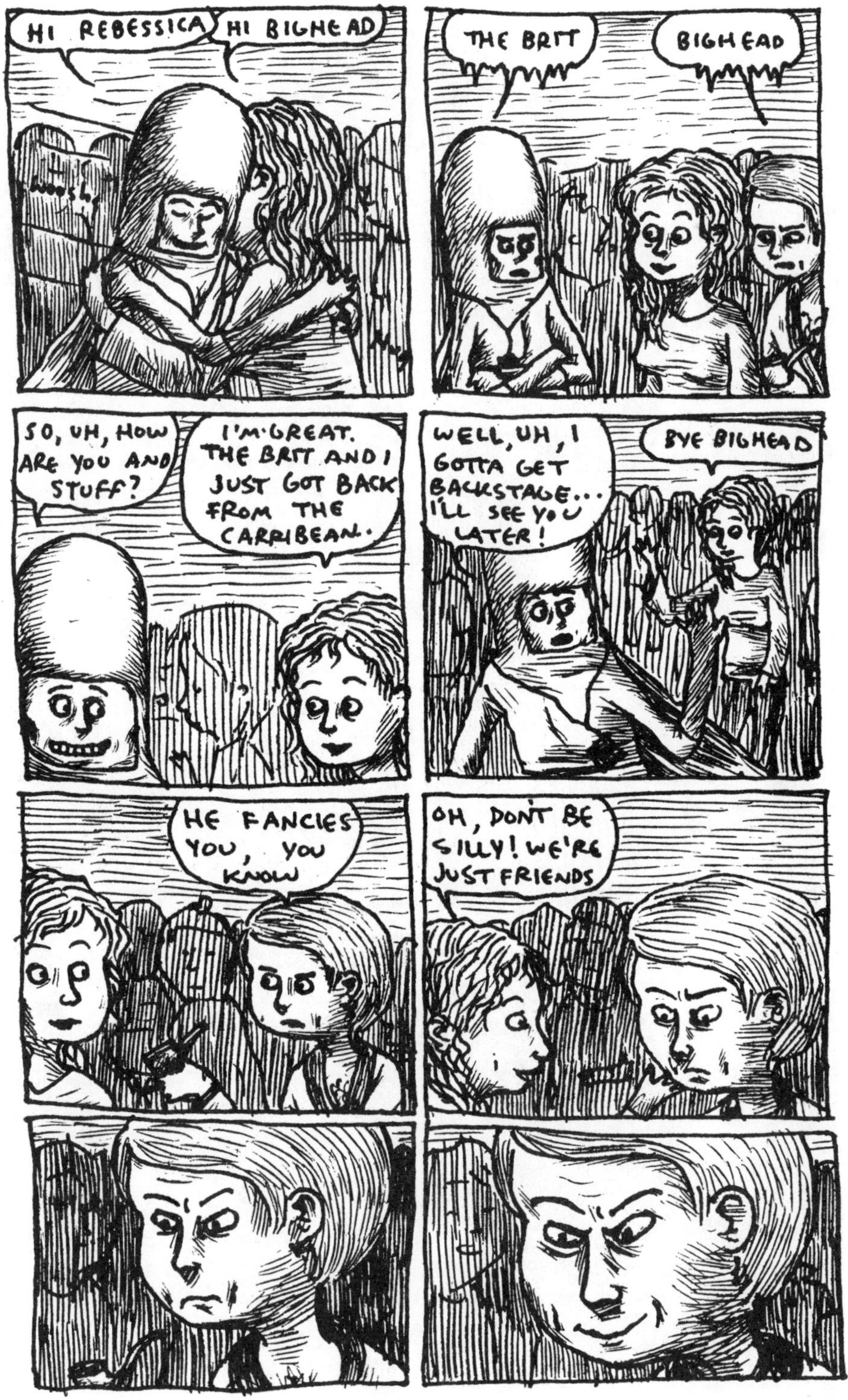
HI REBESSICA
HI BIGHEAD
THE BRIT
BIGHEAD
SO, UH, HOW ARE YOU AND STUFF?
I'M GREAT. THE BRIT AND I JUST GOT BACK FROM THE CARRIBEAN.
WELL, UH, I GOTTA GET BACKSTAGE... I'LL SEE YOU LATER!
BYE BIGHEAD
HE FANCIES YOU, YOU KNOW
OH, DON'T BE SILLY! WE'RE JUST FRIENDS

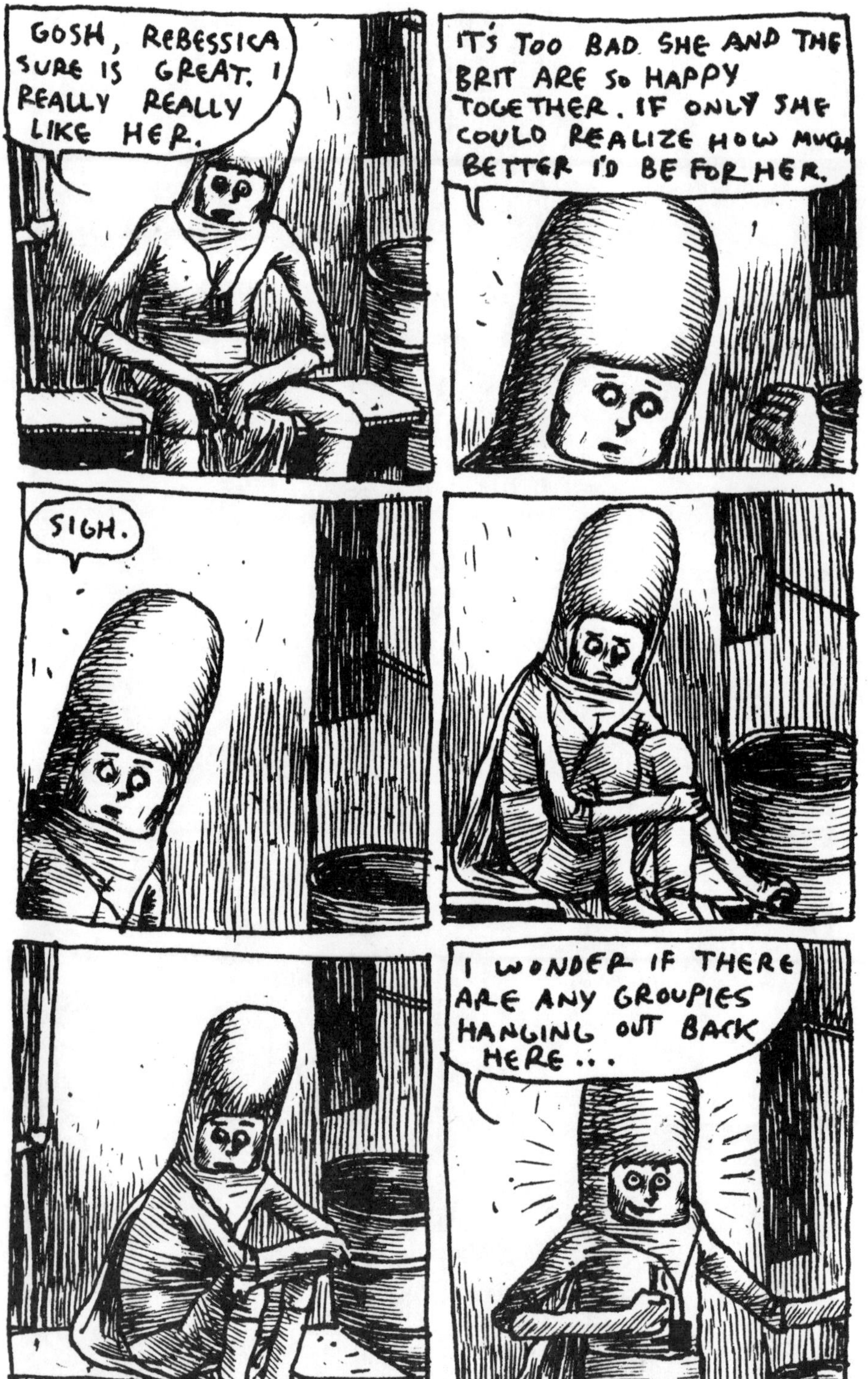
GOSH, REBESSICA SURE IS GREAT. I REALLY REALLY LIKE HER.
IT'S TOO BAD SHE AND THE BRIT ARE SO HAPPY TOGETHER. IF ONLY SHE COULD REALIZE HOW MUCH BETTER I'D BE FOR HER.
SIGH.
I WONDER IF THERE ARE ANY GROUPIES HANGING OUT BACK HERE...

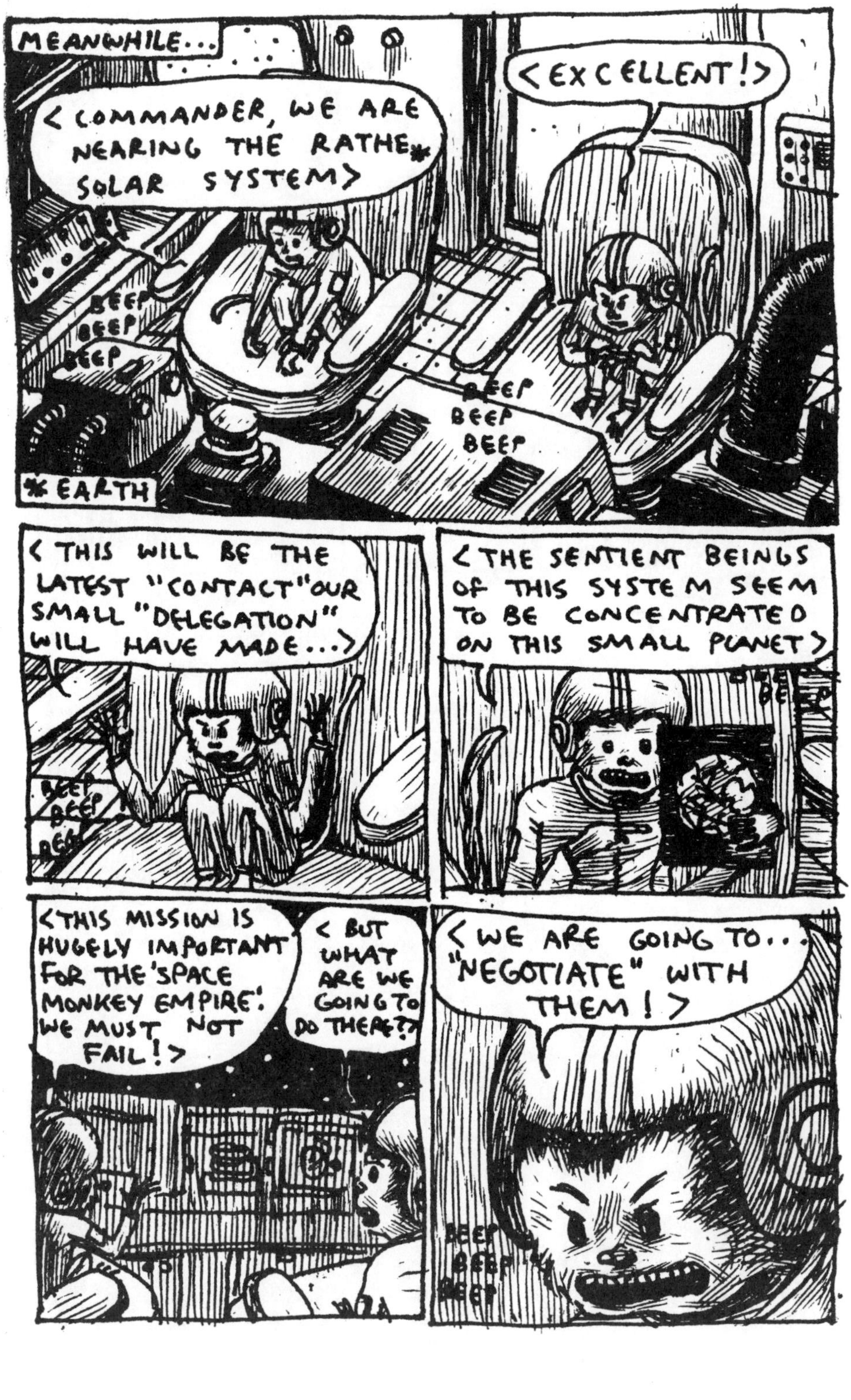
MEANWHILE...
< COMMANDER, WE ARE NEARING THE RATHE* SOLAR SYSTEM>
BEEP BEEP BEEP
BEEP BEEP
* EARTH
<EXCELLENT!>
< THIS WILL BE THE LATEST "CONTACT" OUR SMALL "DELEGATION" WILL HAVE MADE...>
< THE SENTIENT BEINGS OF THIS SYSTEM SEEM TO BE CONCENTRATED ON THIS SMALL PLANET>
<THIS MISSION IS HUGELY IMPORTANT FOR THE 'SPACE MONKEY EMPIRE'. WE MUST NOT FAIL!>
< BUT WHAT ARE WE GOING TO DO THERE??>
< WE ARE GOING TO... "NEGOTIATE" WITH THEM!>
BEEP

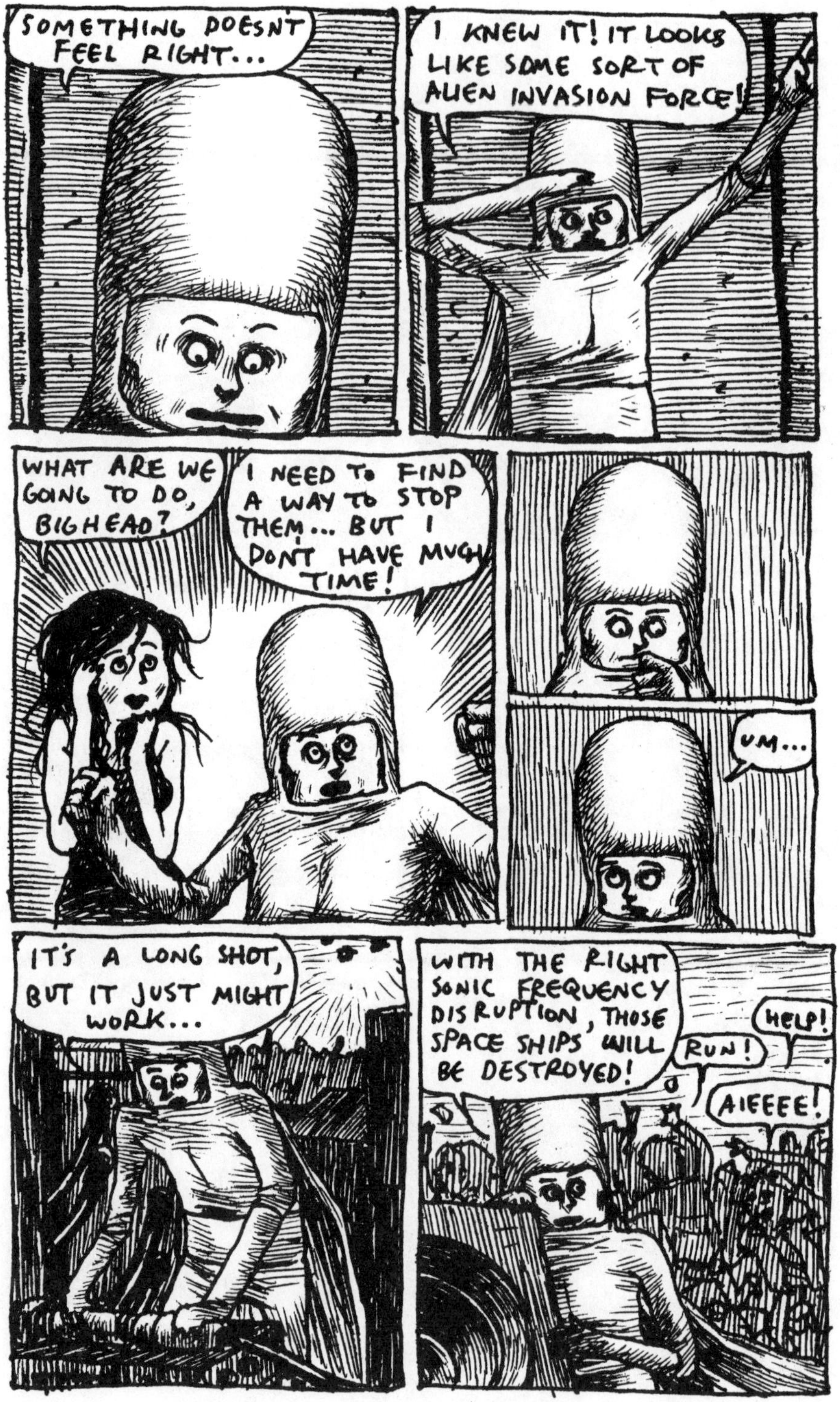

SOMETHING DOESN'T FEEL RIGHT...
I KNEW IT! IT LOOKS LIKE SOME SORT OF ALIEN INVASION FORCE!
WHAT ARE WE GOING TO DO, BIGHEAD?
I NEED TO FIND A WAY TO STOP THEM... BUT I DON'T HAVE MUCH TIME!
UM...
IT'S A LONG SHOT, BUT IT JUST MIGHT WORK...
WITH THE RIGHT SONIC FREQUENCY DISRUPTION, THOSE SPACE SHIPS WILL BE DESTROYED!
HELP!
RUN!
AIEEEE!

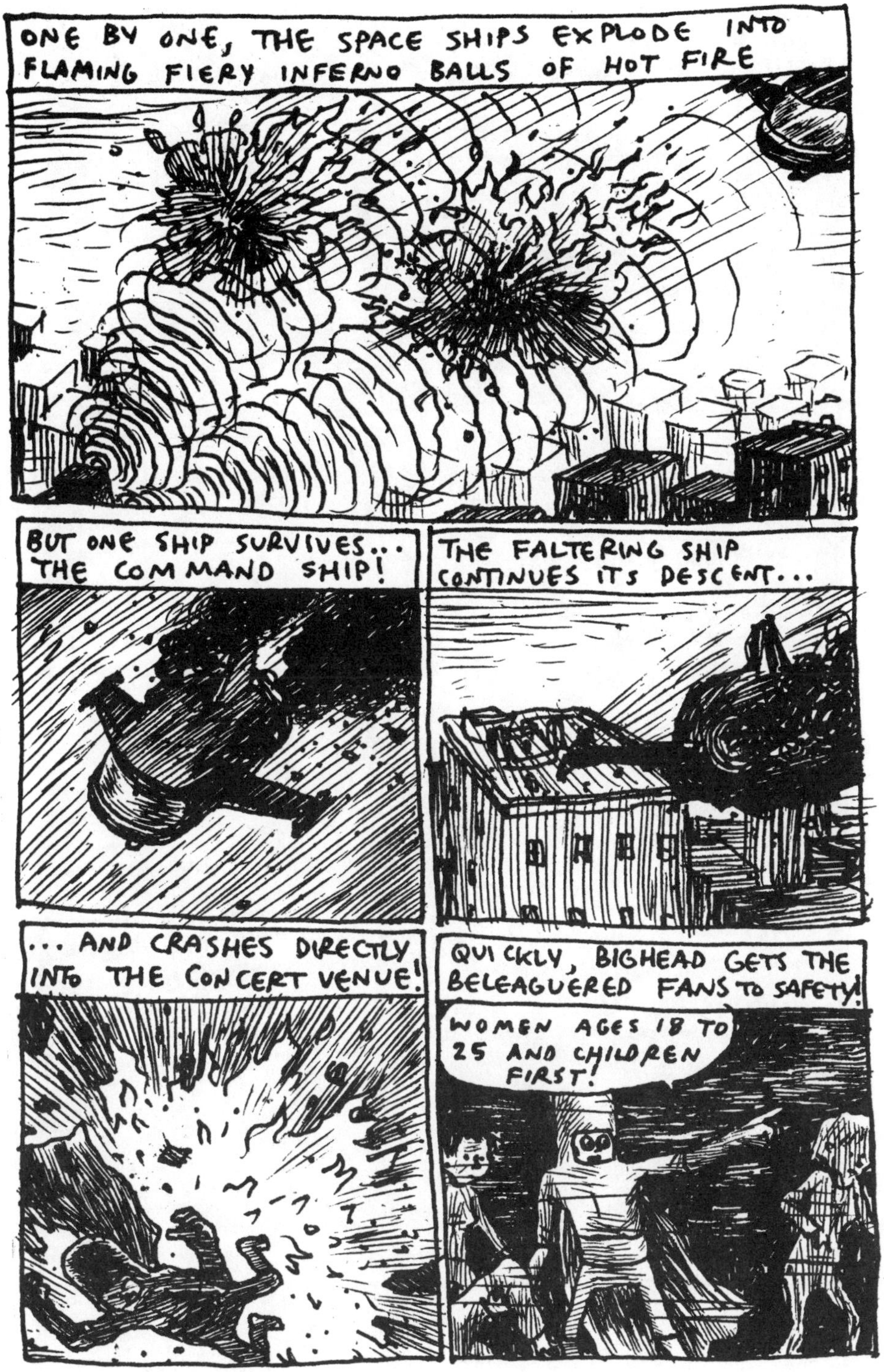
ONE BY ONE, THE SPACE SHIPS EXPLODE INTO FLAMING FIERY INFERNO BALLS OF HOT FIRE
BUT ONE SHIP SURVIVES... THE COMMAND SHIP!
THE FALTERING SHIP CONTINUES ITS DESCENT...
... AND CRASHES DIRECTLY INTO THE CONCERT VENUE!
QUICKLY, BIGHEAD GETS THE BELEAGUERED FANS TO SAFETY!
WOMEN AGES 18 TO 25 AND CHILDREN FIRST!

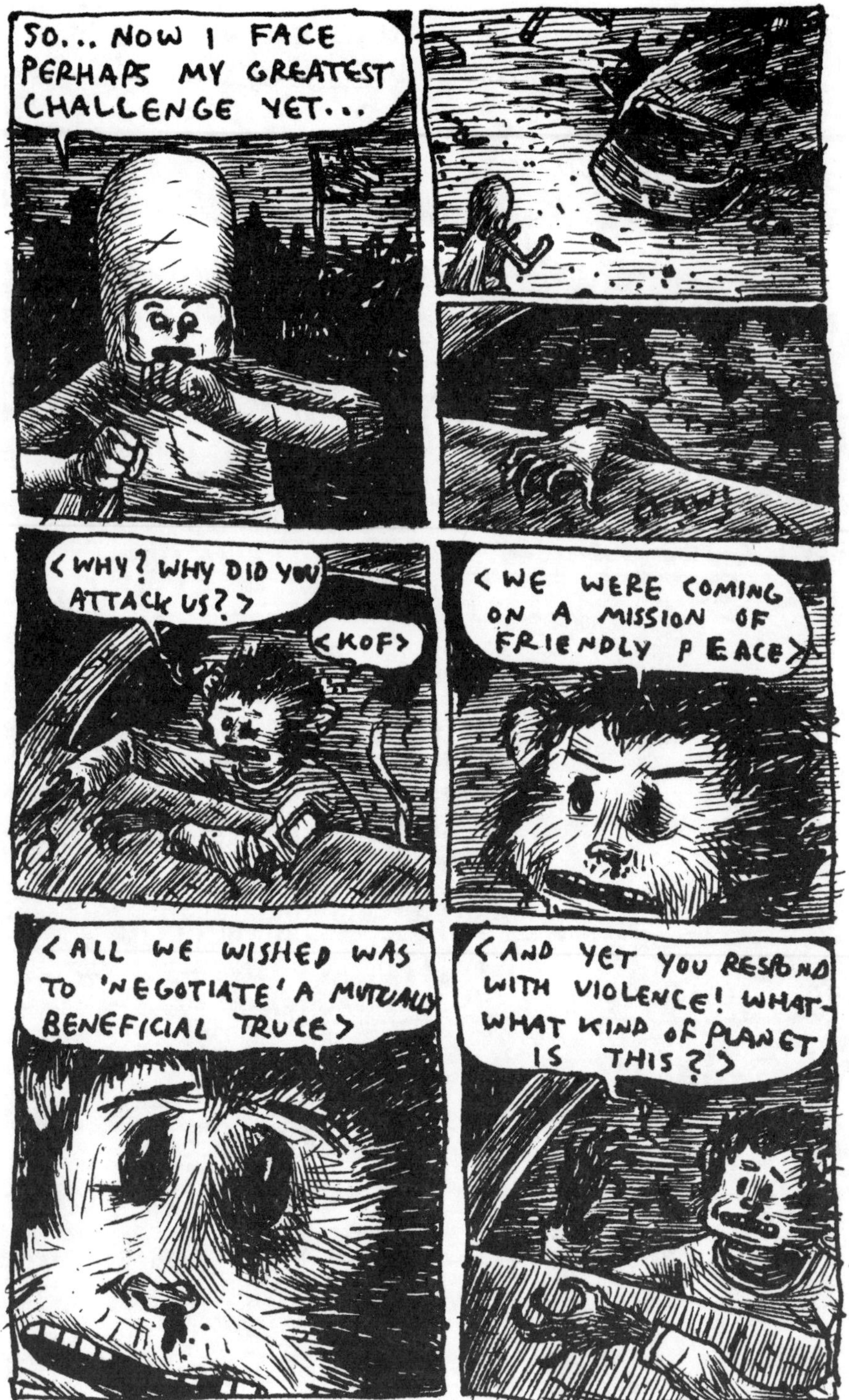
SO... NOW I FACE PERHAPS MY GREATEST CHALLENGE YET...
<WHY? WHY DID YOU ATTACK US?>
<KOF>
<WE WERE COMING ON A MISSION OF FRIENDLY PEACE>
<ALL WE WISHED WAS TO 'NEGOTIATE' A MUTUALLY BENEFICIAL TRUCE>
<AND YET YOU RESPOND WITH VIOLENCE! WHAT-WHAT KIND OF PLANET IS THIS?>

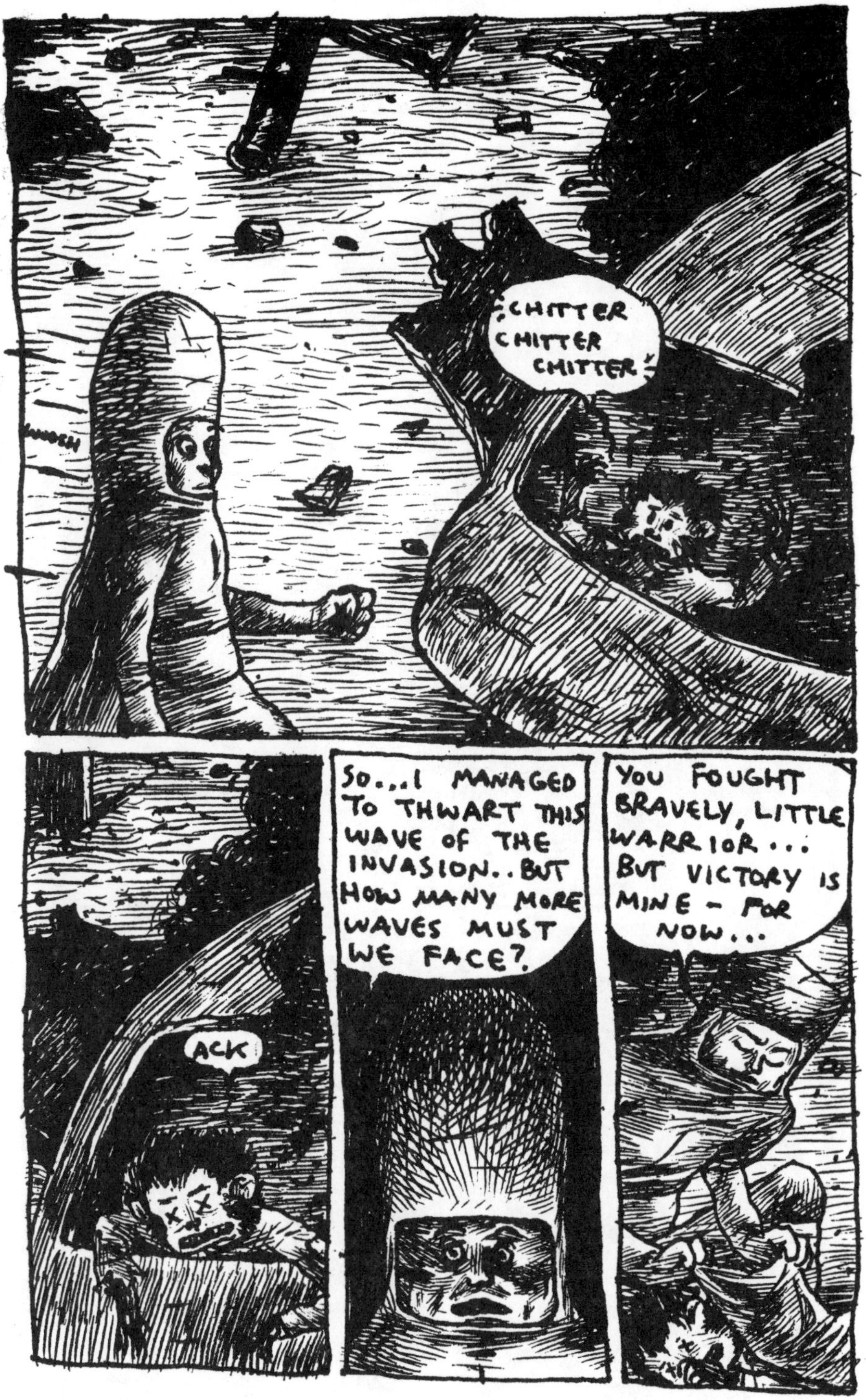
CHITTER CHITTER CHITTER
ACK
SO...I MANAGED TO THWART THIS WAVE OF THE INVASION..BUT HOW MANY MORE WAVES MUST WE FACE?
YOU FOUGHT BRAVELY, LITTLE WARRIOR... BUT VICTORY IS MINE - FOR NOW...

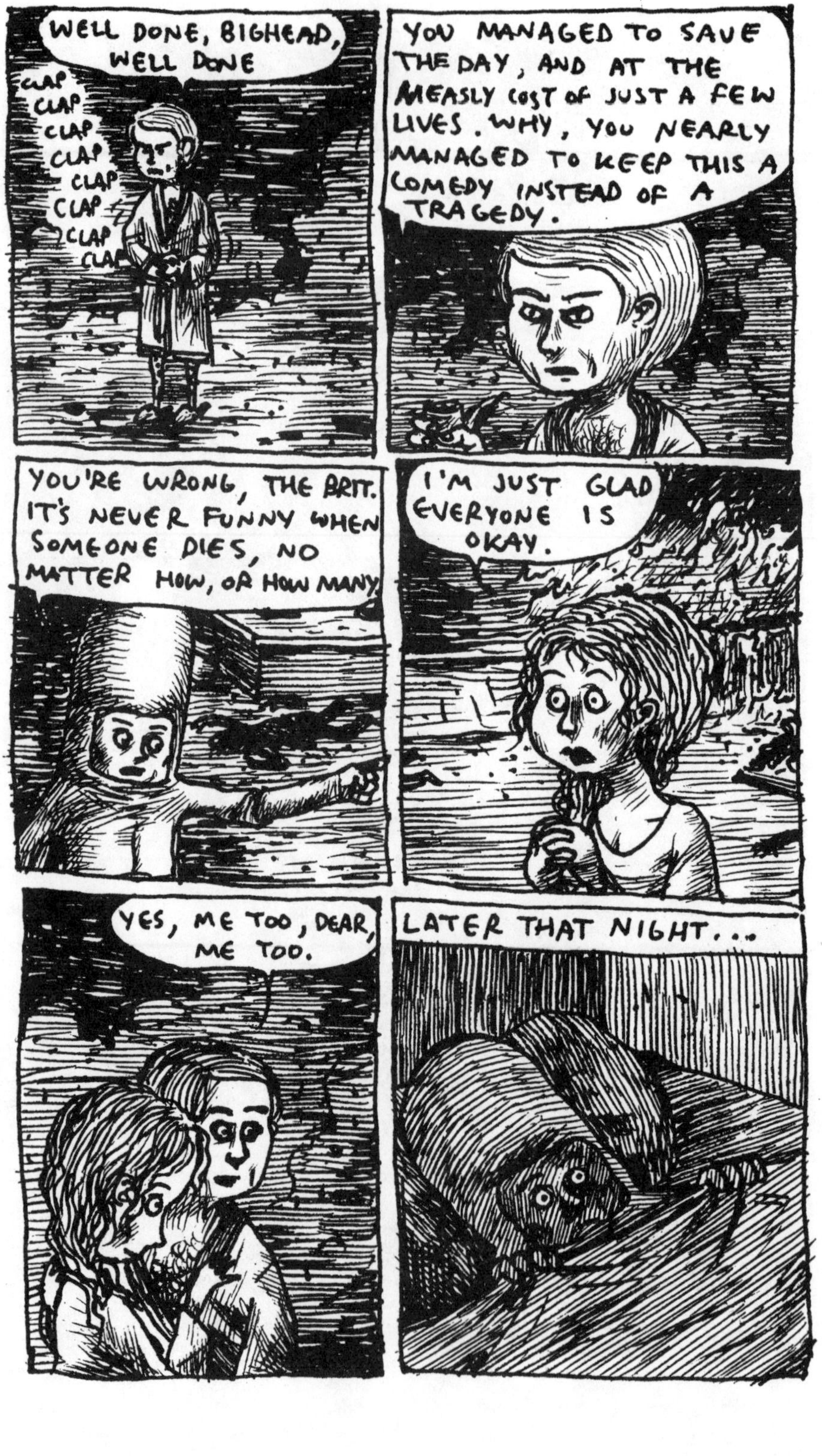
WELL DONE, BIGHEAD, WELL DONE
CLAP CLAP CLAP CLAP CLAP CLAP CLAP CLAP
YOU MANAGED TO SAVE THE DAY, AND AT THE MEASLY COST OF JUST A FEW LIVES. WHY, YOU NEARLY MANAGED TO KEEP THIS A COMEDY INSTEAD OF A TRAGEDY.
YOU'RE WRONG, THE BRIT. IT'S NEVER FUNNY WHEN SOMEONE DIES, NO MATTER HOW, OR HOW MANY.
I'M JUST GLAD EVERYONE IS OKAY.
YES, ME TOO, DEAR, ME TOO.
LATER THAT NIGHT...

TWO

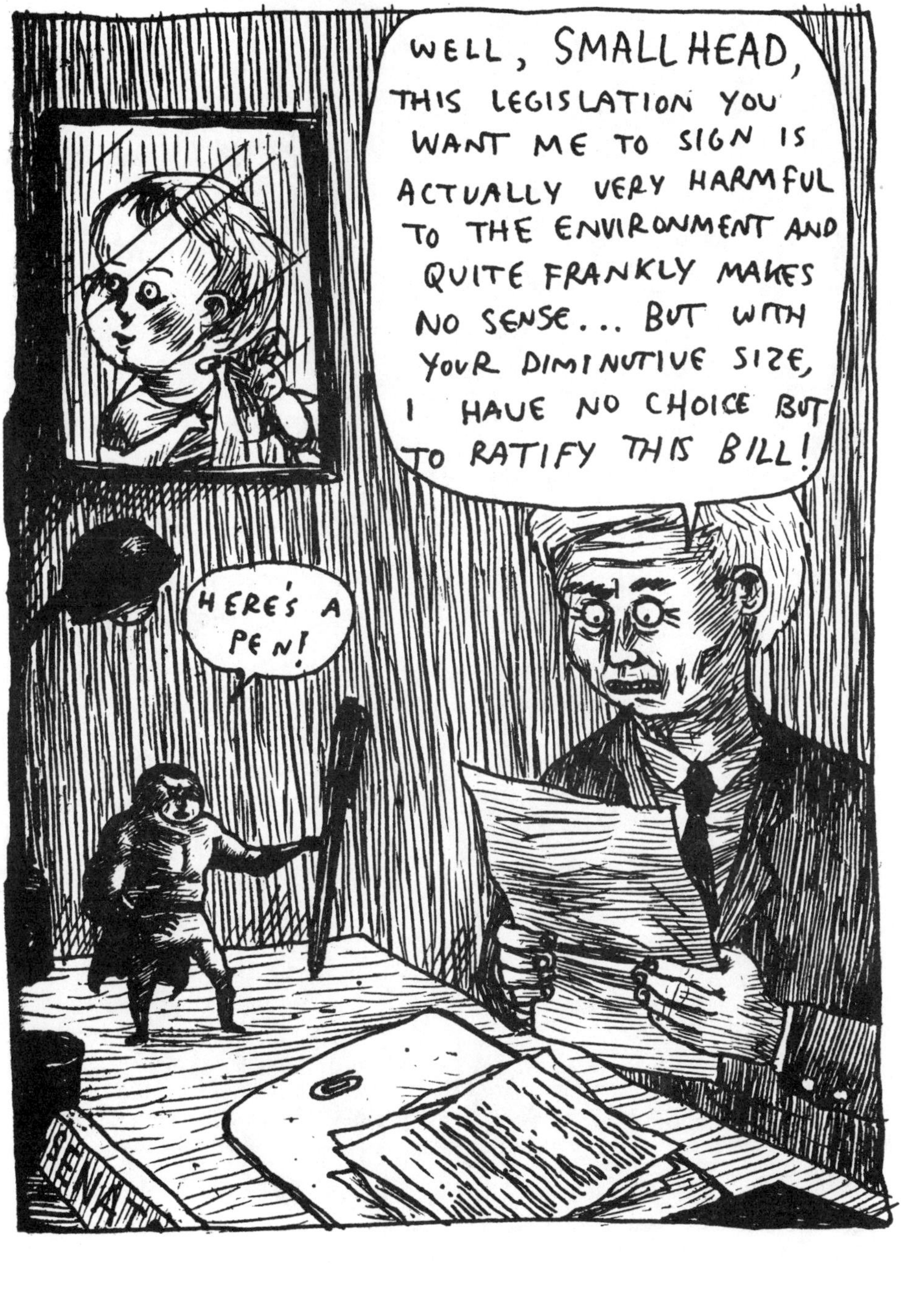
WELL, SMALLHEAD, THIS LEGISLATION YOU WANT ME TO SIGN IS ACTUALLY VERY HARMFUL TO THE ENVIRONMENT AND QUITE FRANKLY MAKES NO SENSE... BUT WITH YOUR DIMINUTIVE SIZE, I HAVE NO CHOICE BUT TO RATIFY THIS BILL!
HERE'S A PEN!
SENAT

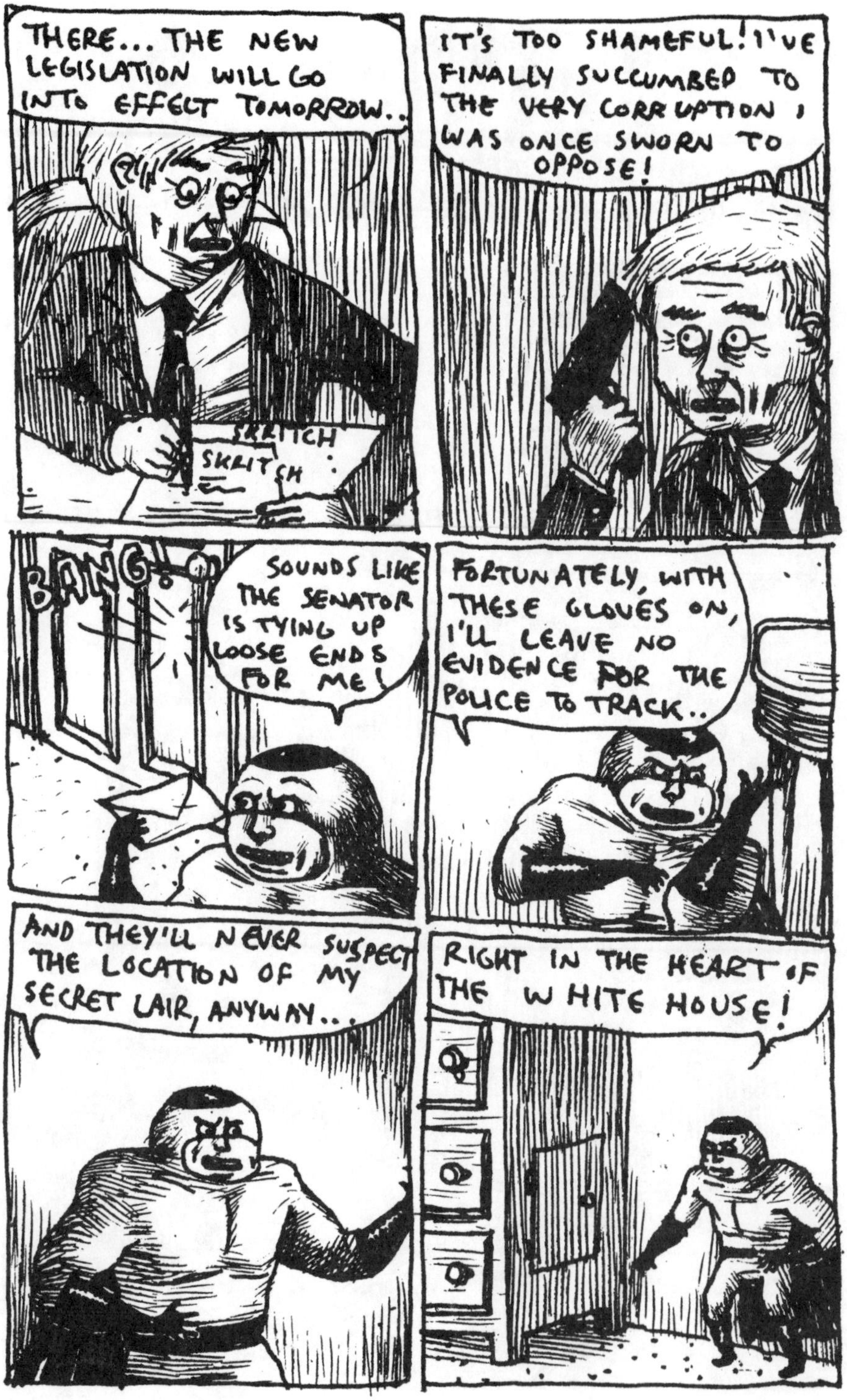
THERE... THE NEW LEGISLATION WILL GO INTO EFFECT TOMORROW...
SKRITCH
SKRITCH
IT'S TOO SHAMEFUL! I'VE FINALLY SUCCUMBED TO THE VERY CORRUPTION I WAS ONCE SWORN TO OPPOSE!
BANG!
SOUNDS LIKE THE SENATOR IS TYING UP LOOSE ENDS FOR ME!
FORTUNATELY, WITH THESE GLOVES ON, I'LL LEAVE NO EVIDENCE FOR THE POLICE TO TRACK...
AND THEY'LL NEVER SUSPECT THE LOCATION OF MY SECRET LAIR, ANYWAY...
RIGHT IN THE HEART OF THE WHITE HOUSE!

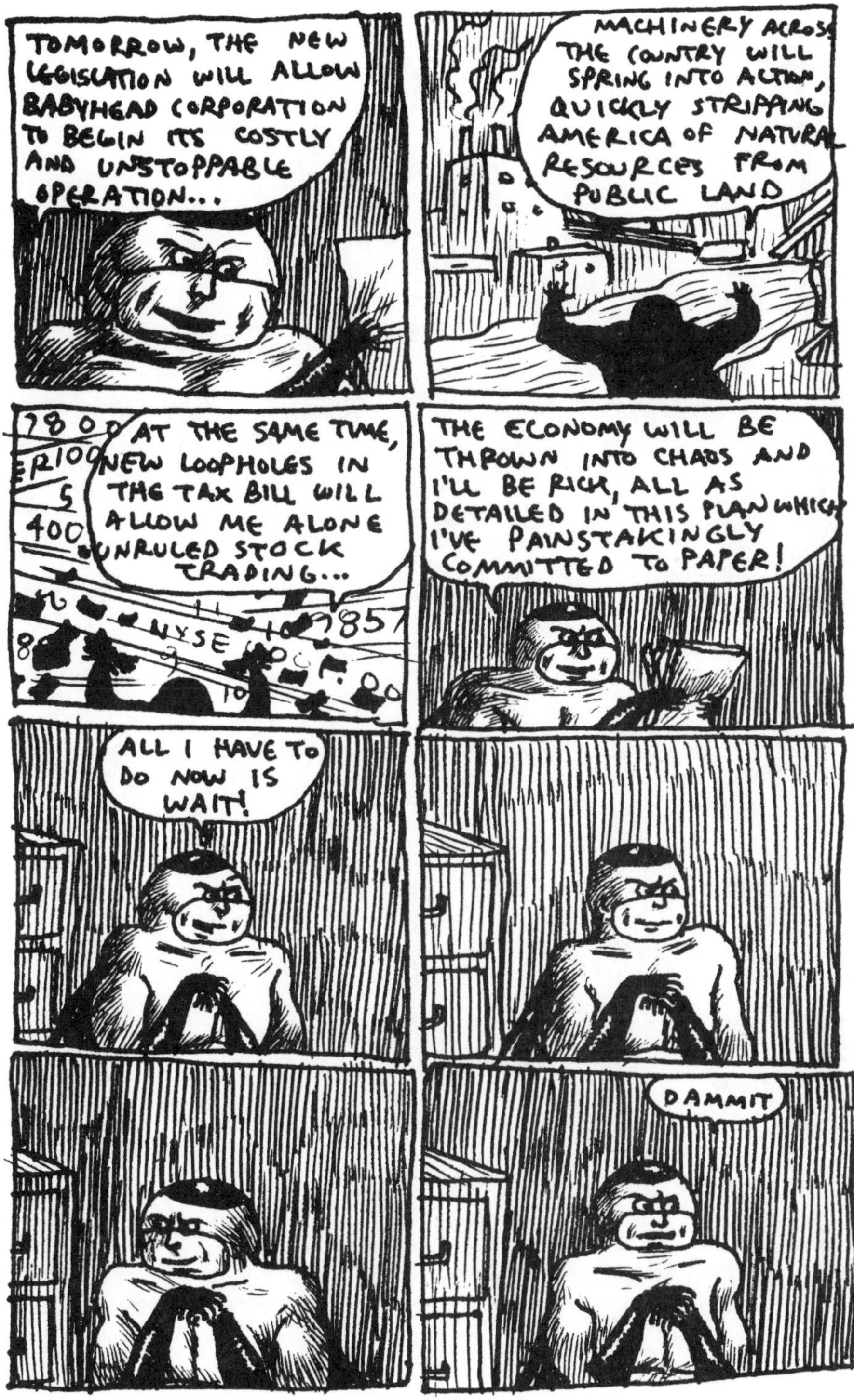
TOMORROW, THE NEW LEGISLATION WILL ALLOW BABYHEAD CORPORATION TO BEGIN ITS COSTLY AND UNSTOPPABLE OPERATION...
MACHINERY ACROSS THE COUNTRY WILL SPRING INTO ACTION, QUICKLY STRIPPING AMERICA OF NATURAL RESOURCES FROM PUBLIC LAND
AT THE SAME TIME, NEW LOOPHOLES IN THE TAX BILL WILL ALLOW ME ALONE UNRULED STOCK TRADING...
NYSE
THE ECONOMY WILL BE THROWN INTO CHAOS AND I'LL BE RICH, ALL AS DETAILED IN THIS PLAN WHICH I'VE PAINSTAKINGLY COMMITTED TO PAPER!
ALL I HAVE TO DO NOW IS WAIT!
DAMMIT

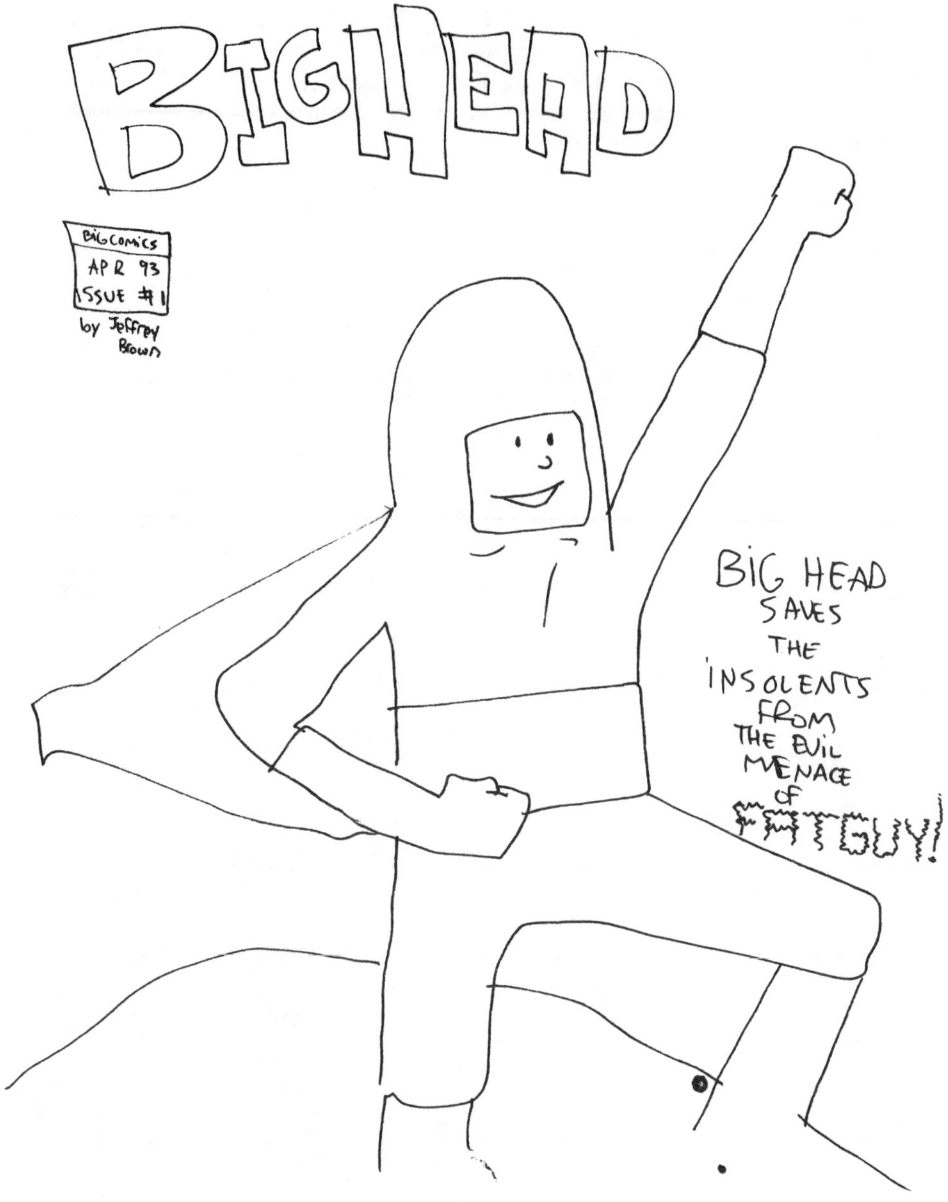

BIGHEAD
BIG COMICS
APR 93
ISSUE #1
by Jeffrey Brown
BIG HEAD SAVES THE INSOLENTS FROM THE EVIL MENACE OF FATGUY!

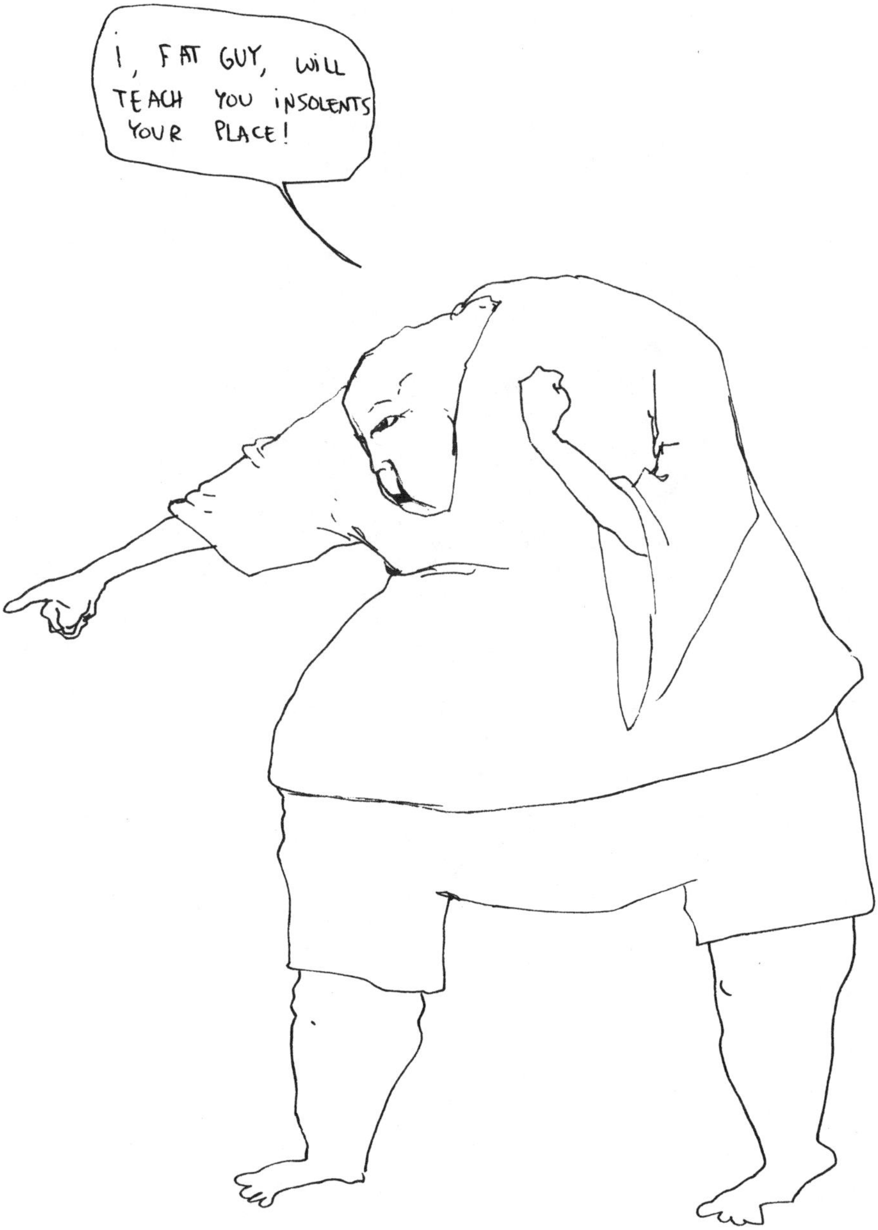
I, FAT GUY, WILL TEACH YOU INSOLENTS YOUR PLACE!

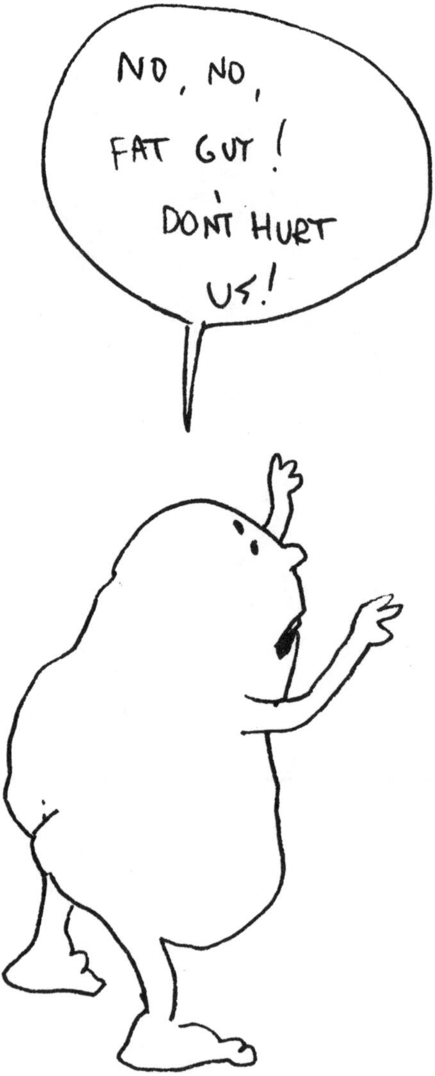
NO, NO, FAT GUY! DON'T HURT US!

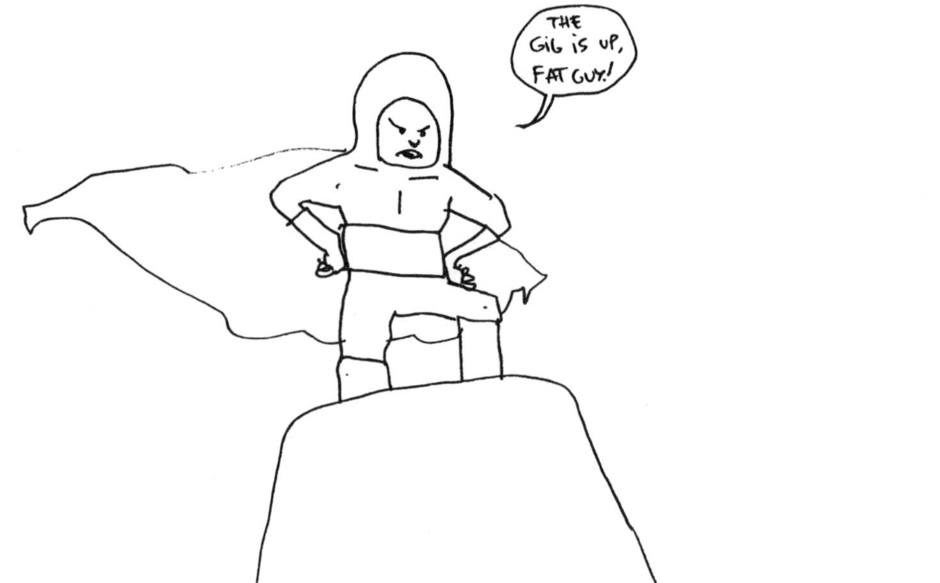
THE GIG IS UP, FAT GUY!

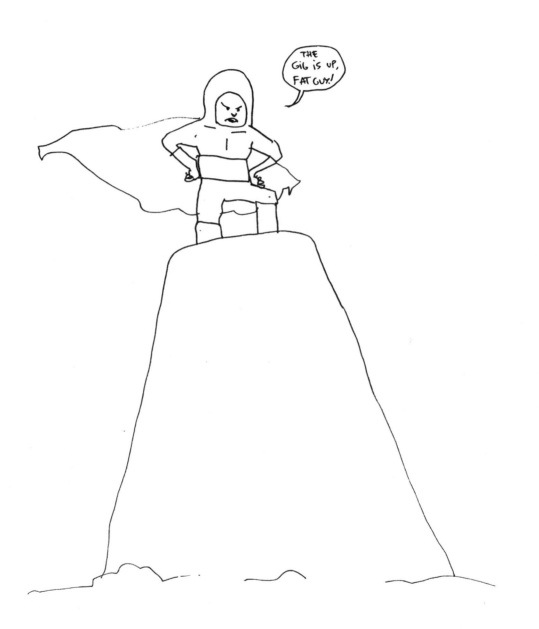

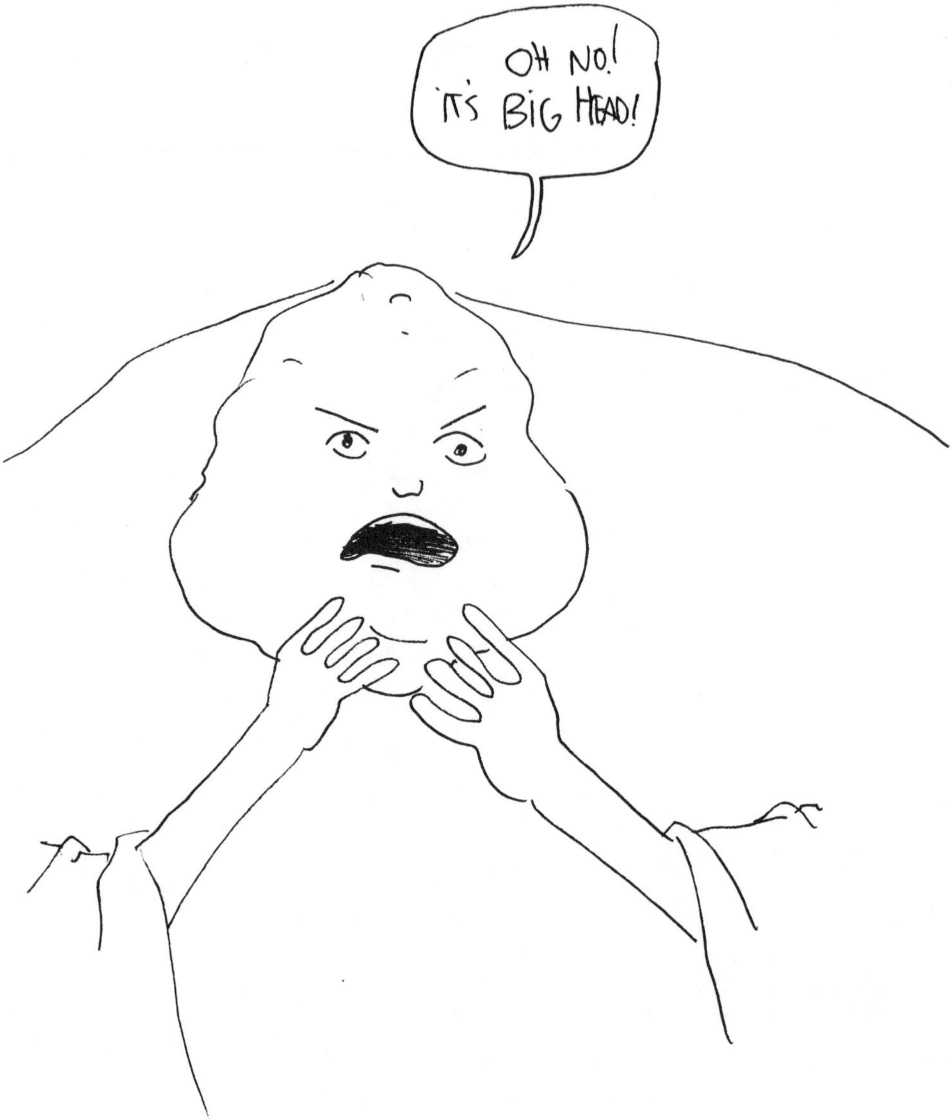
OH NO! IT'S BIG HEAD!

BIG HEAD SAVES THE DAY!

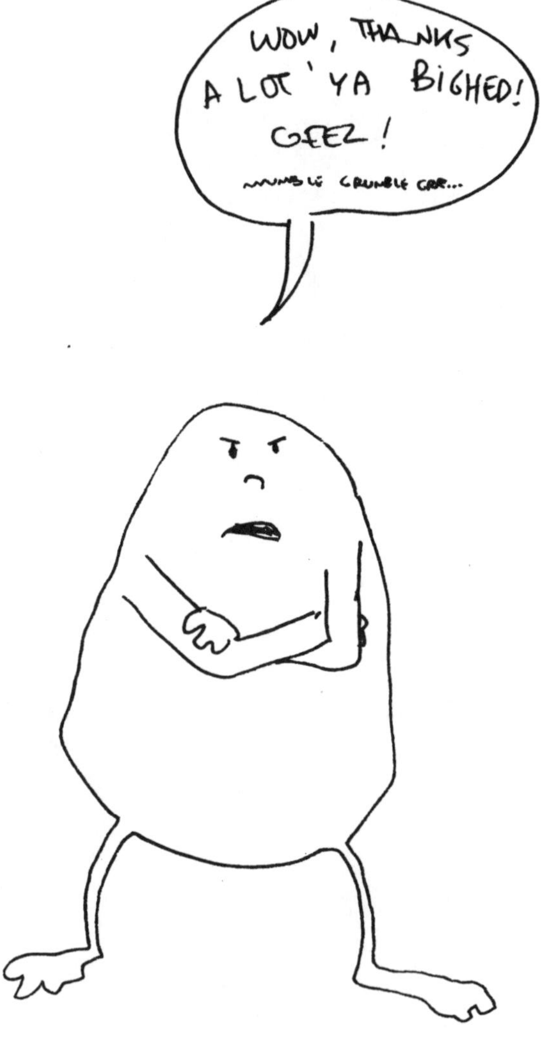
WOW, THANKS A LOT 'YA BIGHED! GEEZ!
MUMBLE GRUMBLE GRR...

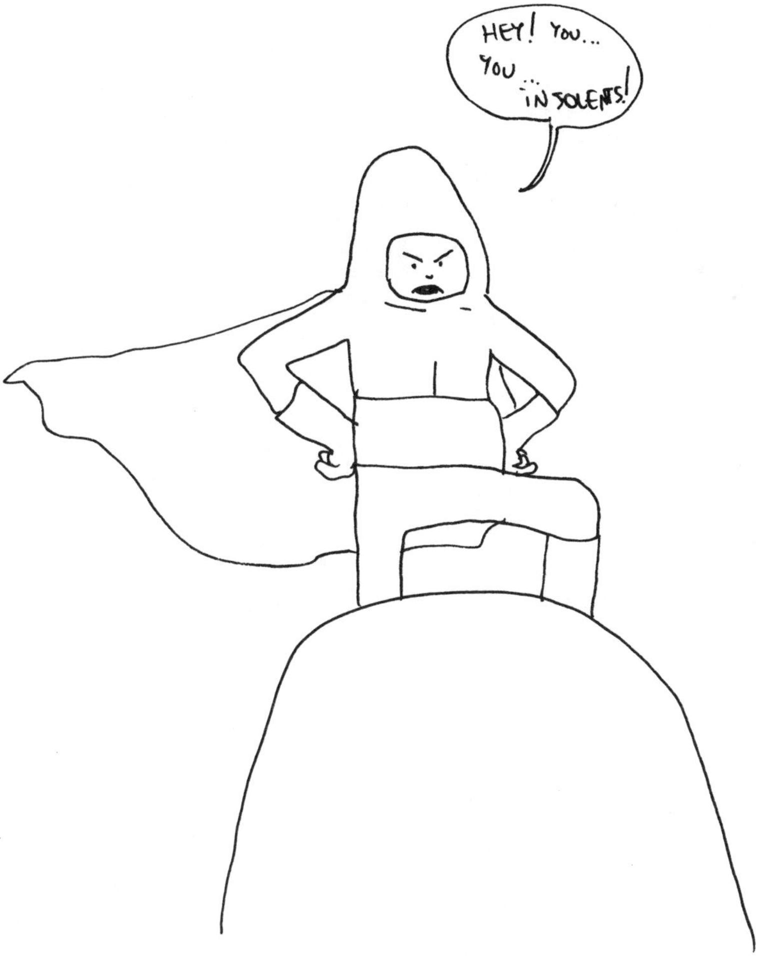
HEY! YOU... YOU... INSOLENTS!

THE END

★ADVERTISEMENT★

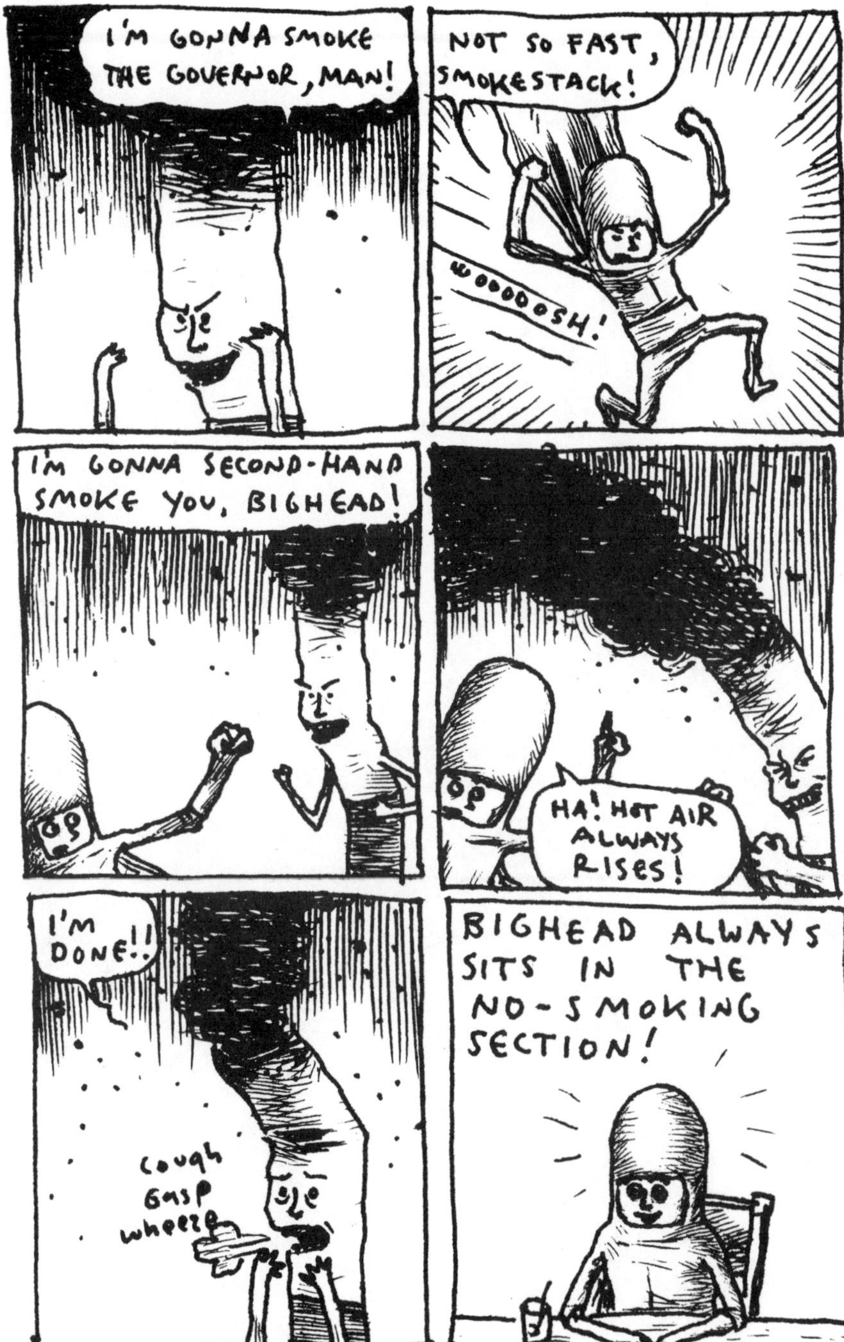
I'M GONNA SMOKE THE GOVERNOR, MAN!
NOT SO FAST, SMOKESTACK!
WOOOOOOSH!
I'M GONNA SECOND-HAND SMOKE YOU, BIGHEAD!
HA! HOT AIR ALWAYS RISES!
I'M DONE!!
cough gasp wheeze
BIGHEAD ALWAYS SITS IN THE NO-SMOKING SECTION!

BIGHEAD VERSUS FAT TONY!

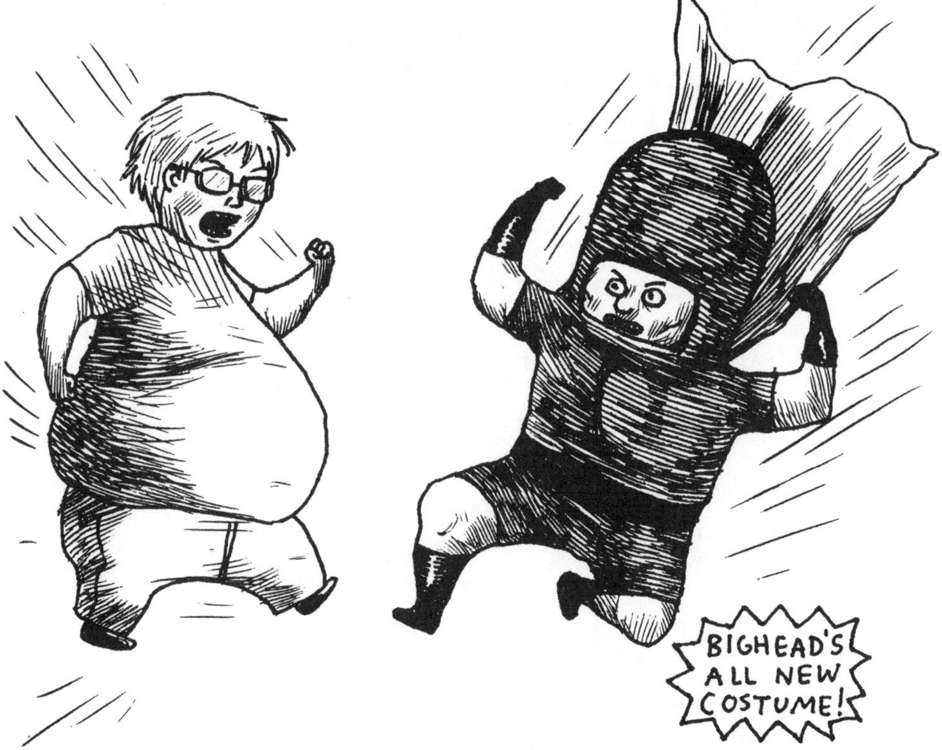
BIGHEAD'S ALL NEW COSTUME!

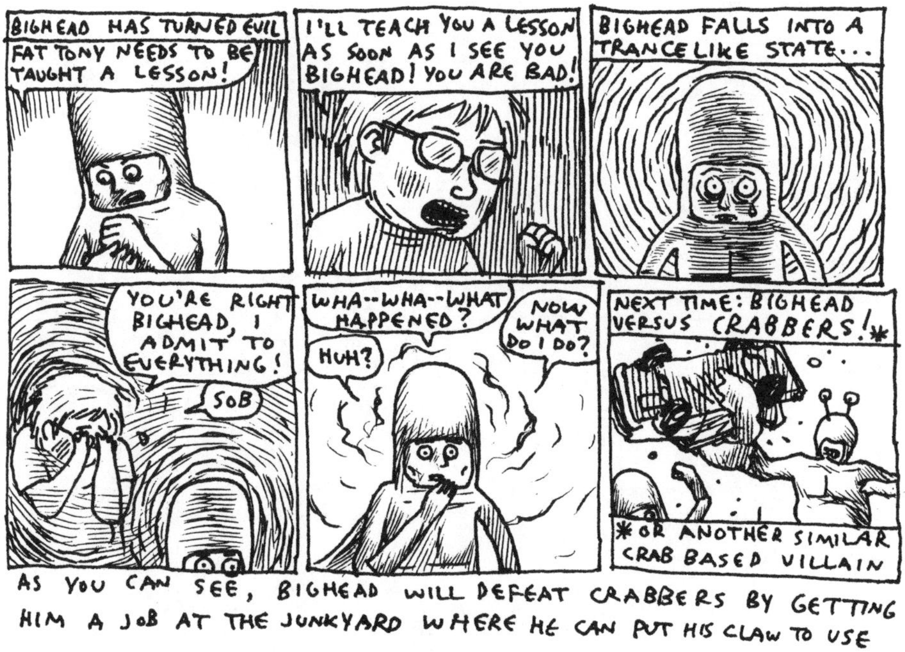
BIGHEAD HAS TURNED EVIL
FAT TONY NEEDS TO BE TAUGHT A LESSON!
I'LL TEACH YOU A LESSON AS SOON AS I SEE YOU BIGHEAD! YOU ARE BAD!
BIGHEAD FALLS INTO A TRANCE LIKE STATE...
YOU'RE RIGHT BIGHEAD, I ADMIT TO EVERYTHING!
SOB
WHA--WHA--WHAT HAPPENED?
HUH?
NOW WHAT DO I DO?
NEXT TIME: BIGHEAD VERSUS CRABBERS! *
* OR ANOTHER SIMILAR CRAB BASED VILLAIN

AS YOU CAN SEE, BIGHEAD WILL DEFEAT CRABBERS BY GETTING HIM A JOB AT THE JUNKYARD WHERE HE CAN PUT HIS CLAW TO USE

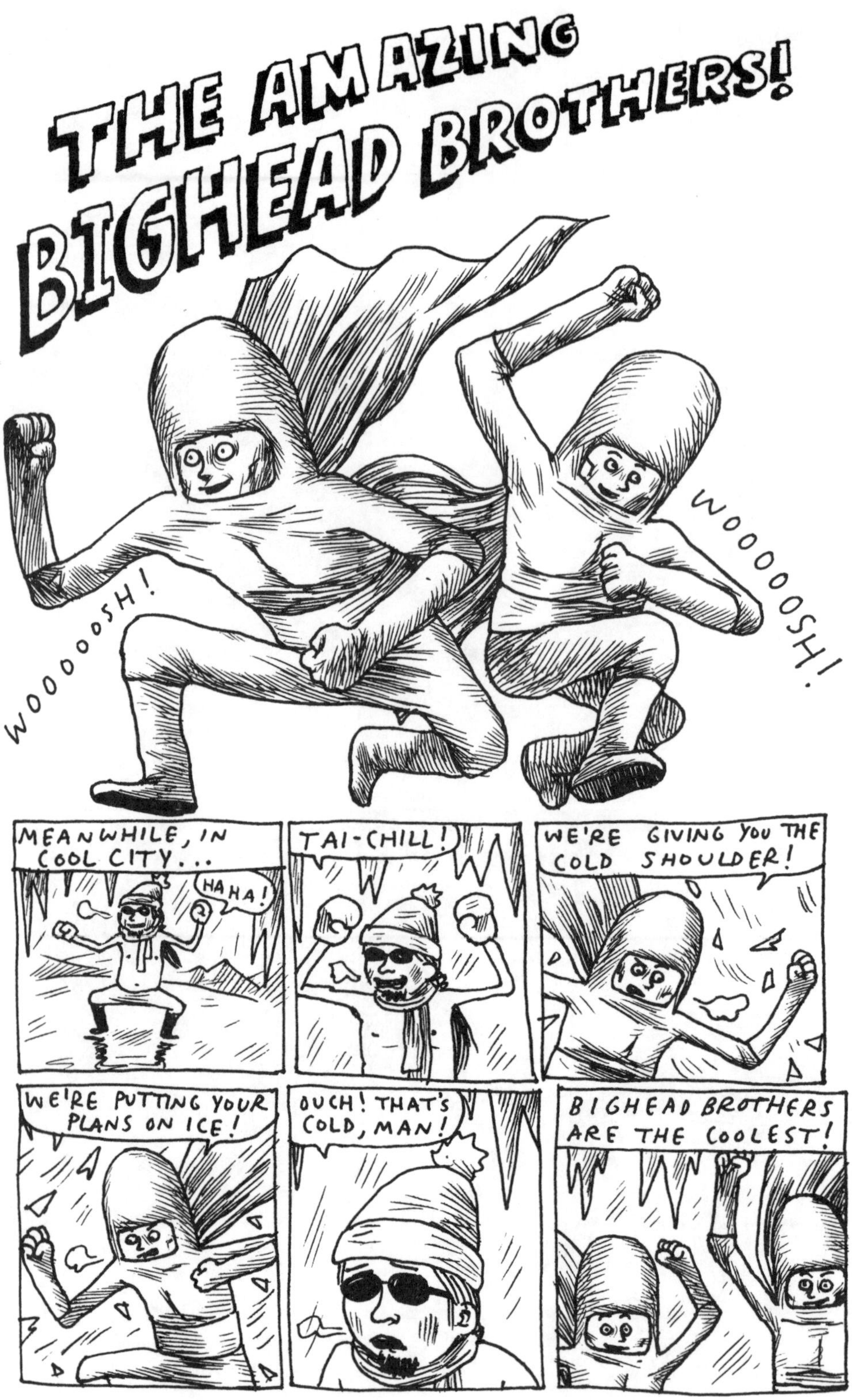
THE AMAZING BIGHEAD BROTHERS!
WOOOOOOSH!
WOOOOOOSH!
MEANWHILE, IN COOL CITY...
HA HA!
TAI-CHILL!
WE'RE GIVING YOU THE COLD SHOULDER!
WE'RE PUTTING YOUR PLANS ON ICE!
OUCH! THAT'S COLD, MAN!
BIGHEAD BROTHERS ARE THE COOLEST!

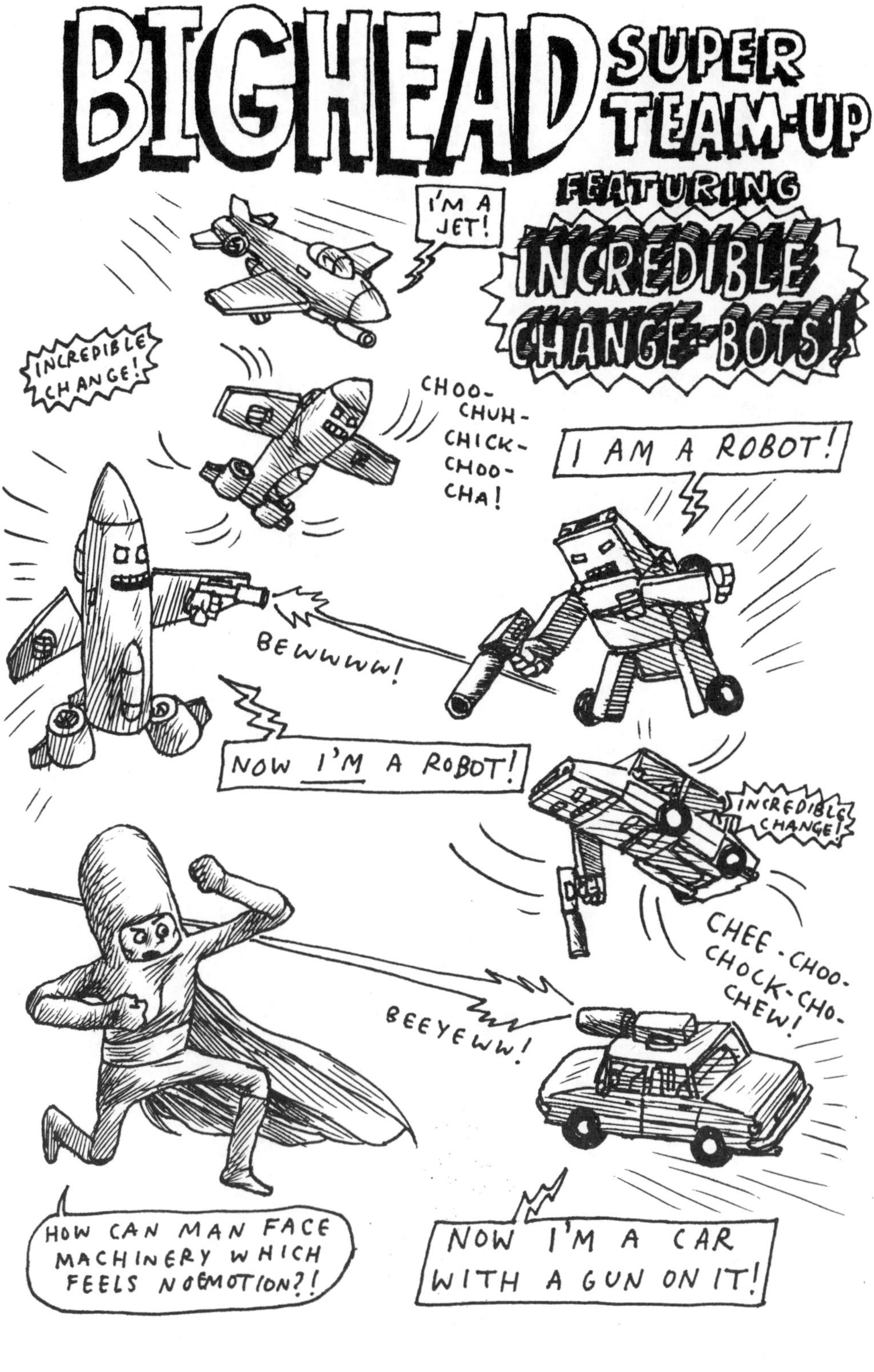
BIGHEAD SUPER TEAM-UP
FEATURING
INCREDIBLE CHANGE-BOTS!
I'M A JET!
INCREDIBLE CHANGE!
CHOO-CHUH-CHICK-CHOO-CHA!
I AM A ROBOT!
BEWWWW!
NOW I'M A ROBOT!
INCREDIBLE CHANGE!
CHEE-CHOO-CHOCK-CHO-CHEW!
BEEYEWW!
HOW CAN MAN FACE MACHINERY WHICH FEELS NO EMOTION?!
NOW I'M A CAR WITH A GUN ON IT!

BIGHEAD in "VIOLENCE--- DON'T PLAY THAT GAME!"

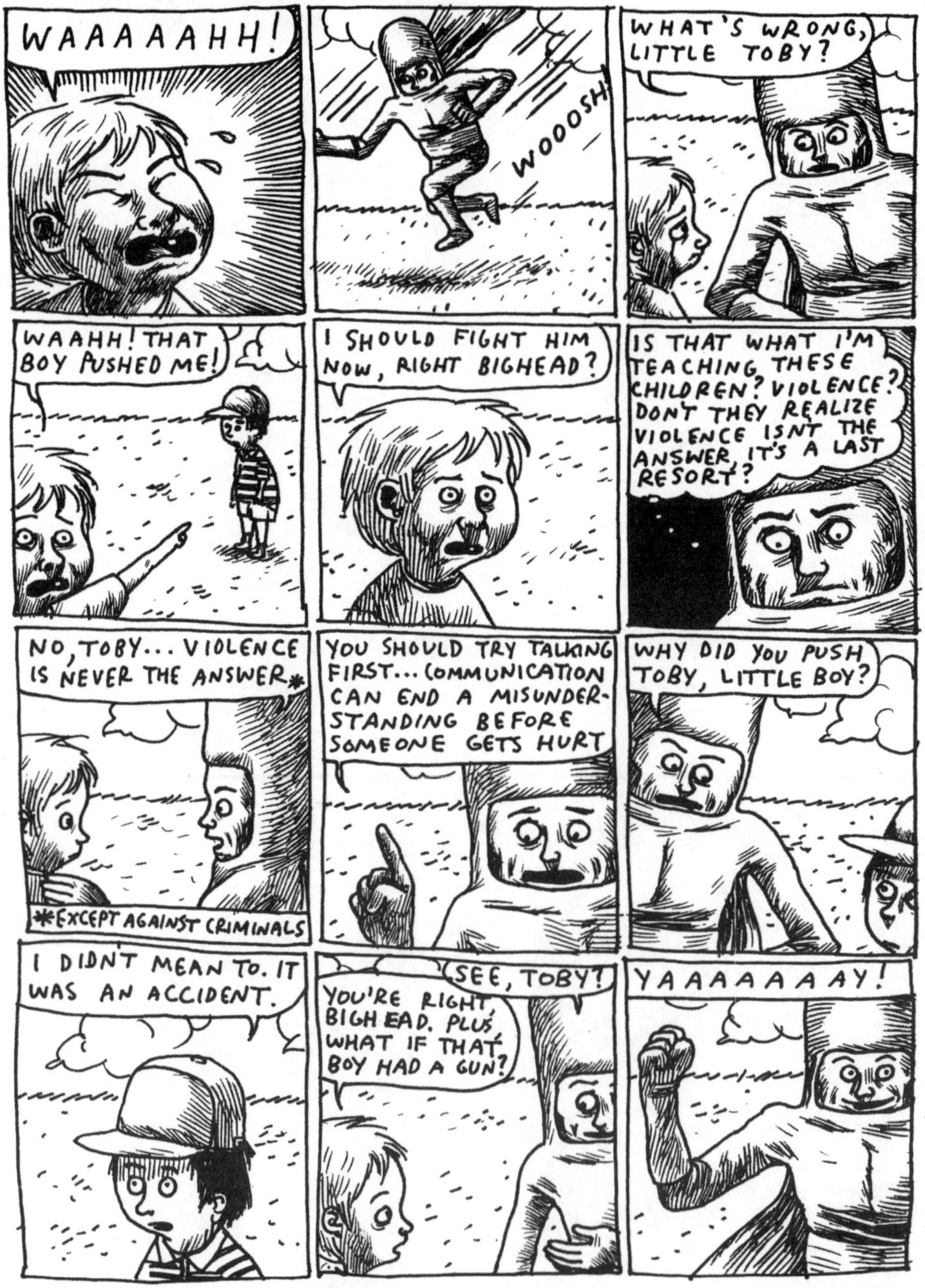
WAAAAAHH!
WOOOSH!
WHAT'S WRONG, LITTLE TOBY?
WAAHH! THAT BOY PUSHED ME!
I SHOULD FIGHT HIM NOW, RIGHT BIGHEAD?
IS THAT WHAT I'M TEACHING THESE CHILDREN? VIOLENCE? DON'T THEY REALIZE VIOLENCE ISN'T THE ANSWER, IT'S A LAST RESORT?
NO, TOBY... VIOLENCE IS NEVER THE ANSWER*
*EXCEPT AGAINST CRIMINALS
YOU SHOULD TRY TALKING FIRST... COMMUNICATION CAN END A MISUNDERSTANDING BEFORE SOMEONE GETS HURT
WHY DID YOU PUSH TOBY, LITTLE BOY?
I DIDN'T MEAN TO. IT WAS AN ACCIDENT.
SEE, TOBY?
YOU'RE RIGHT, BIGHEAD. PLUS WHAT IF THAT BOY HAD A GUN?
YAAAAAAAY!

BIGHEAD

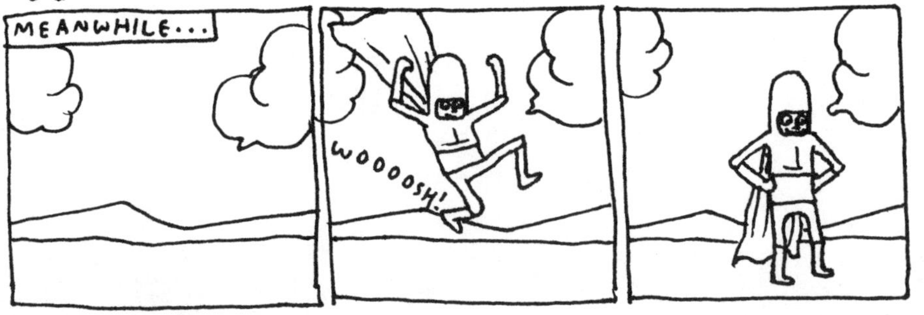
MEANWHILE...
WOOOOOSH!

BIGHEAD

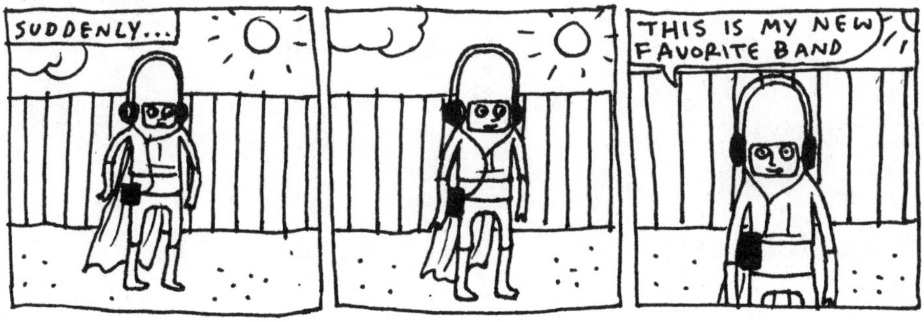
SUDDENLY...
THIS IS MY NEW FAVORITE BAND

BIGHEAD

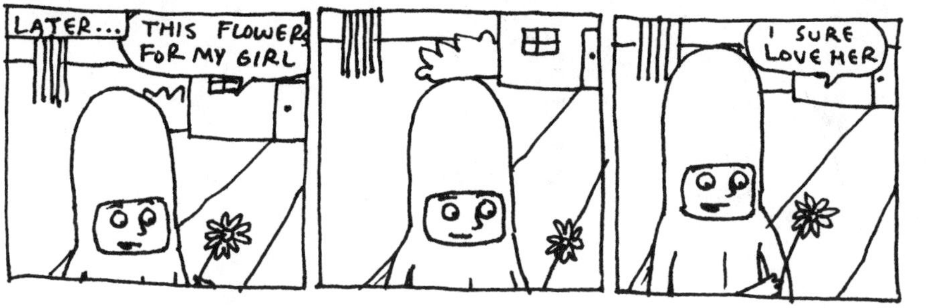
LATER...
THIS FLOWERS FOR MY GIRL
I SURE LOVE HER

BIGHEAD

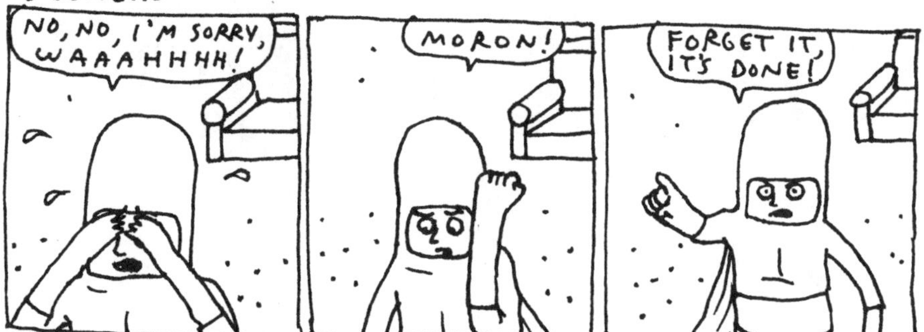
NO, NO, I'M SORRY, WAAAHHHH!
MORON!
FORGET IT, IT'S DONE!

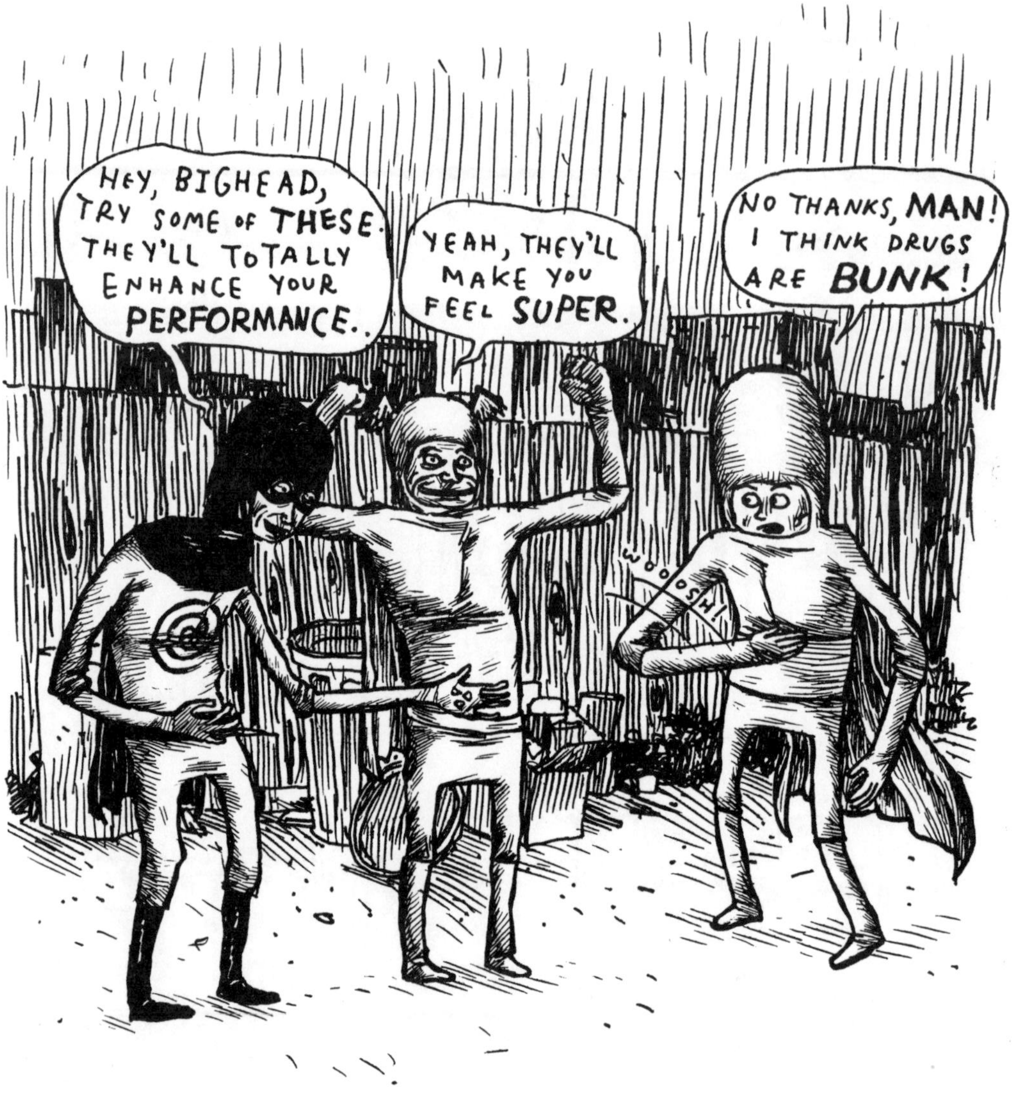
HEY, BIGHEAD, TRY SOME OF THESE. THEY'LL TOTALLY ENHANCE YOUR PERFORMANCE..
YEAH, THEY'LL MAKE YOU FEEL SUPER.
NO THANKS, MAN! I THINK DRUGS ARE BUNK!
WOOOOSH!

JUST SAY NO

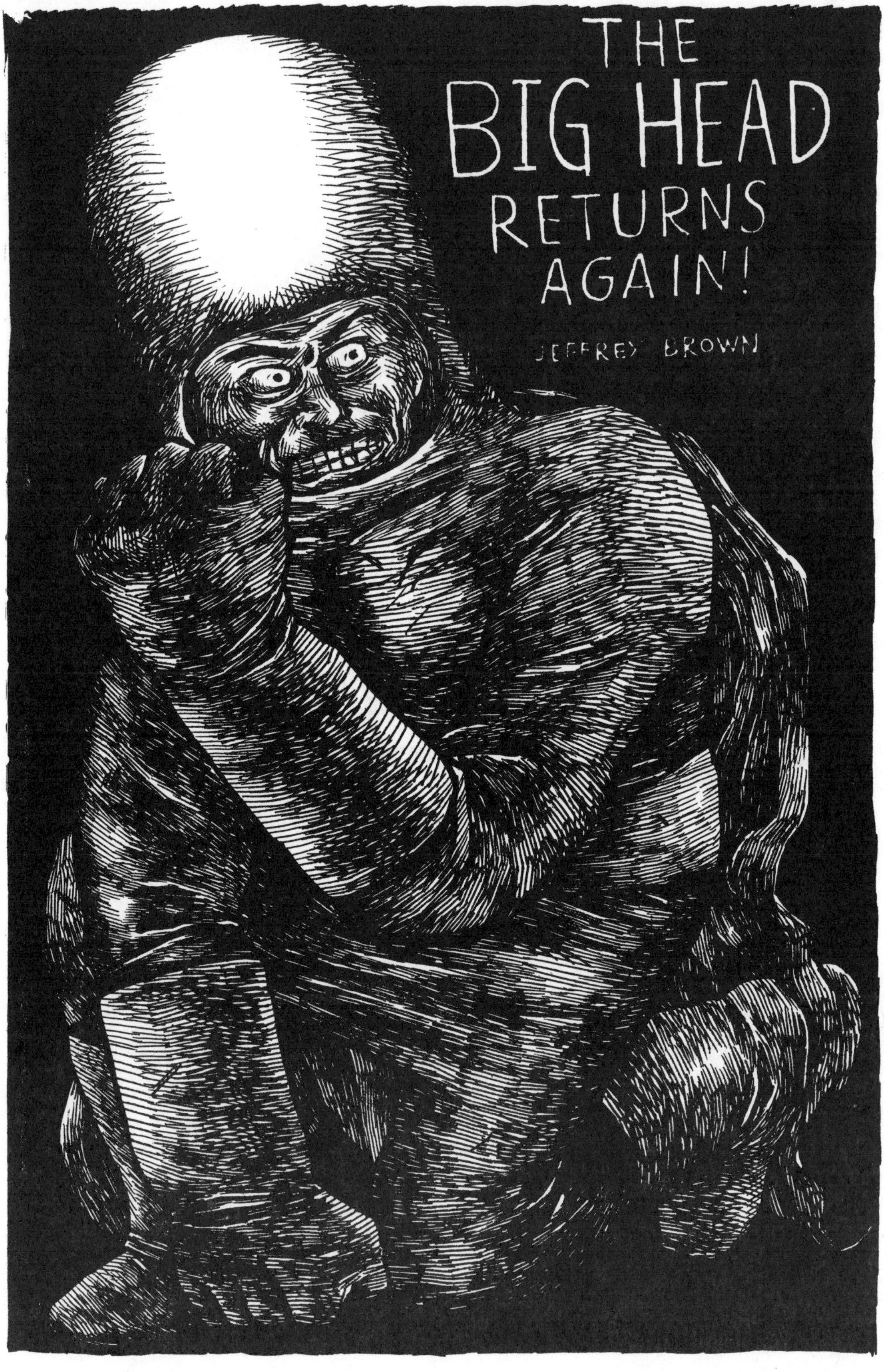
THE BIG HEAD RETURNS AGAIN!
JEFFREY BROWN

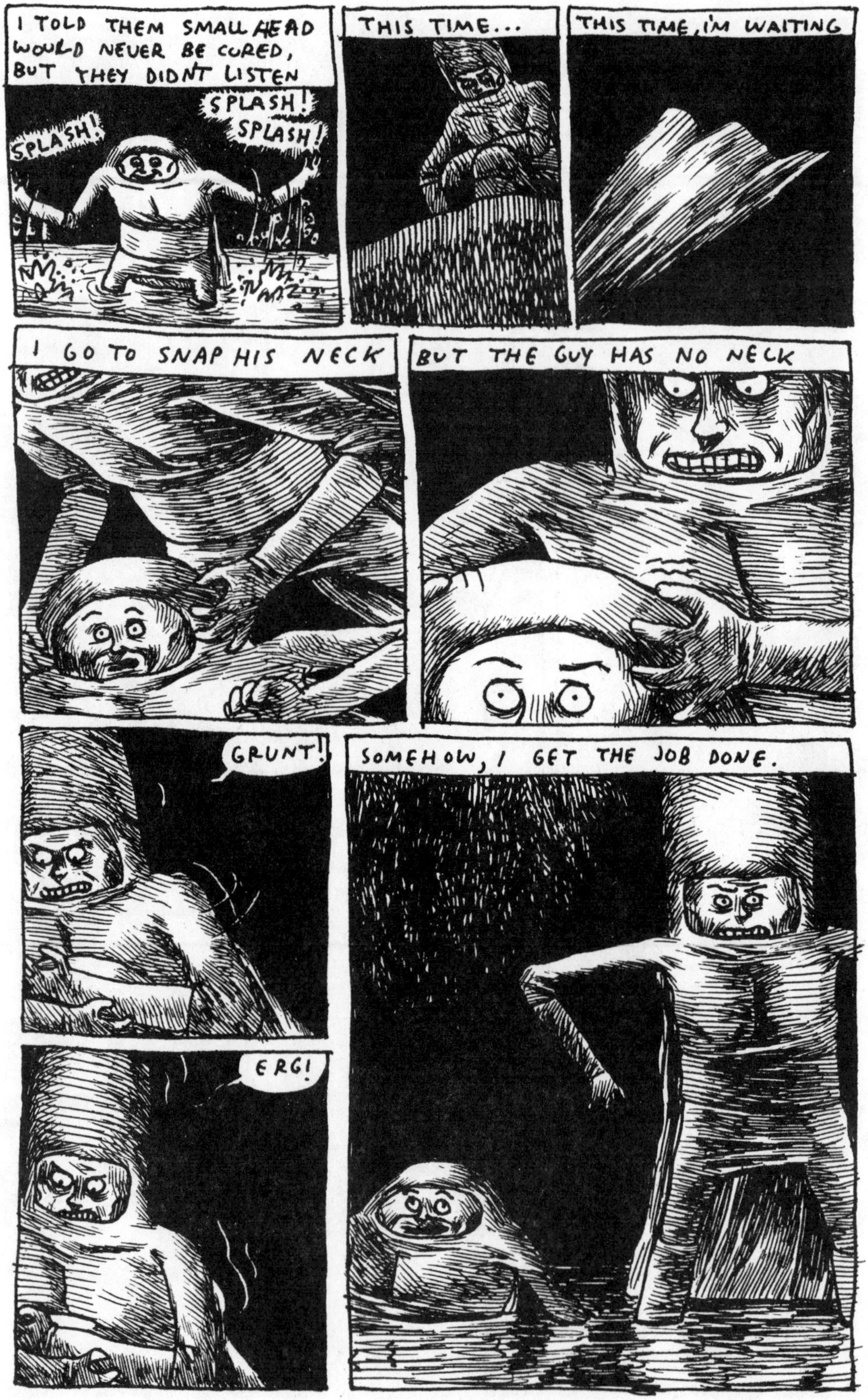
I TOLD THEM SMALL HEAD WOULD NEVER BE CURED, BUT THEY DIDN'T LISTEN
SPLASH!
SPLASH!
SPLASH!
THIS TIME...
THIS TIME, I'M WAITING
I GO TO SNAP HIS NECK
BUT THE GUY HAS NO NECK
GRUNT!
ERG!
SOMEHOW, I GET THE JOB DONE.

HOW TO DRAW BIGHEAD

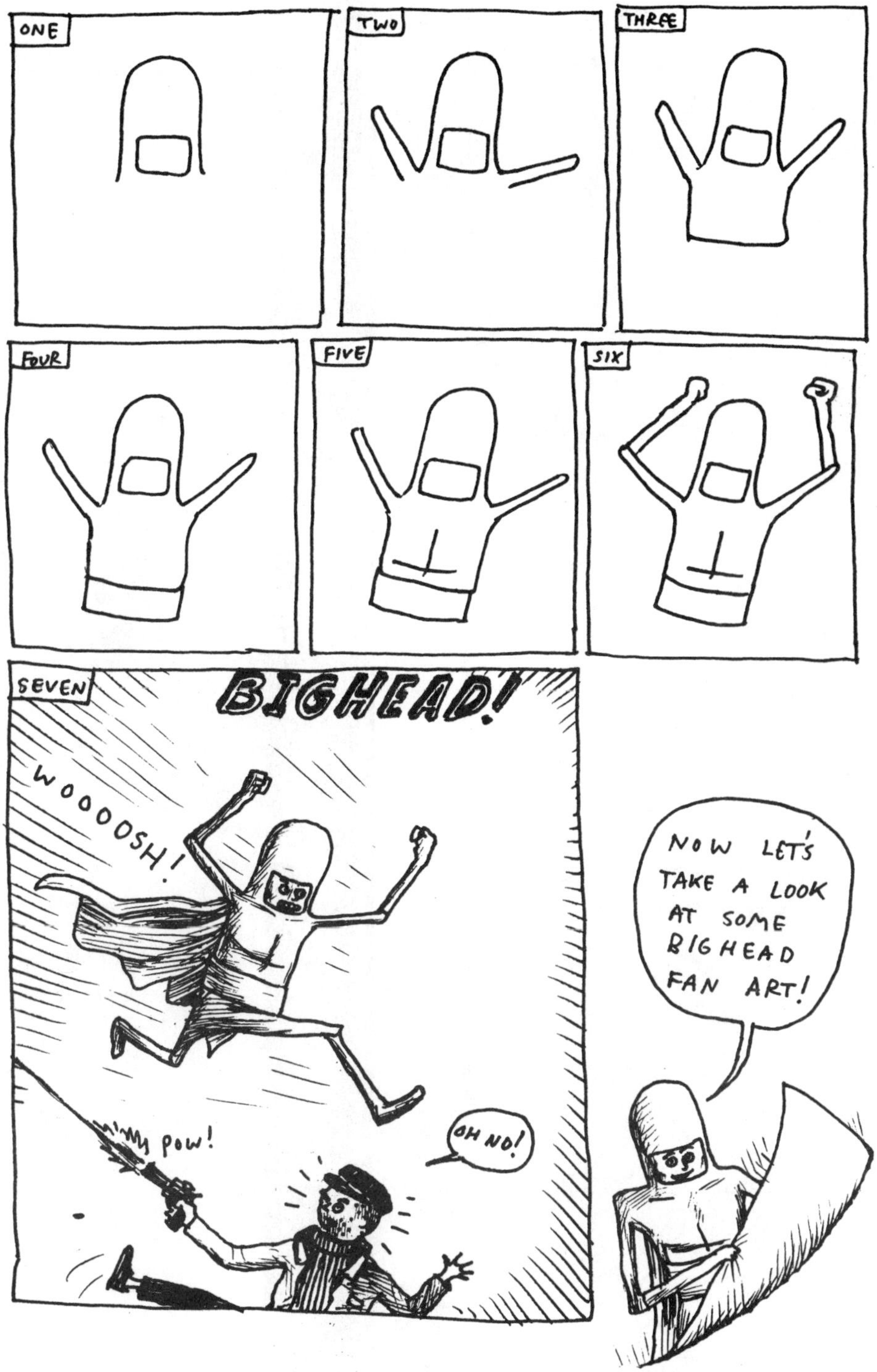
ONE
TWO
THREE
FOUR
FIVE
SIX
SEVEN
BIGHEAD!
WOOOOOSH!
POW!
OH NO!
NOW LET'S TAKE A LOOK AT SOME BIGHEAD FAN ART!

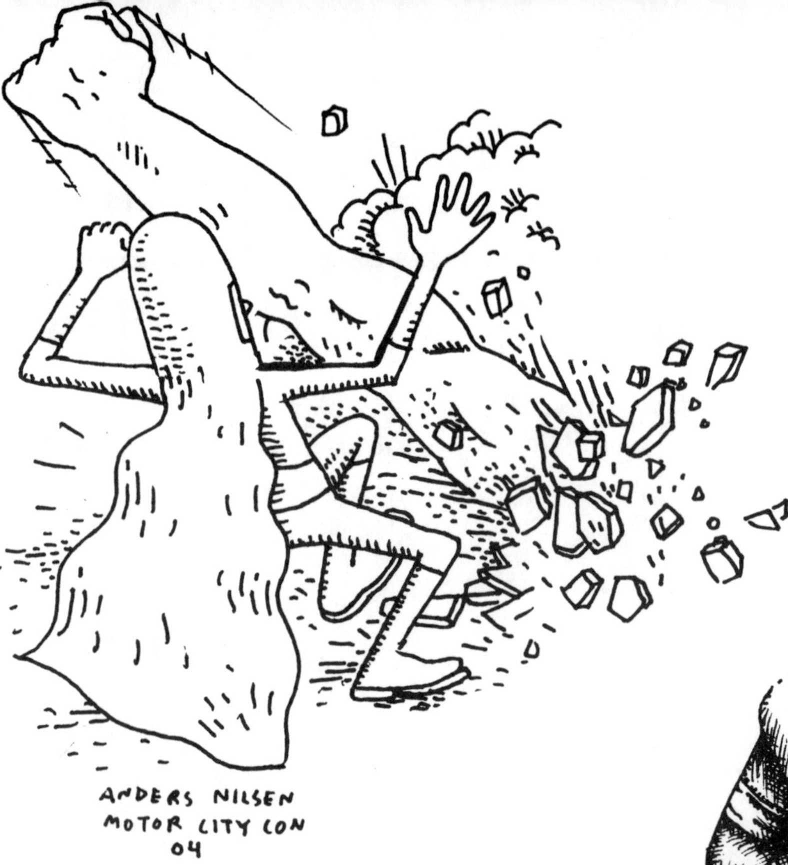
ANDERS NILSEN
MOTOR CITY CON
04

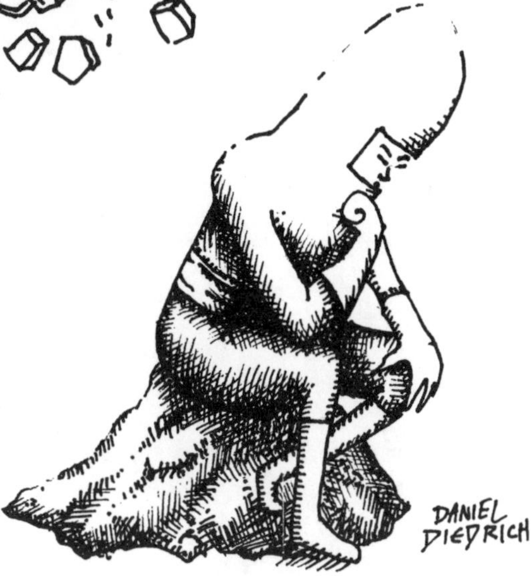
DANIEL DIEDRICH

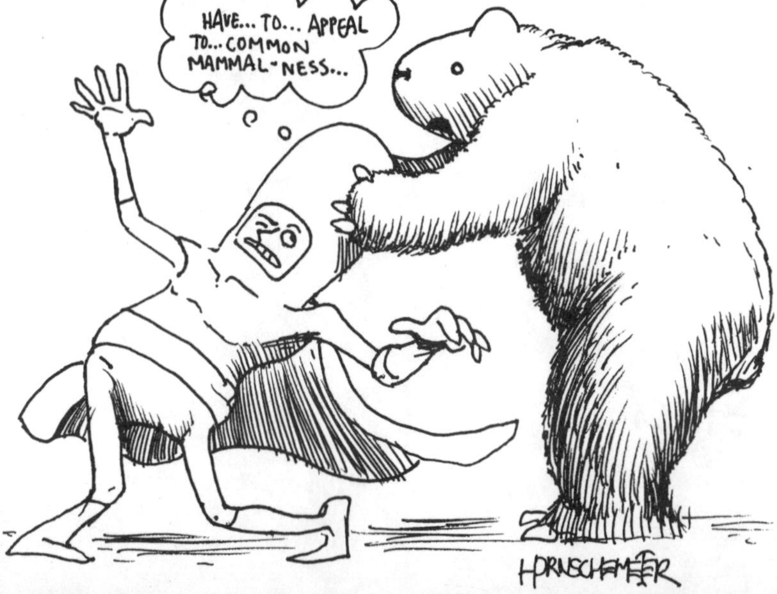
HAVE... TO... APPEAL TO... COMMON MAMMAL-NESS...
HORNSCHEMEIER

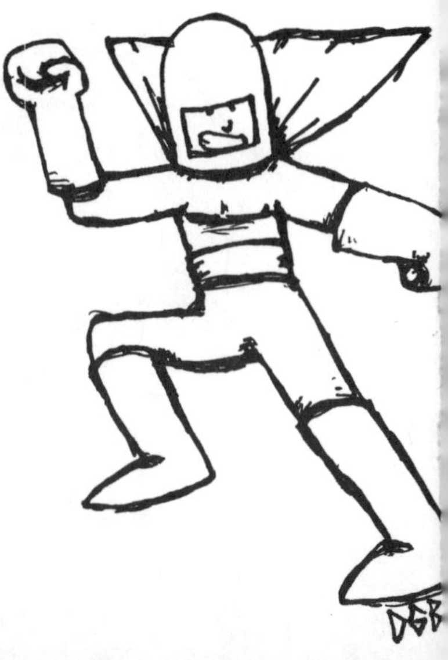
DGB